THE GIRLS OF ROOM 28

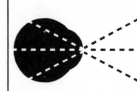 This Large Print Book carries the
Seal of Approval of N.A.V.H.

THE GIRLS OF ROOM 28

FRIENDSHIP, HOPE, AND SURVIVAL IN THERESIENSTADT

HANNELORE BRENNER

TRANSLATED FROM THE GERMAN BY JOHN E. WOODS AND SHELLEY FRISCH

THORNDIKE PRESS
A part of Gale, Cengage Learning

GALE
CENGAGE Learning

Detroit • New York • San Francisco • New Haven, Conn • Waterville, Maine • London

GALE
CENGAGE Learning™

Translation copyright © 2009 by Schocken Books, a division of Random House, Inc.

Grateful acknowledgment is made for permission to reprint the following: *Mein Land* (My Land) by Hanuš Hachenburg. From *1st meine Heimat der Ghettowall?* (Is my home the wall of the ghetto?), edited by Marie Krizkova Ruth, Kurt Jiri Kotouč, and Ornest Zdenek. Translated from the Czech by Lenka Reinerová. Hanau: Dausien Werner, 1994.

Originally published in Germany as *Die Mädchen von Zimmer 28: Freundschaft, Hoffnung und Überleben in Theresienstadt* by Droemer Verlag, Munich, in 2004.

Copyright © 2004 by Hannelore Brenner-Wonsehick.

Thorndike Press, a part of Gale, Cengage Learning.

LIBRARY OF CONGRESS CATALOGING-IN-PUBLICATION DATA

Brenner-Wonschick, Hannelore, 1951–
  [Madchen von Zimmer 28. English]
    The Girls of Room 28 : [text (large print)] friendship, hope, and survival in Theresienstadt [sic] / by Hannelore Brenner ; translated from the German by John E. Woods and Shelley Frisch.
        p. cm.
    "The text of this large print edition is unabridged."
    Includes bibliographical references.
    ISBN-13: 978-1-4104-2183-8 (hardcover : alk. paper)
    ISBN-10: 1-4104-2183-X (hardcover : alk. paper)
    1. Jewish children in the Holocaust—Czech Republic—Terezín (Severoceský kraj)—Personal narratives. 2. Theresienstadt (Concentration camp)—Biography. 3. Holocaust, Jewish (1939–1945)—Czech Republic—Terezín (Severoceský kraj)— Biography. 4. Holocaust survivors—Biography. I. Title.
    DS135.C97A12713 2009b
    940.53'18092—dc22
    [B]   2009033778

Published in 2009 by arrangement with Schocken Books, an imprint of Knopf Doubleday Publishing Group, a division of Random House, Inc.

Printed in the United States of America
1 2 3 4 5 6 7 13 12 11 10 09

For Hester, and for all children

There are stars that twinkle in the sky
although they burned out long ago
and people who bring light to the world
although they are no longer with us
their light shines especially bright
in the darkness of night
they show the way for us all
— *Hannah Senesh (1921–1944)**

IN MEMORIAM

Hans Krása (1899–1944) was the composer of the children's opera *Brundibár,* which was a light in the darkness for the children of Theresienstadt. It will always keep alive the memory of the children who were killed in the Holocaust and their hope for the victory of good over evil.

Hana Epstein ("Holubička")
Eva Fischl ("Fiška")
Ruth Gutmann
Irena Grünfeld
Marta Kende
Anna Lindt ("Lenka")
Hana Lissau
Olga Löwy ("Olile")
Zdenka Löwy
Ruth Meisl
Helena Mendl
Maria Mühlstein
Bohumila Poláček ("Milka")

Ruth Popper ("Poppinka")
Ruth Schächter ("Zajíček")
Pavla Seiner
Alice Sittig ("Didi")
Erika Stránská
Jiřinka Steiner
Emma Taub ("Muška")
*— The Girls of Room 28
who did not survive*

Dáša Bloch
Hana Brady
Petr Ginz
Jana Gintz
Hanuš Hachenburg
Eli Mühlstein
Piňťa Mühlstein
Honza Treichlinger
*— and all the other murdered
children of Theresienstadt*

CONTENTS

FOREWORD

ANNA HANUSOVÁ-FLACHOVÁ
AND HELGA POLLAK KINSKY

With the end of the war, those of us girls of Room 28 who had survived were scattered throughout the world; only a few of us were in contact in the decades following the Holocaust. We did not know what had become of most of our friends.

It took almost half a century for us to find one another again. In October 1991, after the Berlin Wall came down, a few of us met in Prague for the first time since we had lost touch. We came from everywhere — from Israel, the United States, Russia, England, Sweden, Germany, Austria, and Czechoslovakia.

It was an unforgettable moment. Gathered together in the lobby of an international hotel, we laughed and wept and spun in circles of joy as bystanders looked on in amazement.

We were all surprised to find that our feelings had stayed the same as they were back

13

then in the Girls' Home in the Theresienstadt concentration camp. We felt like a family all over again and understood each other marvelously. Since that day we have been seeing one another regularly.

Our great fortune at being together reminded us of all the girls and boys, caretakers, teachers, and doctors who did not survive, and we very much desired to rescue from oblivion those who had lost their lives in the German camps. That was the first impulse for this book.

And then, in Prague, we became acquainted with Hannelore Brenner, and we were set to move ahead. We all agreed to meet at our favorite place, Spindlermühle, in the Giant Mountains. This book is the result.

CHAPTER ONE:
SPINDLERMÜHLE,
CZECH REPUBLIC,
AUTUMN 2000

Every fall since the mid-1990s a group of extraordinary women gathers at Spindlermühle, a little Czech resort just below the headwaters of the Elbe, in the Giant Mountains. For a few days, the atmosphere in this small town is filled with the sounds of their joyous reunion, with songs and laughter, but also with the sad memories of their childhood, more than half a century ago.

The women are in their seventies, and they come from all parts of the globe. The shared vacation, which arose spontaneously out of their pleasure at having found one another again after so many years, quickly developed a momentum of its own, attracting more participants with each passing year. Soon the reunions became a cherished tradition. And while the women enjoy their time together, their hearts are both saddened by the approaching farewells and hopeful as they contemplate future re-unions.

This annual meeting has come to repre-sent the high point of their year. With brac-ing breezes blowing through its forests and the sparkling Elbe River rushing by, Spin-dlermühle radiates enchantment. The women feel rejuvenated as they hike up the mountains or stroll along the rushing stream. They bask in the happiness of being together. Their happiness is palpable to outsiders, who might well wonder what invisible tie binds them. The women them-selves would offer a simple answer: "We feel like sisters, like a family. We're happy when we are together."

Indeed, the women are like sisters, bound by a special fate: Between 1942 and 1944, when they were twelve to fourteen years old, they lived in Room 28, Girls' Home, L 410, Theresienstadt, a fortress town near Prague. They were prisoners of the ghetto, a small group of the 75,666 Jews from the so-called Protectorate of Bohemia and Moravia who, with the incursion of German troops into their country, lost their homes, their prop-erty, and their freedom.

In Room 28, their paths crossed with those of about fifty other girls. They spent their lives, day and night, together in the closest of quarters — thirty girls at any given time confined to approximately 325 square feet. They slept on narrow two- and three-bed wooden bunks, ate their meager rations together, and listened as their counselors read to them when evening fell. Once the lights were out, they would talk about their experiences and share their thoughts and dreams, their worries and their fears.

Time and again, some of the girls would suddenly be torn from their midst and forced to join one of the dreaded transports to the East. New girls would arrive in Room 28 and grow accustomed to this community that had been created by force. New friendships formed, only to be torn asunder again by the next transports — the word itself a metaphor for the constant fear that dominated their daily lives. Under the increasing pressure of these threatening events, the girls would cling together all the more tightly. And then, in the fall of 1944, a devastating wave of transports carried off almost all the girls and boys, putting an end to the children's homes and to Room 28.

It was at that time that Eva Fischl wrote in the album of her friend Flaška, as Anna Flach was lovingly nicknamed by her friends: "When the day comes that you are back in Brno and you are eating a fish,

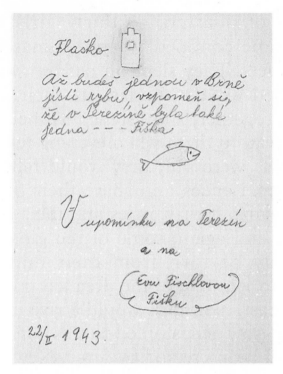

Eva Fischl's page in Anna Flach's album

remember that in Theresienstadt there was also a little fish. Your Eva Fischlová. Fišku." And with a few pencil strokes she added a picture of a fish. Little Ruth Schächter, whom everyone called Zajíček ("Rabbit"), dedicated these words to her: "Don't forget the girl who wrote this, and lovingly stuck by you. Your —"; and here she drew a mother rabbit with seven bunnies, followed by: "Dear Flaška: Will you always remember who lay beside you? And was your good friend????????"

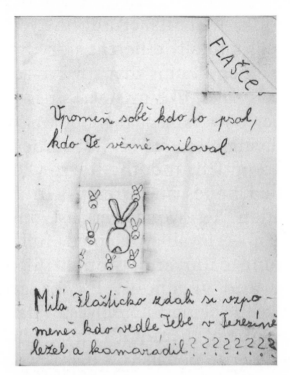

Ruth Schächter's page in Anna Flach's album

At first glance, Anna Flach's little album isn't much different from the kind that many girls keep at that age. Here, too, one finds aphorisms like this one from Goethe: "Relish your good moods, for they are rare." And dedications from friends and relatives: "All the best for your future. Your Aunt Ella in Vienna. July 23, 1940." And a steady stream of pictures and sketches: colorful flowers, a squirrel, a girl peeking through a keyhole, a puppy, an idyllic village street. Only gradually does it dawn on us that this little book, with its crumbling yellowed pages, tells a totally different story from that of most other albums that survive solely for nostalgia's sake, like my own. It is obvious that other powers kept this book alive. In it are the living memoirs of the murdered girls from Room 28 and the sorrow of their unfulfilled hopes and dreams. In Flaška's imagination these youngsters live on as they were then — lovable, talented, full of fantasy, some calm and thoughtful, others athletic and vivacious. Flaška and her friends keep asking themselves: What would have become of them? Of Lenka, who wrote such wonderful poems? Of Fiška, who came up with witty sketches and loved the stage? Of Helena, with her talent for drawing and painting? Of Maria, with her beautiful voice? Of Muška, Olile, Zdenka, Pavla, Hana, Poppinka, and sweet little Zajíček, who was so helpless and in need of protection?

The past lives on. "You can't forget it," says Judith Schwarzbart. "You live with it every day without talking about it, or even giving it a conscious thought. But then all at once something happens. It can come unexpectedly, out of the blue. A remark, a bit of food, a day of remembrance, anything — and suddenly it's all there again. But only just parts of it, never everything at once."

The past comes especially alive when these friends gather, and even more so when they celebrate together. As their annual reunion usually takes place around Rosh Hashanah, the Jewish New Year, and coincides with several of their birthdays as well, there's plenty of reason to celebrate. Flowers and candles adorn the festively set table, there are little speeches and toasts, and gifts are exchanged. Later in the evening the lively conversation is increasingly drowned out by song. And finally all of them sing the songs of their childhood in the Theresienstadt ghetto — Czech folk songs, Zionist anthems, songs from the children's opera *Brundibár.*

A unique atmosphere fills the room at such moments — a blend of gaiety and gravity, of love and friendship, and of gratitude as well. We are thankful, they seem to be saying, that we have our families, that we are mothers and grandmothers, that after all we have gone through, many of our wishes have come true. Their joy is enhanced by the fact that with the end of the Communist era, they are finally able to come together with their relatives and friends in their beloved Czech homeland.

Yet it is at just such moments that the women are aware of how many of their childhood friends cannot share their good fortune. For in their hearts and thoughts these friends are still present. They belong to them just as their own childhood belongs to them.

Anna Flach's album is no mere memento; it is a mission. She sees it as her personal responsibility to keep alive the memory of the murdered girls of Room 28. Whenever she leafs through the pages — and apparently she does so quite often — she sees these girls in her mind's eye, hears their voices, gazes into their sad eyes. *Don't forget me,* they seem to call to her from the past. *Do you remember how we swore to be faithful to one another forever?*

"On one of the first Sundays after the war we shall wait for each other under the Bell Tower in the Old Town Square in Prague." This is what Flaška and her comrades had promised one another when they had to say goodbye in Theresienstadt. They reinforced their promise with words that resonated like an incantation and a secret password.

You believe me, I believe you.
You know what I know.

Whatever may happen,
you won't betray me,
I won't betray you.

They were a community sworn to loyalty and friendship, with its own motto, emblem, hymn, and flag. The flag displays two clasped hands set in a circle. The emblem, which they called the *ma'agal* (the Hebrew word for "circle"), was a symbol of perfection and of the ideals they strove to live by. But what united them above all was their desire for Germany's defeat and their hope that the war would finally end.

Today, more than half a century later, the girls of Room 28 are among the very few who still remember the girls who did not survive.

"We always bring them to mind," Ela Weissberger (née Stein) says on one of our walks in Spindlermühle. "Every time I speak to an audience in America I ask them to join me for a moment in remembering these girls, and all the children of Theresienstadt. Because no one knows these children apart from us, the few who survived. We have them in our thoughts and our hearts, and we see them before us: their faces, their eyes, their personalities, and everything that we experienced with them. That's why we are eager for this book to be published. And we hope that someday we will come together and dedicate the book to younger generations and to future generations, and send them on their way with our wishes for a better life. We hope that they may see that we did our best to pass on our memories and the love that comes with these memories: the love that the adults — our counselors and teachers, the artists, and so many others — gave us in those black days. I believe that a great many children today could use the kind of love we knew back then."

I got to know Ela Weissberger in America in 1996. She was the first eyewitness I sought out in my attempt to learn more about *Brundibár,* the children's opera that was performed in Theresienstadt fifty-five times in 1943 and 1944. An old friend, Frank Harders-Wuthenow, had piqued my interest. A member of the artistic staff of the Bielefeld Opera in Germany, he had discovered *Brundibár* in Prague and brought it to the stage in 1992.[1] From the moment he told me about the opera, questions about its history and the fate of the children who had performed in it never left my mind. And one day, as I held a *Brundibár* program in my hand, I settled on a plan: I would produce a radio documentary on the history of *Brundibár*. Luckily, the special features division of Radio Free Berlin accepted my proposal, and soon afterward I set out to investigate the story.[2]

In the Theresienstadt performances of *Brundibár,* Ela had played the cat, one of the lead roles in this lovely children's opera, originally composed in Prague just before the outbreak of World War II. The creators of *Brundibár,* the Czech composer Hans Krása and his friend, the artist and writer Adolf Hoffmeister, could not possibly have imagined that their work would premiere a few years later in a concentration camp, with an ensemble of young Jewish prisoners. Nor could they have imagined what their work would come to mean to these children and to all ghetto inmates: a symbol of hope and resistance, of faith that good would triumph over evil.

No one living in Prague in 1938 could have fathomed what Hans Krása, a prisoner in the ghetto from 1942 to 1944, was forced to witness with his own eyes: how his opera, along with other art and culture in Theresienstadt, was exploited by the Nazis in their pernicious propaganda operations. Who could ever have imagined that such a thing was possible? That one day the history

25

of a children's opera would also be the story of an infamous deception and of the cruel murder of Jewish children?

My conversation with Ela revealed something surprising. When I raised the topic of *Brundibár,* her eyes sparkled. The very word seemed to prompt a veritable stream of consciousness — a phenomenon I would encounter over and over in my research. Quite evidently, *Brundibár* is a magic word that enlivens heart and soul, and conjures images of bygone times. They were nightmarish, yet *Brundibár* imbued them with visions of a more humane, cultured, and hopeful world.

The hours with Ela passed too quickly, and I left with a strong sense that I had heard only the beginning of a gripping and important story. But how was I to proceed? How could I find out more? As if she had read my mind, Ela said: "I'll be going to Prague again in September. I'll be seeing my old friends there. If you like, you can join us."

Before long, I was able to meet Ela's friends from Room 28 in Prague — an encounter that led to many others in their homes in Brno, Vienna, Israel, and England. I learned about their childhoods, their experiences in Theresienstadt, and the period after they were transported to the East, to Auschwitz, where so many vanished from their midst. The abyss of horror into which these young people gazed on their journey through hell, the cataclysm that tore at their souls — never before had I experienced the tragedy of the Holocaust so directly and starkly as during those meetings. My sense of time seemed to have been suspended, the lines that normally separate today from yesterday suddenly appeared random and irrelevant, and I was all too painfully aware of the truth that we never leave the past behind. "If we had stayed in Room 28 until the end of the war, I think many things would have turned out differently." I clearly remember Judith Schwarzbart's words: "We would be happier people today. But most of us had to leave on the transports. And what happened then was so terrible that you just want to forget it."

It was during these interviews that I realized that I had to do everything in my power to pass on the torch of memory. This book draws primarily on the experiences of ten of the fifteen surviving girls from Room 28, who took part in our annual September meetings: Anna Flach, Helga Pollak, Ela

Stein, Judith Schwarzbart, Eva Landa, Marta Fröhlich, Hanka Wertheimer, Handa Pollak, Eva Winkler, and Vera Nath. Two former counselors, Eva Weiss, from England, and Eva Eckstein, from Sweden, happily joined these gatherings with "their girls" when their health permitted. Three of the girls — Eva Stern, Marianne Deutsch, and Eva Kohn — opted not to participate in the annual reunion in Spindlermühle. But Eva Stern and Marianne Deutsch welcomed me into their homes. Eva Heller and Marianne Rosenzweig, both of whom live in America, would have liked to come to Spindlermühle, but were unable to do so.

I consider myself extremely fortunate to have become part of this circle of friends and to have witnessed their happiness at being together. It has taught me a remarkable lesson: In recalling periods marked by the deepest of horrors, memory can be merciful, and happy recollections can be extracted and sheltered within our hearts, providing strength during times of adversity. Moreover, it is even possible to share and pass on this healing energy, provided that, like the girls of Room 28, we base our lives, against all odds, on the principle of love.

"When I think of those truly evil years of

The finale of the children's opera Brundibár. *This still is from the infamous Nazi propaganda film about Theresienstadt directed by Kurt Gerron (1944), unofficially dubbed* The Führer Gives the Jews a City.

the war and the Holocaust, one bright, shining point of light always emerges in my memory — our Children's Home in the ghetto, our Room 28," recalls Eva Landa. "I was in Theresienstadt for eighteen months. That isn't long in the life of an adult, but in the life of a twelve-year-old, it is practically an eternity.

"I came to Theresienstadt in 1942, when I was eleven. By the time I left the ghetto on

29

a transport to Auschwitz in December 1943, I felt almost grown up. Parting from Theresienstadt was very hard for me. I left behind my friends and the community we had fashioned with so much care. However, I took with me the memories of our striving for a better and more just world. I did my best to be brave and not to betray our ideals.

"Our little community helped me to overcome many hardships. Sadly, only fifteen girls from Room 28 were fortunate enough to survive. In the 'Theresienstadt Hymn,' we all sang: 'If you wish, you will succeed, hand in hand we'll be as one, on the ghetto ruins we'll all laugh one day.' These prophecies never came true. No one could laugh on those ruins. But we who survived remember our childhood in Room 28 of the children's home at Theresienstadt with a gentle smile."

"How did we handle it?" Judith Schwarzbart wonders. "How did we manage to get along and help one another — about thirty girls at that difficult age between twelve and fourteen? Why did we voluntarily attend to our studies? How did we keep our room clean and our hair washed under such trying circumstances? I now realize that our counselor Tella pulled off a miracle, as did the other counselors."

"They were like second mothers to us," Flaška says. "Room 28 was a little island that protected us and made it easier for us to bear the loss of our homes — and in many cases, the separation from one or both parents."

The adults who were responsible for caring for the children did everything they could to create a refuge for them. "We wanted to make a home for our youngsters, a place where they were taken seriously, where they were allowed to be young, where they weren't constantly confronted with the major issues of the day," Fredy Hirsch, the legendary Zionist youth leader, wrote in mid-1943, one year after the children's homes were established. "We wanted to give them a reasonably lovely place to call home in the midst of misery piled upon misery."[3]

No one could have predicted what lay ahead for the prisoners in Theresienstadt. They could only hope that they would survive until the war was over, and in the meantime try to prepare for that day, both physically and mentally. "Over the last year and a half we have seen traditionally inviolable notions of human society reevaluated in a way that many of us do not understand," Fredy wrote. "In this world we built

31

Children's Homes. The attempt had to be made to rescue children from the devaluation of what is good." And he concluded with these words: "I believe that someday these children will look back fondly on the home that we tried to provide for them in Theresienstadt. How terrible it would be if Theresienstadt were to represent an irrevocable spiritual and physical defeat for our youth."[4]

It is horrifying to contemplate that the lives of most of the children of Theresienstadt ended in the gas chambers of Auschwitz; still, it is comforting to know that Fredy Hirsch's hopes found fulfillment in the lives of those children who survived.

"It was truly a privilege to live in the Girls' Home, L 410," Marianne Rosenzweig writes. "I consider the time I spent in Room 28 the best time in Theresienstadt. Although we were young, and although hunger, cold, and fear defined our lives, we remained honest and decent and always had high moral values. And we developed very deep friendships of the sort that would have scarcely been possible under normal circumstances."

"I believe that Room 28 made me a tolerant person capable of forming friendships with a wide range of people," says Handa Pollak. "We lived in a little room with about thirty children, and we all came from very different backgrounds. Some were spoiled, some were quarrelsome, some egotistic, some good, and some less so — but that's how life is. Everyone has a different character. And we learned to get along, to listen to one another. We learned to live together — because there was no other choice."

Flaška's album contains the following words, which were written in farewell by Margit Mühlstein, a social worker in the Girls' Home. They would become Flaška's guiding principle in all her actions: "Our years in Theresienstadt will have been for nothing if we ever oppress so much as a single person in our own lives."

It seems as though there was no other place in those days where education was taken more seriously and where pedagogical ideas and goals were put into practice with more determination than in Theresienstadt. Part of the reason was, of course, the unique situation that had forcibly confined almost the entire Jewish population of a nation, including its intellectual elite (artists, teachers, scientists, Zionist activists). The key to this educational success was the combined effort of adults who valued the children's well-being over their own lives. Among them were Fredy Hirsch, Walter Eisinger, Rudi Freudenfeld, Ilse Weber, Kamilla Rosenbaum, Ella Pollak, and the Viennese artist and art instructor Friedl Dicker-Brandeis, from whose classes at Theresienstadt more than three thousand children's drawings were saved.

"There is a certain irony of fate," writes historian Livia Rothkirchen, "in the fact that the coerced society of Theresienstadt struck the final chord in a life shared by three ethnic elements — the Czech, German, and Jewish communities — that had influenced and enriched one another on Bohemian soil for several centuries and that had played a significant role in the development of the culture of European thought. . . . Wrenched from the nourishing soil of their homelands and placed in the most difficult circumstances, Czech and German Jews, generally thought to be assimilated and incapable of defending themselves against the Nazis, found their way back to their own human and spiritual values in Theresienstadt, of all places."[5]

What remains are the works of those who contributed to the unique cultural milieu of Theresienstadt, to striking this last chord in so resounding a fashion that even today, some sixty years later, its echo can still be heard in the works of musicians and composers such as Viktor Ullmann, Gideon Klein, Hans Krása, Pavel Haas, Rafael Schächter, and Karel Ančerl; in the works of artists such as Otto Ungar, Leo Haas, Bedřich Fritta, Peter Kien, Karel Fleischmann, and Alfred Kantor; in the cabaret songs and poems of Karel Švenk, Leo Strauss, and Walter Lindenbaum. And it is captured in unforgettable performances — of Giuseppe Verdi's *Requiem* and of Hans Krása's children's opera, *Brundibár* — which embody the essence of the culture of Theresienstadt.

Those who were children at the time could not possibly have fathomed the almost superhuman determination needed to create this cultural environment. Still, many of them would surely have grasped the meaning of Viktor Ullmann's words: "I must emphasize that in no sense did we sit weeping by the rivers of Babylon, but, instead, our will to create culture matched our will to live." But to understand what extraordinary powers these adults had to summon to realize these outstanding achievements while gazing into the abyss — this was most certainly beyond the realm of a child's comprehension.

Only years later would they be able to make sense of an old parable that was known among some of the ghetto inmates: The inhabitants of a valley are told that within two days their hometown will be flooded by a natural catastrophe. There is no escape. No chance to be rescued. So the rabbi calls his faithful to the synagogue and tells them: "Ladies and gentlemen, we have exactly forty-eight hours to learn how to live under water."

This book recounts these "forty-eight hours." While enduring unimaginable suffering, the children of Theresienstadt also studied, played, danced, sang, did gymnastics, created art, wrote poems, and appeared in theatrical productions. This is why many of those who survived, particularly those whose road to survival also took them through the death camps, remember Theresienstadt as a last instance of humanity, a place where there was still love, education, art, and culture.

The renowned musician and conductor Karel Ančerl, one of the few musicians in Theresienstadt who survived the Holocaust, wrote in his memoirs: "Yes, the Nazis almost succeeded in exterminating the Jews. However, they did not succeed in exterminating the idea of the human dimension of humanity."[6]

Abraham Weingarten, Hanka's husband, captured the spirit of this book when he said to me in Spindlermühle: "We are witnesses to a miracle. Everyone here, apart from you and me, experienced the Holocaust first-hand and survived. Those girls are now grandmothers. Each has a unique personality, temperament, and outlook, and each has traveled a different road. But despite all these differences and despite the scars that life has left on them, just look at how cheerful they all are, how they laugh and sing, how happy they are here together. Life has proved stronger. Isn't that a miracle?"

CHAPTER TWO:
SAYING GOODBYE

One day in late August 1938, a little brown-haired girl stood frozen in place on the balcony of an old apartment house in a desolate neighborhood of the Moravian capital city of Brno, her gaze fixed on a figure that was slowly walking away. Her eyes remained riveted to the spot long after the figure had vanished from sight. After what seemed an eternity, time that is etched into her memory, she went back inside, into a large dim room in a musty old building that now served as a boardinghouse. Sobbing, she buried herself in one of the empty beds in the deserted room. Her world was falling apart.

Helga Pollak was eight years old when she left Vienna and became a stranger in a strange land, when her childhood came to an end in an inhospitable boardinghouse in Brno, when she said goodbye to her mother, unaware that more than eight years would

Helga Pollak, circa 1941

elapse before they would be reunited.
Czechoslovakia (as it was called then) was
still a country at peace. To Helga's mind,
the ever-increasing persecution of Jews that
she had experienced in Vienna was not a
serious danger, or at least not a life-
threatening one. She was only vaguely aware
of the fact that she was Jewish.

More than sixty years later, these images
live on in Helga Pollak's memory. "At the
end of August, my mother, who had come

from Vienna to Kyjov, where I was spending the summer, brought me to a boardinghouse in Brno. I can still see her walking away. I was standing on a balcony, watching her go. I wept. No one in that gloomy boarding-house paid any attention to me. The young women who were living there like me, in a sublet room containing four or five beds, were, I suppose, working somewhere or attending classes. They all spoke Czech. The only person who was around during the morning was a maid from the countryside, but she didn't speak to me, either. How could she have? I didn't speak Czech back then, and she didn't know any German. I felt totally abandoned."

Up to this point, nothing in her life had ever hinted that anything like this could happen. Born in Vienna on May 28, 1930, the only child of Otto and Frieda Pollak, Helga had led a sheltered childhood. Her father was the owner of a large and well-known concert café on Mariahilfer Strasse called the Palmhof. She had grown up in a spacious apartment in the same building, and had been tenderly cared for by her mother and her governess, Johanna. The adults kept her out of the café in her early years. "Going to the café was something very special for me," she recalls.

The Palmhof, a concert café Otto Pollak operated with his brother Karl from 1919 to 1938

Otto Pollak, who came from the southern Moravian town of Kyjov/Gaya,[1] had moved to Vienna and joined the army in 1916, where he saw action in a field artillery unit and was so severely wounded that one leg had to be amputated. A disabled veteran, he was awarded a silver medal for bravery, first

41

and second class, at the end of World War I — a circumstance that would later save his life.

In 1919 Otto and his brother Karl opened the Palmhof in Vienna and devoted great energy to running it. Otto loved the café atmosphere and personally waited on his guests, among them prominent artists such as the operetta composer Franz Léhar, the tenor Richard Tauber, and the actors Hans Moser and Fritz Imhof. Well-known musical groups often performed there, and the concerts were broadcast live weekly on RAVAG, the Austrian radio station. Once a year, Otto went in search of performers, both throughout Austria and abroad. Sometimes the musicians he discovered would make their Viennese debut at the Palmhof, then go on to play in major symphony orchestras.

Vienna became Otto Pollak's second home, and he felt so closely bound to it that even when dangerous times loomed, it took quite a while before he seriously considered leaving Austria — although there were ample reasons to do so. As early as 1934 — in connection with an attempted putsch by Austrian National Socialists and the assassination of Engelbert Dollfuss, the Austrian chancellor — the Palmhof became a target of vandalism by members of the then-illegal Austrian Nazi Party. Two attacks were carried out against the café, the first a smoke bomb that went off in the checkroom during a Sunday tea dance, and the second an incendiary bomb that exploded beside a cellar window in the middle of the night. "I'll never forget the blast of that bomb," says Helga. "I was four years old at the time. The bomb could have caused devastating damage, and it was only due to good luck and the fact that it was so poorly positioned that no one was injured and no more serious damage was done to the building. But many windows were shattered."

Four years later, the situation in Austria had come to a head. In the meantime, Otto Pollak and his wife, Frieda, who was fourteen years his junior, had divorced amicably. Helga remained with her father in his apartment on Mariahilfer Strasse. Her mother, who had taken an apartment of her own, visited her every day and continued to assist Otto Pollak in running the Palmhof. But it was the governess, Johanna, who looked after Helga most of the time and became a second mother to her.

That is why Helga always associates the memory of two crucial events with the image of her governess. The first took place on the evening of March 11, 1938. "I was in the living room. Johanna had turned on the radio and was listening intently to a speech. It was the abdication speech of Kurt Schuschnigg, the Austrian chancellor. I can still remember his final words precisely — 'May God protect Austria,' he implored. That was the first time I ever saw Johanna cry."

Early the next morning, Helga stood with her governess at the window overlooking Mariahilfer Strasse. "I saw soldiers marching up the street. And there were lots of swastika banners hanging from the windows of other buildings. An officer came up to my father and asked whether he would serve the soldiers. And my father said, 'No. This is a Jewish business.' To which the officer replied that this was of no interest to him; he cared only about his men. Suddenly the café was full of soldiers. A few days later, the Palmhof was shut down."

With the appearance of German troops, greeted jubilantly by a majority of the population, a new and invigorating self-confidence blossomed in the hearts of thousands of Austrians, a feeling fueled by hatred of *jüdische Untermenschen* ("Jewish subhumans") and by pride in belonging to the *arische Herrenrasse* ("Aryan master race") that had come to power. In an instant, the anti-Semitism that had been smoldering for decades became a raging wildfire that spread across the country with pogrom-like excesses. Jews were harassed, mistreated, and beaten. Eventually, they were fired from their jobs, robbed of their possessions, and expelled. The scale of Nazi terror on Austrian soil assumed even greater proportions than the attacks then rampant in Germany. Thousands fled across Austria's borders or scrambled to get visas so they could emigrate.

Until then, religion had not played a significant role in the lives of the Pollaks. They were assimilated, liberal Jews, and they rarely celebrated Jewish holidays. Helga's first sustained encounter with Judaism was during the Jewish religious instruction class she attended in grammar school. But now, in these changing times, her parents gave serious thought to their Jewish roots. In April 1938 Otto, Frieda, and Helga Pollak attended synagogue for the first time and participated in a Passover seder.

In order to assert control over the random acts of terror, the new rulers launched official actions of their own. A first transport of 151 Austrians, a group of so-called *Schutzhäftlinge* ("prisoners in protective custody"), among them sixty Jews, had already reached the Dachau concentration camp. In May two thousand more Jews were arrested and taken to various concentration camps. On May 20, 1938, the Nuremberg Race Laws were implemented in Austria as well. Now violence and fear began to dominate everyday life.

However much Helga's parents tried to shield her from the darkness of this new time, each day Helga felt it creep farther into her life. Jewish students had to sit on special "Jewish benches" in school. Children who had previously been friendly with Helga now turned their backs on her. The mob controlled the streets. "One day on the way home from school, a couple of boys I didn't know blocked my way and shouted, 'You Jewish pig!' I remember that I was crying and that a policeman — it was Herr Lahner, who lived in our building — took me by the hand and comforted me and walked me home."

Helga's teacher, Dora Neuss, still treated her with affection. At the end of the school year she wrote in Helga's poetry album: "When fate turns against you, don't fret. The moon must wane before it can wax again. Your teacher, Dora Neuss, who will miss her little laughing dove very much."

That year, Helga could hardly wait for summer vacation to begin. She usually spent it with her father's family in Kyjov, near the Austrian border. There, in a stately house on Market Square, lived her grandmother Sophie, together with her father's sister, Aunt Marta, Marta's husband, Uncle Fritz, and their two children, Trude and Josef, whom everyone called Joši. Trude was fifteen, and Joši was twelve. Helga would play with them and the neighborhood children in the big yard behind the house, where there were chickens, a rabbit hutch, and a large shed with all sorts of tools.

More than ever, Helga found her thoughts racing ahead to the summer. Kyjov was an enticing adventure; even the little shop that Aunt Marta ran in the house was great fun. "There were all sorts of intriguing things there: sewing needles, sweaters, toys, baby carriages. At Christmas she displayed dolls in the shop window, and in the storage room in the back, the boxes of dolls were stacked to the ceiling — one doll prettier than the next. Sometimes my aunt would tell me to pick one out. That made me happy — for me, Kyjov was a magical place."

This was true in 1938 as well. Helga spent the last lovely summer of her childhood there. Then, at the end of August, her mother came to see her, bringing two momentous decisions along with her baggage. In view of the disastrous events befalling the Jews of Austria, Helga's parents had decided that she would stay for a while with their relatives in Kyjor. But because she did not speak any Czech, she would have to attend the German school in Brno and live there during the school year — on her own, in a boardinghouse if need be. Frieda tried to make her eight-year-old daughter understand that this was for her own good: to keep her safe from the persecutions in Vienna, and to ensure that she continued to receive a good education so she would have a good future.

A few days later, mother and daughter left for Brno. Once Frieda had the feeling that Helga would be well taken care of at the boardinghouse, she bid her goodbye. "You're a smart girl, you'll manage," she said, trying to instill courage in her daughter. And with that, she left. What had begun as a carefree summer vacation turned into an exile.

Helga spent the ensuing days in a state of apathy. If someone addressed her, she was unable to reply. Even if she had been able to speak Czech, she could not have explained her predicament, because she did not understand it herself. She began to sink into a deep depression.

Informed of this by the owners of the boardinghouse, Helga's father, with the help of his relatives in Kyjov, quickly found a family to take her in, but nothing really changed for Helga. "The Wittmanns were a distinguished family, living in a beautiful apartment. They were really very kind to me. But I always felt like a stranger. And I wasn't allowed to speak with their fourteen-year-old daughter. I wasn't even allowed in her room to play with her toys."

About two weeks later, someone near and dear to her finally arrived. Her cousin Joši came for a visit with one of his friends, and the two boys took Helga to the movies. As they were saying goodbye, Helga burst into tears. How she longed to go back with them to Kyjov! Luckily, when Joši returned home, he convinced his parents to send a telegram to Helga's father in Vienna, telling him about Helga's distress.

The very next day, Otto Pollak took the train to Brno. "It was a beautiful day; the sun was shining. My father's visit came as a complete surprise. No one had said a word to me. I can see him before me, sitting on a park bench, trying to decide what he should do, while I did my best to persuade him to take me back to Kyjov."

That evening, Otto wrote a letter to Helga's mother.

Brno, September 11, 1938

Dear Frieda,

. . . Frau Wittmann went upstairs to announce my arrival to Helga. An indescribable cry of joy echoed through the stairwell. Helga, in a new summer dress, white shoes, and stockings, ran down the steps toward me.

There are no words for our joy at seeing each other again. Frau Wittmann left us alone. Helga stood in front of me and said with a serious look on her sweet young face: "I've been thinking, Papa, that the moment you stood before me I would tell you that I don't want to stay here any longer. I just want to be in Vienna with my parents or in Kyjov with Aunt Marta."

There is no describing the mature and collected way the eight-year-old little imp had thought things through, and the depth of soul she revealed.

Tears kept coming to her eyes, and as I sat down out in front of the house she said to me: "For all I care they can take away all the parks in Vienna. I'd rather be at home just spinning in circles in a corner of my room than running around in a park here. When Mama left, I tried hard not to cry so that she wouldn't be so sad on the train. But I cried afterwards."

When I told her that Ilse Kalinhof had gone to Palestine, she declared that she'd rather be a little beggar girl traveling the world with her parents than a rich girl living with strangers. She asked about Helga Weiss, and said: "She's lucky; she can be with her parents."

Then she told me that Joši had visited her and that she couldn't help crying when they said goodbye. And when I asked whether Joši had cried, too, she said that he was very sad, but that he hadn't ever had to live with strangers.

It went on like that for hours. It took everything in my power to stand firm when she begged me to make a decision. I shall wait a few days so that I can figure out in peace and quiet, rather than in the heat of the moment, what measures to take regarding the future of this extraordinary child. I sat in the dark outside the house with a heavy heart and gazed for a long time up at the brightly lit window of what I assumed was the room of my girl, who

Postcard from Frieda Pollak to her daughter Helga: "Ostende, March 25, 1939. My darling little girl! In an hour this beautiful little ship will take me across to England. You will soon be making the same journey,

means everything to me . . .

Warmest wishes, your Otto

Two days later, the decision had been made. "We took a taxi all the way from Brno to Kyjov — I was overjoyed! I bounced up and down until my head banged against the roof of the car — that's how happy I was! I can still see the landscape as it passed by us."

Because of the language barrier, Helga had to repeat the second grade. But she didn't care. She was glad to be with her relatives again. She learned Czech easily, made rapid progress in school, and soon felt very much at home in Kyjov.

Under the care of her relatives, Helga barely noticed the menacing events that were brewing in Europe. She was too young to grasp the impact of the disastrous Munich Agreement signed by Germany, France, Italy, and the United Kingdom in September 1938, followed by Hitler's occupation of the Sudetenland, a predominantly German-speaking area on the fringes

---

and then you will be just as happy as I am now. A thousand kisses for my darling and my warmest greetings to your dear Aunt Marta, Grandma, Uncle Fritz, Uncle Karl, Marienka, Trudel and Joši. Your Mama."

of Czechoslovakia.[2] And she could not see the imminent danger in the German army's advance into the vicinity of Kyjov. But she did notice that with each passing day people were becoming increasingly restless and frightened.

When, on March 15, 1939, the Wehrmacht formally occupied the so-called rest of Czechia and set up what they called the Protectorate of Bohemia and Moravia, not much changed for Helga and her family right away. Far more dispiriting was a postcard she received from her mother, who was on her way to England.

On June 21, 1939, the anti-Semitic Nuremberg Race Laws, which had been enacted in Germany on September 15, 1935, were instituted in the Protectorate of Bohemia and Moravia as well, and Helga was becoming increasingly caught up in the fate from which her parents had tried so desperately to shield her. But there were still ways to leave the country. Jewish organizations such as Hechalutz and Youth Aliyah offered agricultural training abroad and thus managed to help young people escape to Great Britain, Denmark, and the Netherlands. Children's transports were also being organized to bring thousands of young refugees to England. Helga was scheduled to leave from Prague on one of the upcoming children's transports.

In the summer of 1939 a seamstress even came to the house to take Helga's measurements and provide a wardrobe for her trip to Great Britain. Helga got new skirts and blouses, a dress, and a coat, each with her name sewn into it in case something went wrong and she landed in a children's home instead of joining her mother right away.

But in the early hours of September 1, 1939, the German battle cruiser *Schleswig-Holstein* opened fire on the Westerplatte Peninsula near Gdansk. The German army invaded Poland, and World War II began. New laws were passed that reduced the freedom of movement for Jews, one decree at a time, to an absolute minimum. Then the borders closed, and Helga's dream of a journey to England was shattered.

One year later — Helga had just completed the third grade — Jewish children were expelled from public schools. Once again her family found it necessary to send Helga back to Brno, this time because the Jewish school there was now the only type of school she was still allowed to attend. In order to ensure that Helga got the best possible care, her family placed her in the local

Jewish orphanage, where she met a good many other children in a similar situation. Helga's uncle delivered her to the orphanage shortly before the school year started.

"It was a nightmare. No one was there to receive me, no counselor, no office or service employee, no one at all. I slept in a large, dark room surrounded by about forty empty metal beds. Many children, I learned later, were in the hospital with scarlet fever; others were still on vacation."

After a few days the children returned. But Helga's situation did not improve. "We didn't have much to eat. To get anything in the morning you had to run to the kitchen, where two serving girls doled out bread. That was all we got, dry bread, and maybe, if you were among the first, a little marmalade. Sometimes my cousin Joši, who by then was also attending school in Brno, waited for me after classes to give me a little wedge of cheese. I couldn't stand it in that orphanage. I wanted out no matter what."

Helga got her way and eventually found shelter with a couple who lived near the Jewish school. The woman took care of her young boarder lovingly, and Helga soon felt comfortable there, especially because Ruth Steiner — a girl her age, the daughter of an ophthalmologist — lived nearby. She became Helga's first friend.

Then came the spring of 1941, and with it a decree that made it illegal for Jews in the Protectorate to travel. Without asking anyone, Helga packed her things, went to the train station, and bought a ticket to Kyjov. It was still light when she arrived at her relatives' home toward evening. Her aunt was feeding the chickens in the yard and was astonished when she suddenly saw Helga standing in front of her, clutching her suitcase. "Here I am again," she said.

In the spring of 1941 Otto Pollak was still living in Vienna. His café had been Aryanized and his assets confiscated. He had been forced to give up his beautiful home on Mariahilfer Strasse, along with its valuable furniture, and to move to another place. He had witnessed the Kristallnacht pogrom of November 9–10, 1938, when forty-two synagogues and small houses of worship in Vienna were set on fire and plundered, and countless Jewish businesses and homes were confiscated or destroyed. Of the 6,547 Viennese Jews arrested that night, approximately 3,700 ended up in the Dachau concentration camp; some were murdered on the spot.

The Nazi terror triggered a mass exodus

57

of Jews from Austria. By May 1938, one hundred thousand had fled the country, many of them escaping illegally to neighboring countries. With the outbreak of World War II, Jews still living in Germany and Austria found that almost all their escape routes had been cut off.

Meanwhile, Poland, with its Jewish population of more than three million, quickly became a laboratory for the Nazis' anti-Jewish policies. Early experiments in uprooting Jews throughout the country evolved into a strategy of forcing them into ghettos established in towns and cities. By late 1941 the Nazis were experimenting with ways to get rid of the weakest and, for them, least productive Jews in these ghettos. They perpetrated the first murders of such people — using gas, in specially adapted trucks — in December 1941 in Chelmno, not far from the large ghetto in the city of Lodz.

At the same time, an even more threatening new type of Nazi anti-Semitism had begun with the invasion of the Soviet Union in June 1941. Mass shootings of Jewish men and boys of military age were now commonplace, and soon expanded to include women and children. Hundreds of thousands died in this way within months. By the fall of 1941, the Nazis had begun deporting Jews from Germany by train to the ghettos and the new killing fields of the East. A war of conquest and annihilation unprecedented in history would leave twenty-seven million Soviet citizens dead and come very close to bringing about the realization of Hitler's "Final Solution."

Otto Pollak barely escaped deportation in the summer of 1941. He had received no transport order, but was simply seized on the street by the SS and forced onto a transport that was about to depart. Still, his luck held. At the last moment, a storm trooper who had frequented Otto's café pulled him off.

After this experience, Otto redoubled his efforts to leave Vienna for Kyjov. On September 2, 1941, the Viennese police granted him rare permission to resettle in the Protectorate of Bohemia and Moravia. A week later, he arrived in Kyjov. "I was tremendously happy," Helga recalls. "We were already living in very close quarters, since by then a great many Jewish children were residing in Kyjov. All the Jews from the neighboring areas had to resettle there. But we managed somehow."

People were forced to share their homes with other families. Apartments that had housed one family now sheltered several.

The house on Market Square was no exception. In one room Helga's cousin Trude, who had married and was expecting a child, was living with her husband, Hermann. Another room was occupied by a family named Taussig. Joši slept in the kitchen. The third room was shared by Aunt Marta and Uncle Fritz and, separated only by a folding screen, Helga and her father.

On September 19, 1941, a decree was issued ordering all Jews above the age of six living within the German Reich to wear a six-pointed yellow Star of David with the word *Jude* ("Jew") inscribed in black. "It is the Führer's wish," Heinrich Himmler wrote to SS *Obergruppenführer* Arthur Greiser, the Nazi governor of the Wartheland region, in a letter dated September 18, 1941, "that both the Old Reich and the Protectorate, moving from west to east, be emptied and freed of Jews as quickly as possible."[3]

Far from Kyjov, in Prague's beautiful old Hradschin castle, SS *Obergruppenführer* Reinhard Heydrich, the newly appointed *Stellvertretender Reichsprotektor* (deputy Reich protector), had set up his offices and convened a secret conference. At the first meeting, the participants, among them

Adolf Eichmann and Karl Hermann Frank, discussed actions to be taken regarding the Jewish population in the Protectorate. The minutes from the October 10, 1941, meeting include the following:

Concerning the possibility of creating ghettos within the Protectorate: . . . In Bohemia one option . . . is the occupation of Theresienstadt by the Central Office for Jewish Emigration. After evacuation from this temporary assembly camp (whereby the Jews will have already been severely decimated) to the East, the entire area could be expanded to build a model German settlement. . . .

The transport to Theresienstadt would not require much time, two to three trains with 1,000 persons each could be sent to Theresienstadt per day. . . . As well-tested methods have shown, the Jew can carry up to fifty kilos of nonbulky luggage and — in order to ease matters for ourselves — food for fourteen days and up to four weeks. Straw will be strewn in the empty rooms, because the installation of beds would occupy too much space.

The larger apartments in the good buildings are reserved solely for the

Gestapo, the Jewish Council of Elders, the Food Storage Office, and, of course, the guard units. The Jews will have to dig their own quarters in the ground . . .[4]

At a second meeting, on October 17, 1941, the following measures were agreed upon:

Concerning the Jewish Question:
. . . In the meantime, Jews from Bohemia and Moravia are to be collected in a provisional camp for later evacuation. . . . 50,000 to 60,000 Jews can be comfortably accommodated in Theresienstadt. From there the Jews will be sent to the East. Consent has already been obtained from Minsk and Riga for 5,000 Jews each.

After total evacuation of all Jews, Theresienstadt will be settled by Germans, following a precise plan and thereby becoming a core of German life. It is a very favorable location for this plan. Thus it will become yet another vanguard, perfectly modeled according to the ideas of the Reich Führer SS, as Reich Commissar for the Strengthening of the German People's National Identity.

Under no circumstances can even the slightest details of these plans reach the wider public.[5]

Also brought up during the discussions was the issue of creating a second temporary holding center, in addition to Theresienstadt, in order to evacuate the Jewish population of Moravia. "The expansion of an existing Jewish village into a ghetto for Moravia is quite possible and would present no great difficulties." It was Kyjov that they had in mind. But this measure soon proved unnecessary, given the speed at which transports of Jews from Theresienstadt were rolling eastward.

Deportation to the East, extermination through hard labor, the creation of regions free of Jews — these were the initial cornerstones of a Nazi program that ensnared the Jewish population of Central Europe in its deadly grip. After October 23, 1941, Jews within the Nazi sphere of influence were officially prohibited from emigrating. There was now almost no chance to escape.

In early December 1941 the Soviet Army's counteroffensive put an end to German hopes of a quick military victory in the East, and the Japanese surprise attack on Pearl

Harbor led to Germany's declaration of war on the United States on December 11, 1941. What was planned as a European blitzkrieg expanded into a war on a global scale. The moment for Hitler to rage against "the Jews" for conspiring to entrap Germany in a world war had come. The very next day, as Nazi propaganda minister Joseph Goebbels recorded in his diary, Hitler made it unmistakably clear to the party's senior representatives that as regards the "Jewish question," he was resolved "to make a clean sweep."

> He had prophesied to the Jews that if they ever brought about a world war again, they would experience their own annihilation. That was no empty phrase. The world war is here, and the annihilation of the Jews must necessarily follow. This question is to be regarded without sentimentality. We are not here to have sympathy with the Jews, but only with our German people. If the German people sacrifice the lives of another 160,000 men on the Eastern front, those who have caused this bloody conflict will have to pay for it with their own lives.[6]

Shortly thereafter, on January 20, 1942, a now-infamous secret conference took place in a villa in the Berlin suburb of Wannsee. Its purpose was to coordinate the efficient implementation of the Führer's wish for a "final solution to the Jewish question." The host was Reinhard Heydrich, head of the Reich Security Main Office, the central office overseeing the entire Nazi security and police apparatus. The invited guests, high-ranking SS officers and civilian officials in charge of the German Reich and its occupied territories, proved to be willing executioners. The entire Jewish population of Europe was now fated for extermination.

In the Czech lands, beginning in September 1941, Reinhard Heydrich had swiftly crushed a growing resistance. Four thousand Czechs were taken prisoner, and 402 were executed in the first few months of his rule.

The Czech government in exile in London, the Czech resistance back home, and the British secret services agreed on a daring retaliation. On May 27, 1942, Czech fighters attacked Heydrich's official car as it made its way into Prague. Heydrich was fatally wounded and died on June 4, 1942. After Heydrich's death, Hitler ordered brutal revenge. It fell upon a village ten miles west of Prague called Lidice, whose inhabitants were accused of helping the assassins. The buildings in Lidice were demolished, all the men were shot, and the women were sent to the Ravensbrück concentration camp. Most of the children were murdered in Chelmo.

The search for the conspirators expanded in all directions, including into Kyjov. "After Heydrich's assassination, all the residents of our house in Kyjov were ordered out into the courtyard late in the evening," Helga recalls. "It was already dark, and most were in their pajamas. The SS from the concentration camp at Svatobořice, where Czechs were imprisoned, searched all the apartments and beat up several people, including an aunt of my father's, Frieda Freud, who was handicapped and could barely walk, and thus brought the rage of the SS down on her."

By this point, Adolf Eichmann was presiding over the Jewish section of the Reich Main Security Office. He had already ordered the deportation of fifty-five thousand Jews from the territory of the Reich, which included "Ostmark," as Austria was called after its annexation, and the Protectorate of Bohemia and Moravia. Starting in March 1942, forty-five trains (twenty-four from Germany, six from Vienna, and fifteen from Theresienstadt), each carrying a thousand people, headed for ghettos that had been established in Lublin, Poland. The systematic deportation and murder of Jews was well under way.

The Jewish population of Kyjov had so far been spared in these transports, but everyone felt a sense of foreboding. They prepared themselves and took comfort in the thought that, as Czech Jews, they would most likely be resettled or, in the Nazis' official language, "evacuated" to the Theresienstadt ghetto. At least, they reasoned, it was a town in their native land, less than forty miles from Prague. With a little luck, they would be able to wait out the war there.

On July 27, 1942, the education of Jewish children was officially outlawed, and private instruction was secretly organized throughout the Protectorate. Helga and her friends were able to continue their education, and, despite the shadows cast by these dismal events and a sense that the walls were closing in on them, she still led something resembling a normal life. But this was not to last much longer.

In the winter of 1942–43, Helga opened for the first time the diary her father had given her and began to make entries.

This photograph shows Helga (second row, first child on the left) with her teachers and other pupils in her class in Kyjov. It was taken sometime during the second half of 1942, after schooling for Jewish children had been prohibited and could take place

Sunday, January 17, 1943

I've spent my last day in Kyjov, a day of hectic activity. We've packed our food in bread sacks and shopping bags. I doubt that my aunt has sat down for a single second today (she doesn't sit down anyway, even if she's not preparing to travel). I'm now sitting at my desk. I am very tired. But that doesn't matter! This is my last day at home, so I have to write about it! Within twelve hours the whole house will be deserted (I will not hang my head; I'm going to leave my home with head held high!). Now I'm going to sleep. I have to get up very early in the morning. I'll lie down with my clothes on, since I don't have anything left to cover up with.

Two days later, when Helga and her family arrived in Uhersky-Brod, she continued her account:

Tuesday, January 19, 1943

It was a miserable trip. I got up very early, but only just in time to get ready. I had so many clothes on I could hardly

---

only secretly in homes. Next to Helga is Jiri Bader (1930–1944), the son of a prominent Jewish family and a friend of Helga's. Like most of the people pictured here, he did not survive the war.

move. We used the sled to get to the train, with Uncle Karl, Maria, and me pulling, and with Papa, Aunt Trude, and Lea sitting on it. So much snow had fallen, we were glad just to make it to the train. We hastily searched for our luggage. Amazingly, there was little commotion. I thought everyone would be a lot more out of control. There wasn't enough room on the train to sit. My father fell trying to board. Frau Dr. Schönthal (who's not Jewish) helped him get up. She was sobbing.

As the train pulled out, we started to sing patriotic Czech songs. A policeman standing beside the train was very touched and walked the whole length of the train wishing every one he knew a safe and happy return. An hour and three quarters later we arrived in Uhersky-Brod. I didn't have to carry my rucksack there. We loaded it onto a truck. Papa, Trude, and Lea rode along, too.

By the time we arrived at the high school where we were quartered, I thought I'd collapse. Frau Webschovska brought me to my aunt. We're lying on mattresses.

Helga was feeling more and more miserable. The last days in Kyjov, the rigors of a trip in the cold and snow, and the conditions at the assembly camp had completely exhausted her. "It is awful here, probably even worse than in Theresienstadt," she noted on January 20. "The food makes you want to throw up, and I have a sore throat today. I saw the doctor and he gave me a powder to make me sweat."

Helga's condition grew worse. Early on the morning when they were to travel from Uhersky-Brod to Theresienstadt, her temperature reached 102.2 degrees and the doctor diagnosed tonsillitis. It was in this same condition that Helga arrived at eight o'clock on the morning of January 23 in Bohušovice, from which point they had to march to Theresienstadt, forty-five minutes away. "If the walk had lasted fifteen minutes longer," she later wrote, "I'm certain I would have collapsed."

In Theresienstadt, Helga and her family were assigned to an attic in the Hamburg Barracks, where the exhausted girl was finally able to stretch out on an old mattress on the cold floor. Her eyes closed immediately. She could not and did not want to see anything more that day. After that dreadful journey, here was the terrible reality of the ghetto: ugly old barracks, blocks of unfriendly, virtually indistinguishable buildings, streets laid out in a grid pattern,

Jews arriving in Theresienstadt: Like these deportees, Helga Pollak had to complete the last part of her journey from Bohušovice to Theresienstadt on foot.

ditches, trenches, and barricades. And there were so many people — sick, hungry, and emaciated, young and old, all living in miserable quarters.

Where had she ended up? What was happening to her? And why?

CHAPTER THREE:
DAILY LIFE IN THE CAMP

On January 23, 1943, when Helga, her father, and their relatives arrived in Theresienstadt, this northern Bohemian garrison town about thirty miles north of Prague on the Eger River had already served as a concentration and transit camp for Jewish prisoners from the Protectorate of Bohemia and Moravia for more than a year. The previous six months had also seen the arrival of thousands of Jews from other European countries, primarily Germany and Austria.

One hundred eleven thousand, seven hundred fifty-six men, women, and children had been sent to this place since the first transport of Jewish prisoners arrived on November 24, 1941. Most went on to be deported by the thousands to places farther east. On January 9 and 15, 1942, the first two transports left Theresienstadt for Riga, each carrying 1,000 prisoners, followed by more transports to the extermination camps of Izbica, Piaski, and Sobibór, and to other destinations in Poland. Two thousand prisoners left in March 1942, 7,000 in April, and 3,000 in May. Only 175 people from these transports survived.

By July 3, 1942, the original population of Theresienstadt had been evacuated completely to make room for new deportees. They came mostly from Germany and Austria, and, as 1943 wore on, also from Denmark and the Netherlands. In September 1942, Theresienstadt's population swelled to a peak of 58,652 — in an area comprising little more than three hundred acres, in a town whose prewar population had numbered about 3,500 civilians plus roughly the same number of soldiers. Barracks that had housed 320 soldiers now had to accommodate more than 4,000 people. The Hamburg Barracks alone held 4,346 people, which came to just over sixteen square feet per person.

Many people in Theresienstadt died of hunger, illness, heat, or psychological trauma. In July 1942 the average daily death toll was 32. In August it went up to 75, and by September it had climbed to 131, with a high of 156 reached on September 18. The total number of deaths recorded between

August and October 1942 was 9,364.

But death alone, which the Nazis cynically termed "natural decimation," did not create enough room for all the Jews constantly arriving on new transports. For the SS that was no problem: They simply increased the number of transports from Theresienstadt to the East. Between September 19 and October 22, 1942, ten transports containing 19,004 people, most of them elderly, left Theresienstadt on what were called "old people's transports." With the exception of a single individual, they all ended in the Treblinka death camp. Only 3 people from those transports survived the war. After October 26, 1942, nearly all transports led to Auschwitz.

Of the 50,871 prisoners who had been deported from Theresienstadt to the East during 1942, only 327 would eventually be liberated. Theresienstadt had long since become just a way station on a long journey to death.

Helga, of course, had no knowledge of any of this when she arrived in Theresienstadt in January 1943, or of the Wannsee Conference in Berlin a year earlier, or of the secret meetings in the Hradschin castle in Prague in October 1941. Not even the adult prisoners, including the members of the Zionist

At the end of the eighteenth century, on the order of the Hapsburg emperor Joseph II, a fortress was built at the confluence of the Elbe and the Eger rivers, about thirty miles north of Prague. The emperor called it Theresienstadt after his mother, the empress Maria Theresa. The fortress was intended to block any advance of the Prussian army on Prague, which was then part of the Austrian Empire. In 1846 the town was given its own municipal government and coat of arms. But by 1888 Theresienstadt was no longer of any strategic military importance, and its designation as a fortress was rescinded. It remained a garrison town, however, with a growing civilian population. After the Nazi occupation of the Sudetenland in October 1938, Terezin (as it was called when

76

organizations and the leaders of the Jewish community in Theresienstadt, knew anything about these meetings and their purpose: to define precisely the role of Theresienstadt as an "old-age ghetto," a "model ghetto," and a transit camp for further evacuations of the Jews to the East.

The Jewish leaders in Theresienstadt who formed the Council of Elders worked in the belief that their actions would help ensure the survival of Theresienstadt's Jews until the end of the war. In doing so, they unwittingly reinforced the Nazi myth that Theresienstadt was an autonomous, democratic, self-governing Jewish settlement. But it quickly became apparent to Jakob Edelstein, the first chief Jewish elder, "just what sort of wind was blowing in the Theresienstadt Ghetto."[1] Edelstein and the other elders

---

the independent republic of Czechoslovakia was formed in 1918) found itself on the border between the so-called rest of Czechia and Germany, and it became a refuge for the waves of people fleeing the Sudetenland. The arrival of the "construction commando" in late November 1941 marked the beginning of the transformation of Terezin (renamed Theresienstadt) into a concentration camp for Jewish prisoners. The building to the right of the church is the Girls' Home L 410.

The Girls' Home L 410 in Theresienstadt. The arrow points to Room 28.

were bitterly disillusioned when it became clear that the Nazis had no intention of allowing the Jewish Council to act as anything more than an instrument in the hands of the actual camp administration — the SS commandant's office under the leadership of Dr. Siegfried Seidl. Indeed, only eight days after Helga's arrival, Edelstein was abruptly and unexpectedly replaced by Paul Eppstein, the former chairman of the Reich Representation of German Jews in Berlin. Edelstein was demoted to Eppstein's deputy.

A few days after her arrival in Theresienstadt, Helga was assigned to live in the Girls' Home. Having known nothing but disruption in her life over the past few years, she was now going to have to find a place for herself in another new world. "I can still remember it very clearly," she recalls. "All alone, without my father, carrying my suitcase in my hand, I walked to the Girls' Home L 410, passing through its ugly entryway. On the ground floor was an office, and someone told me that there was a place available on the third floor, in Room 28. They sent me up on my own. I stood in the doorway, not daring to go inside. I was so self-conscious that I probably sounded brusque when I said, 'Hello. I am Helga Pollak and I'm supposed to live here.' "

A crowd of girls looked back at her in surprise from every corner of the room, while she stood on the threshold. *How did she get here, this strange girl?* their eyes seemed to be asking. *And why was she sent to us when our room is already overcrowded?*

To this day, Helga relives the memory of the feeling that came over her as she stood there. There was a big lump in her throat. More than anything, she wanted to turn on her heel and walk away. But where would she go? So she just stayed where she was, unmoving and uncertain. "Why there was no counselor to receive me and introduce me to the others, I really don't know," she says. "Ordinarily, that's how it was done. But for some reason that wasn't the case with me." Helga is still puzzled by it. "If someone had introduced me, my initiation into Room 28 would definitely have been easier."

Finally there was some movement. A young woman who appeared to be just as surprised by Helga's arrival as were the girls directed her to an open bunk.

"My suitcase is downstairs. Can anyone help me bring it up?" Helga asked. And, in fact, one of the girls jumped up and helped her carry the heavy suitcase up the three flights of stairs.

Friday, January 29, 1943
I've moved into the Girls' Home. It's a sunny room in a building that previously housed the military administration. The building is next to the church, the windows of the room look out on Market Square. I wish I could gaze out of the window all the time because I can see beautiful mountains. When it's clear, I can see a cross on top of one, and a castle on top of another.

The girls haven't made a good impression on me. When I went downstairs, they

Helga made this sketch of her diary. The entry for March 10, 1943, reads, "I'm longing for Mama now. That's why I put her photo in my diary, and I imagine that when I'm writing, I'm writing for her."

told the counselor to make sure I didn't move in. The counselor tried, but it didn't do any good. I'm lying on a mattress on the second level of a three-level bunk. It's all weighing me down. I'm very tired, so I'll stop writing.

The feeling of being a stranger weighed upon Helga for quite a long time, and the ease with which the other girls got along only reinforced it. They had evidently known one another for a good while. Some were close friends, some were always at the center of things and set the tone for the room, and others stayed in the background. And there were the troublemakers. Helga was baffled by this tangled network of relationships.

There was Anna Flach, whom they all called Flaška, a girl with a very outgoing personality. She shared a bunk with Ela Stein, who had black hair and dark eyes and was definitely a vivacious and chatty sort of person. Lenka Lindt, with her gentle expression and her levelheaded way of talking, seemed more mature than the others. Handa Pollak piqued Helga's interest as well. She was a quiet girl with beautiful dark eyes. Handa had a middle bunk, which she shared with Eva Landa, a strikingly pretty girl from Prague. In the top bunk was lively, blond Eva Winkler.

Helga quickly realized that she had been given a bad spot — the middle bunk of a triple-decker just to the right of the door. Beside her lay Marta Kende, a pale girl of Hungarian descent. She had a way of letting Helga know that it didn't suit her to have a new neighbor, and she reacted peevishly if Helga so much as touched an inch or two of her space, which was hard to avoid in this cramped area. Housed in a space of barely 323 square feet were an equal number of girls.

Two girls who seemed to be the youngest slept on the lowest bunk beside the window: Maria Mühlstein and a girl who was obviously the pet of Room 28. Her name was Ruth Schächter, but everyone called her by her nickname, Zajíček, which means "bunny" in Czech. Helga was surprised to find out that nearly all the girls had nicknames. Eva Fischl answered to Fiška ("Fish"), Ruth Popper to Poppinka, and Anna Flach to Flaška ("Little Bottle"). There was a Didi, Alice Sittig; an Olile, Olga Löwy; and a Rutka, Ruth Gutmann. Many of the nicknames, like Zajíček's, were taken from the animal realm. There was a girl called Kuře ("Chick") and one called Prasátko ("Piglet"). Next to Marianne Deutsch, who was usually called Marianka, lay little Hana Epstein, who went by Holubička ("Dove").

Sometimes the girls teased little Hana. "Come here, Holubička, play our little dove," they would call. Then they all would sing the Czech folk song "Vyletěla holubička ze scaly" ("A Little Dove Flew out of the Rock"). And, merry as a little bird, Hana would jump about the room to the applause and shouts of her roommates.

Helga watched it all as if through a telescope. Everything around her seemed unreal. It was not her world. She didn't belong here. It seemed to her that there was no place for her. She crept into her shell. "The girls don't like me — I know it," she wrote in her diary on February 14. "But that doesn't bother me here in Theresienstadt. I don't care about them. But I care about Frau Sander. I'm as fond of her as if she were my aunt."

Mimi Sander was her father's girlfriend from Vienna. It had come as a great surprise to Helga to be introduced to Mimi shortly after her arrival in the attic of the Hamburg Barracks. She had heard a great deal about this woman from her father, but she had never met her. And here she was, standing right in front of Helga. "To think this is where we've met. I can't believe it," Helga wrote in her diary. "She looks just the way I pictured her."

Helga's father and Mimi Sander, her relatives from Kyjov — especially Lea, the one-year-old daughter of her cousin Trude — these were the people to whom Helga felt attached and with whom she spent as much time as possible. In Room 28, she still felt like a stranger.

Wednesday, March 3, 1943

It's been so long since I've written any-thing, and so much has happened in the meantime! I was in bed for a week. I had a bad cold and couldn't write because I had conjunctivitis. Now I can write again without my eyes hurting so much. Lea has pneumonia. I saw her yesterday. She looks like a little wax doll.

Friday, March 5, 1943

I've been given two inoculations for typhoid, which is why I'm lying in bed. Papa hasn't been to see me yet either. Evening: Mimi was just here. She brought me goulash with potatoes. Papa won't be coming today, he's too tired.

Sunday, March 7, 1943

Nothing special happened the whole day. Lea is still just as sick. It's Masaryk's birthday today.[2] My favorite counselor told us all about him.

Monday, March 8, 1943

We got up at 6:30 this morning because we had to do a thorough housecleaning. I'm not tired at all, though I worked hard enough. We tossed our pillows and mat-tresses out of the third-story windows down into the garden, where we beat

85

them. And afterward I cleaned thirty pairs of house shoes and fifty pairs of regular shoes. All by myself! Lea is doing worse. Yesterday evening she got her second blood transfusion. I found some dextrose for her. What a circus we've just had here. Some kids hid one girl's pillow, and she's been crying for a whole hour now.

Before I went to bed, I happened look out the window. I'll never forget my impressions at that moment for as long as I live. A mountain with a village on its slopes. Above the mountain, a red sky, all the shades of the setting sun. The sky was still very blue, and in about the middle was a crescent moon, and beside it a star, and off to one side in the shadows towered Castle Hasenburg. I closed the shutters quickly. I couldn't bear the sight any longer, I felt uneasy. I'm locked up in here — with such magnificent nature so near! Freedom! How happy I'd be if I could live deep in the woods, in a cabin or in a tent, all alone, and could experience freedom.

As of February 1943, the Girls' Home L 410 had been in existence for a little less than six months. Occupying a former military administration building that was right next to the church on Market Square, it had provided, since its opening on September 1, 1942, lodging for about 360 girls who were allocated rooms — subunits called "Homes" — according to their year of birth.

The Girls' Home was directed by Rosa Engländer, Walter Freund, and Karel Huttner. Several counselors were assigned to each room, but one bore the overall responsibility. In Room 28 that person was Ella Pollak. At her side were Eva Weiss, a few years younger than she, and others who would help out as needed.

On the other side of Market Square, in what had been the Theresienstadt school, was the Boys' Home L 417. It had been founded before the Girls' Home, on July 8, 1942. Other homes had also been established on the same pattern: the Toddlers' Home L 318, several homes for apprentices, as well as Home L 414, which lodged children primarily from Germany and Austria. Homes L 410 and L 417 were reserved mainly for the children of the Protectorate.

Of the approximately five thousand children and teenagers up to the age of sixteen who were then living in Theresienstadt, only a fraction lived in these homes. Babies and toddlers spent the nights with one of their parents, usually the mother, and were cared for during the day — depending on their age — in toddlers' homes or nurseries. A sizable number of children between the ages of eight and sixteen stayed with the adults in the large general barracks. There wasn't enough room for all of them in the Children's Homes, where the living conditions were a bit better.

"We were aware that material conditions are of crucial importance for a young person who is still in the developmental stage," Otto Zucker, a member of the Council of Elders and deputy to Edelstein, wrote in mid-1943 in his report on the occasion of the first anniversary of the Boys' Home L 417. "Those conditions must be as favorable as possible if we are to have a strong and healthy generation that is physically up to the tasks that the future holds for the Jewish people."[3]

Lodging these young people in what the Germans called youth homes improved their overall situation and allowed for the implementation of specific pedagogical objectives. Otto Zucker summed up the program this way: "An education of the young individual for communal life: We are convinced that this education to foster a collective orientation, to help young people find their way in the community, subordinating individual interests to the interests of the community and letting each individual develop within the framework of the community's organization is an essential part of today's educational tasks."[4]

The entire staff of the Youth Welfare Office and, above all, Jakob Edelstein and the Council of Elders were of one mind regarding their obligation to and special responsibility for the welfare of the young ghetto prisoners. During the earliest days of the ghetto, a fundamental decision had been made — that the welfare of the young had priority over that of the old. For the young people this meant better food, better and more hygienic living conditions, and special medical care. But for the older people, of course, this meant greater privation and hunger — "bread was literally being taken from their mouths."[5]

"This may have been somewhat unusual and cruel toward the elderly," said Ze'ev Shek, the Zionist youth leader and a founding member of the Hechalutz movement, in his testimony before an Allied investigative commission on June 29, 1946, "but given the circumstances then it was an entirely correct solution, favoring the future. . . . The Council of Elders' decision was applied in all the lodgings, in the kitchens and in the streets. Everywhere, special care was given to the children."[6]

On March 9 Helga attended a puppet theater for the first time in Theresienstadt. "It was very beautiful for Theresienstadt," she recalls, "and it had definitely required a lot of work and effort to make all the puppets. The piece was called *The Enchanted Violin.* Someone played a violin and someone played a harmonium (though not very well)."

That brief bit of enjoyment was quickly forgotten. "The pneumonia is spreading," Helga wrote in her diary that same evening, after a visit to her cousin Lea. "The doctor thinks that if her heart has held out this long, it will keep holding on. But Dr. Fischer is doubtful that Lea will survive."

Lea was thirteen months old when she arrived in Theresienstadt, and she became sick within a day. Hers was not an isolated case; the ghetto was a breeding ground for infections. And then there was also the psychological shock. Even today just a catchphrase can bring back all the scenes that Judith Schwarzbart associates with her first days in the ghetto: "The Hamburg Barracks was dreadfully overcrowded, and everything was in great confusion. The older people wanted

Eva Stern and her father, Dr. Walter Stern. Eva was born in the northern Bohemian town of Žatec. When she was six months old, her family moved to Brno, where her father started a pediatrics practice.

peace and quiet, the children wanted to play, there was constant shouting, arguing, and noise. Everyone was cold, and everyone was hungry. There were lice, and my beautiful long hair was cut off. I fought awfully hard to stop them from doing it — to no avail. They cut it off."

A short time later, Judith developed a high fever accompanied by persistent vomiting. The doctors didn't know what to do. There was no change in her condition for days. Then Dr. Walter Stern came up with the right diagnosis: jaundice. "It was Theresienstadt's first case of jaundice. It was followed by a dreadful jaundice epidemic. I came down with it three times. My sister did, too. She almost died of it."

Judith recovered but kept getting sick again. "I lay in the quarantine infirmary with jaundice and scarlet fever for six weeks. I survived. When I came down with typhoid, my father took me in — he lived in the shed of the garden he tended. I didn't want to eat or drink anything. I just begged for a piece of lemon — oh, how I wanted a lemon! And my father brought me half a lemon. Where he managed to find it I don't know. But he was great at finagling."

A talent for "organizing" things, as everyone in Theresienstadt quickly learned, was essential in the daily struggle for survival. But that alone was often not sufficient for dealing with all the dangers and securing that which was essential for survival. The doctors in particular, facing all but insurmountable difficulties, were painfully aware of this. There was neither enough medical equipment nor enough of the essential medicines to help fight the rampant disease. This is clearly evident from a report written in July 1943 by Dr. Rudolf Klein, who was responsible for medical care in the Boys' Home L 417:

From July 1942 until the end of 1942 . . . the homes experienced a substantial epidemic of scarlet fever. . . .

In August and on into early autumn there were epidemics of various forms of diarrhea, followed by numerous cases of infectious jaundice, whereas German measles, mumps, measles, chicken pox, whooping cough were of less concern to us and our patients, except for complications that came with cases of German measles, all of which took a bad turn, but fortunately the patients were restored to health. [There were] several cases of pneumonia and middle ear infections that required surgery.

One great concern was the serious flare-up of typhoid toward the end of January 1943. Around fifty children fell ill in the course of two months, some of them with very severe cases.

As regards the numbers of illnesses recorded per day, there were periods in which thirty to thirty-five percent of the children lay ill — with several different illnesses. A difficult burden for us to bear, since several of those on our already small medical staff were ill at the same time.[7]

Dr. Klein was able to report that "fortunately" all the boys who had fallen ill with typhoid recovered, but the numbers for

Drawing by Helga Weiss of the Girls' Home, Room 24. In February 1943 she noted in her diary: "Typhoid is rampant everywhere in Theresienstadt. The hospitals are overflowing. They cleared one whole building and turned it into a hospital for typhoid cases. You see signs everywhere: 'Beware: Typhoid!' There's a sign at every water tap and well: 'Don't forget to wash your hands!' — But there's hardly ever any running water. On the door of L 410 there is a big sign: 'Beware: Danger of Infections.' Everyone flees on the spot."

Girls' Home L 410 were very different. There, typhoid revealed its most devastating side.

"Lilka's sister has died," Helga Weiss, a resident of Room 24, wrote in her diary during this period. "Lilka herself has typhoid, too. Vera, Olina, and Marta are in the infirmary. Milča was taken to Hohenelbe Barracks yesterday. They say she's dying. 'What's wrong, Hanka? Why are you crying so bitterly? What! Dáša?' — 'Dáša and Jana . . . they're both dead!' "[8]

Dáša Bloch and Jana Gintz were inseparable friends. "They often said that nothing but death could separate them," a girl from Home 16 remarked when describing her indelible impressions of the Girls' Home in October 1943:

Life in the Home went on peacefully and everything was as usual. Until the typhoid epidemic broke out. The first cases were Dáša and Jana. They were taken to the hospital on February 1, 1943. But they weren't kept together. Jana was taken to the Hohenelbe Barracks, Dáša to the typhoid infirmary at L 317. On the morning of February 5, we learned that they had both died the day before, both around six in the evening. Their wish came true, unfortunately far sooner than either wanted. When we were told of their death, none of us could say a word or even cry at first. We knew that they were very sick, but it never would have crossed our minds that they would not be coming back to us. After a while we lit a candle at the head of their bunks. We stood stock-still, and I think all of us prayed.[9]

Helga Pollak's diary continues:

Wednesday, March 10, 1943
I was on call all day and I am very tired. . . . Lea is doing a little better. She drank three ounces of milk with dextrose. I hope she survives.

Thursday, March 11, 1943
We had almost the whole afternoon off. I went to see Frau Sander and then I visited Lea. She's doing better. She slept the whole night through, drank a lot of buttermilk, and when we showed her a picture book, she laughed for the first time in months. Then I went to see Papa, and we talked about what presents I could give for Purim, because we girls in the Home want to make presents.

Ah, I almost forgot: I want to write down

what we get to eat. Every day the soup is lentil soup. Bad potatoes and gravy that's almost always burned. Almost every evening there's margarine and black ersatz coffee. About twice a week there's some kind of noodles for lunch. Every third day we get a little piece of bread, which has to last for three days. When we first arrived, it seemed a lot to me. I gave almost my entire bread ration to Papa. But now it's not enough for me.

Friday, March 12, 1943

I'm awfully tired, and glad that tomorrow is Saturday and that I'll have half a day off. I'm sewing presents for Purim, out of paper! — What silliness.

In the afternoon I got together with Trude, who was taking Lea for a walk. Lea is not even half of her former weight. She's doing a little better. May God make her healthy again!

Yesterday I was invited to an eight o'clock theater performance in the Home of the children born in 1931. It was on the second floor here in our house. I don't know what the fairy tale is called. It has five parts, and they put on just the first part. The sequel is to follow soon. It was very pretty. It's about a king and a forest giant. The girls danced Czech folk dances. — I remembered how my mother took me to the ballet school in Vienna when I was five years old. I also remembered having danced the czardas in a Hungarian folk costume before my parents and relatives. How beautiful it was back then! Together with Mama and Papa! I lived like a princess. Now Mama is so far away from me. But I'm glad that at least things are better for her, and she doesn't have to live through what we're living through here.

Two months after her arrival, Helga had become a well-functioning cog in the mechanism of Room 28. "I was on cleanup duty yesterday with a group of very lazy girls, so that I had to do almost everything myself," Helga jotted down on March 18. "We did a poor job of sweeping up at noon, and so our punishment was to do everything all over again. But now I'm lying in bed and have all that behind me, and I'm looking forward to an afternoon off tomorrow."

The days weren't always that filled with work. But even without cleanup duty, daily life was hard enough, especially early in the morning. The wake-up call sounded every day, usually at seven: "Get up, girls!" And that meant going downstairs to the big, cold, ugly washroom on the ground floor and standing in line to use the primitive toilets — there were only two to three toilets per floor, which meant two toilets for about 120 girls. Then came a thorough hand washing with a squirt of Lysol in a special basin, watched over by Frau Salus, who was in charge of the toilets and constantly repeated the little rhyme: "Wash your hands before you eat / And when you get off the toilet seat."

Every morning the beds had to be aired according to strict rules and in daily rotation — some at the window, others on the bunks themselves or on the table. Then chores were assigned, according to the "*Torahnoot* Plan" (*torahnoot* is Hebrew for "service") that was posted on the door. It listed who was responsible for what chore on what day. Generally that meant fetching the midday meal, cleaning duty, and what was known as "being on call."

For many girls, early morning was the least pleasant part of the day, especially when it was cold and gray outside. Who wouldn't rather go on sleeping and dreaming — especially dreams that blotted out the present and brought relief and strength to the mind? Only the children who were clearly ill were allowed to stay in bed until one of the pediatricians, Dr. Stern or Dr. Fischer, arrived and decided what was to be done. Those with minor symptoms might sometimes be allowed to spend the day in bed, while those who were more seriously ill were placed in a room in the Girls' Home that had been specifically set up as an infirmary, or *marodka,* as it was called in Czech. That actually wasn't the worst thing that could happen. At least in the smaller groupings one could find some peace and quiet, which was close to impossible in the large rooms.

And what added to the appeal of being diagnosed with a minor illness was the much better chance of enjoying a few extra "bonuses." These were doled out by Margit Mühlstein, the social worker assigned to L 410. Even if they amounted to nothing more than two or three spoonfuls of oatmeal or wheat grits, they at least offered some respite from the monotonous daily fare that came from the children's kitchen:

MONDAY: soup, millet; evening: a little piece of bread

TUESDAY: soup, potatoes, turnips; evening: soup

WEDNESDAY: soup, potatoes, goulash, a small piece of bread; evening: a small piece of bread

THURSDAY: soup, dumpling, gravy; evening: sausage, soup

FRIDAY: soup, pearl barley; evening: buns

SATURDAY: soup, potatoes, turnips; evening: soup

SUNDAY: soup, buns with icing; evening: twenty grams of margarine, a teaspoonful of marmalade

This children's menu comes from the diary of fourteen-year-old Šary Weinstein, who added the following commentary: "The list of foods doesn't look all that bad. But the food is horribly prepared, and the soups are the same every day. They look like water from a mop pail, ugh. I've never eaten soup in my life, and I'm certainly not going to eat the soup here. We have black coffee for breakfast (it's dishwater) and nothing with it."[10]

The packages that Helga and her father received at regular intervals from a relative in Kyjov became increasingly important events in Helga's life. On March 16 they got a package with bread, sausage, cheese, and gingerbread. The next one arrived on April 1: "I got another package today, a real nice one. It made me so happy. If it weren't for Maria's packages I'd often go hungry. This package contained a cauliflower, three apples, three wedges of cheese, four bouillon cubes, salami, potato flour, and an eighth of a pound of butter. Here I am writing about food again! But it made me so happy." The fact that she had to share her little packages with eight other people — her father and other relatives — did not diminish her happiness.

Many children — Flaška, Zajíček, Judith, among others — could only dream of such packages. They had no one to send them anything, and they had no choice but to get by on the standard rations from the kitchen. They quickly learned that the piece of bread doled out every third day needed to be handled with utmost care. Each time they received it they wondered: Should I eat it all in one sitting because I'm so hungry? Or should I make it last for three days? Or for two days, and go hungry on the third?

By then it no longer made any difference that the bread was painfully lacking the familiar smell and taste of fresh bread, or that it was being delivered on old wagons that were similar to the ones used to transport corpses. Anyone who had been in Theresienstadt for even a few days appreciated bread more than ever. It even func-

A bread wagon. Such wagons also served as hearses. Drawing by Helga Weiss

tioned as the ghetto's unofficial currency. You could exchange a piece of bread for all sorts of things — a tomato, a cigarette, a few sticks of wood, a garment, a piece of paper. Or even an hour of private instruction.

The old and infirm were in no position to make such deals. They owned nothing and were so hungry that they didn't know how to help themselves. Helga witnessed their dilemma firsthand. When she visited her uncle Eugen in the Sudeten Barracks on

March 16, she saw potato peels being tossed out of the kitchen, "and ten people threw themselves onto that little pile, fighting for it. To Papa and me it looked like what happens when you throw three bones to eight dogs, and the dogs bite each other to get at the bones."

Saturday, March 13, 1943

Today, as on every Saturday, we stayed in bed until eight o'clock. I woke up early and it was such a wonderful feeling. All the girls were asleep, the window was open, and the birds were chirping, just like the ones I had so loved listening to at home.

Monday, March 15, 1943

Sirens started howling in the middle of the night, waking me up. I couldn't remember quickly enough what it was, and thought that the sirens were telling us we could return home. What a strange sound the sirens had. To my ears it was like the howling of jackals or wolves. I've learned since that the howl of sirens means there are enemy planes approaching.

Tuesday, March 16, 1943

We worked until 11:30, giving our room a thorough cleaning. I got out of other duties for the afternoon, and for the first time in my life I did laundry. This Theresienstadt is a school for life.

Yesterday there was a real ruckus. Helena grabbed a crust of bread from another girl, who then took revenge by hiding Helena's pajama tops, which then set her howling. The counselor didn't know what to do and called in the director of the Girls' Home, Frau Engländer. She calmed Helena down, and everything was back to normal. But I could not help laughing, even with Frau Engländer there.

Wednesday, March 17, 1943

I was on duty the whole day, which didn't exactly please me. I didn't even get to visit Papa at noon. I played dodgeball until three o'clock, and afterward went to a children's recital. Six- and seven-year-old girls danced and did gymnastics, but some were my age, too. Some of the big girls made a mess of it, but the little ones were all agile and charming. I was especially taken by a girl my age who tap-danced.

The biggest event of the day was that I went half into hysterics. I was rearranging my suitcase, picked up a wad of cotton, and a mouse fell out! I stood there petrified, looking down at my suitcase. After a while I pulled myself together and called the counselor, then ran away. Laura, the counselor, caught the mouse and threw it out the window down into the garden, where the girls dug a little grave for it.

Friday, March 19, 1943

I've put together a plan for what I'll be doing tomorrow. At one o'clock I'll visit Mimi Sander, whom I haven't seen for three days now. I'm going to get some of my clothes back from her, because she has no room for them, and put them in my suitcase, and then go to Papa. I'm looking forward to Purim. We're going to have a *žranice* — a blowout banquet.

Thirty-year-old Ella Pollak was the girls' main counselor. They called her Tella, which was a combination of *teta,* which is Czech for "aunt," and Ella. Tella and Eva Weiss, who was ten years her junior, spent most of the day with the girls. One of the counselors — usually Lilly Gross or Laura Šimko — always spent the night with them.

Ella Pollak, born on June 13, 1913, in Liberec/Reichenberg, was an imposing figure. She was a piano teacher, had studied music at the Prague Conservatory, and in the mid-1930s had joined the Zionist youth movement Hechalutz. Her parents and two of her brothers, who had been able to emigrate to Palestine in time, had tried in vain to get her to do the same. But Tella saw it as her duty to remain in her country and stand by the children. Until her deportation to Theresienstadt she worked as a *madrichah* (Hebrew for "counselor") in the illegal system of education put together by Zionist organizations in Prague.

When she arrived at Theresienstadt with one of the first transports at the end of 1941, Tella continued her work. Along with Eva Weiss, who came from Brno, she spent the first half of 1942 caring for a group of girls quartered in Room 104 of the Hamburg Barracks. The girls — Eva Winkler, Pavla Seiner, Eva Landa, and Ela Stein — were later transferred to Room 28. Also in the group was twelve-year-old Handa Pollak, in whose life Tella was soon to play an important role because of Handa's father, Karel Pollak.

Karel and Tella first met in Room 104 of the Hamburg Barracks. (The surname that they shared was a common one.) Karel was drawn to Tella — a good-looking woman with green eyes, thin lips, and black upswept hair — and the attraction was mutual. When Room 28 in the Girls' Home was created

Karel Pollak and Tella Pollak

and both Tella and Handa moved there, Karel Pollak had a twofold reason to stop by, which he did whenever possible after a day of work in the fields.

The girls called Karel Pollak "Strejda," which is Czech for "uncle." "He was always there for us," the girls recall. "He was always ready to help and comfort us. Or explain something to us. He always had a kind word."

"He was perhaps the only man liked by everyone who knew him," Handa says of her father. "He had studied in Halle in Germany and graduated with a degree in agriculture. He knew everything there was to know about nature and farming. He was the only teacher I ever had who was able to introduce me to the mysteries of mathematics. He had a great sense of humor, and he loved silly jokes that would make him laugh so hard that tears would come to his eyes. He loved to sing, even if not quite on key, and was very clever with his hands. That was his main job in Room 28, rebuilding our bunks for us. The day they did their count of us out in the Buhošovice Hollow in November 1943, he was the first to get back home and heat the stove for us so that we could get warm again."

Handa Pollak was a quiet girl with beautiful dark eyes. She loved her father very much, and she missed her mother. Her parents had divorced when she was four years old, and Handa had grown up in Olbramovice, a little village south of Prague, with her father. But in recent months Handa had been living with her mother, until, one day in 1941, she was torn away from her.

Handa and her father had to leave their home in 1939 and had been living, mostly apart from each other, with a series of relatives in Prague. In the meantime, Handa's mother, together with her sister and her sister's husband, had built a house in Prague-Dějvice. When they moved into it in

1940, they took Handa with them. But larger political events soon caught up with them. "The Germans wanted our villa and insisted that my mother and her brother-in-law sign a document stating that they had 'voluntarily' handed the villa over to the Third Reich," Handa recalls. "We heard that the Germans wanted the villa for Karl Rahm, whom we were soon to get to know as the commandant of Theresienstadt. But my mother and Uncle Joroušek wouldn't consent, which was why over the next several months they were both constantly summoned to appear before the Gestapo. They were threatened: 'If you sign, you'll be protected. If not, something bad may happen to you.' They didn't sign."

There were other, similar cases, for which the Germans devised the simplest solution — they put the people whose real estate or property they wanted in the next transport. Handa's mother and her brother-in-law Joroušek (his wife had died some weeks earlier of blood poisoning) were placed on the list of one of these "capitalist transports," as they were called. "I can remember the day I said goodbye to my mother. We were both very unhappy. No one knew what lay ahead. I had a premonition that some dark, awful place awaited her. But none of us thought that things would be as awful as they later turned out to be."

Left behind without mother and father was four-year-old Jarmilka, the daughter of Handa's relatives. She was taken in by another family, but they were unable to protect her. Jarmilka found herself in the very next transport. "It was horrible. She was all alone. We brought her to the assembly point. We asked another family to look after her. She cried terribly. The transport was headed for Lodz. We never heard from her again."

And Handa would never hear from her mother again, either — not one letter, not one message. It was only after the war that she learned of her mother's fate. She had worked as a laboratory assistant in the Lodz Ghetto, which saved her from being transported to Auschwitz-Birkenau. But when she saw that all her friends and comrades were being deported while she, as a "protected" person, was left behind, she decided — having always been a woman of principle — to give up her work. And with the very next transport she, too, was taken to Auschwitz.

In 1943 the Jewish holiday Purim fell on March 21, the first day of spring. "I woke up at six o'clock," Helga noted. "It was so quiet all around. The sun was shining, and the birds were singing."

Purim is one of the happiest of the Jewish holidays. It commemorates Queen Esther's rescue of the Jewish community in Persia some twenty-five hundred years ago from the murderous plans of prime minister Haman. The adults had spent the previous days preparing the children for the holiday. Both Tella and Margit Mühlstein told them the story of Purim and explained its significance in Jewish culture. Margit, who was Maria's mother, was very religious. To this day, in the minds of the girls of Room 28, the Jewish Sabbath and the holidays — Purim, Pesach, Rosh Hashanah, and Hanukkah — are linked to the image of this woman.

"We never observed the Sabbath at home," Ela Stein says. "It was Frau Mühlstein who first taught me how to light candles on Friday evening and how to pray. And she did it in such a special way — very solemn."

"Whenever she sang, the room would grow very quiet," Flaška recalls. "She had a voice like honey."

Frau Mühlstein helped infuse the Girls' Home with a little of the spiritual radiance that Purim brings with it. But it was equally important to do justice to the lighter side of the holiday — to eat, drink, and celebrate the happy ending of the story. Eva Weiss was perfect for this task.

Everyone liked Eva, an athletic young woman who was so unaffected and open with the girls. She was not yet twenty years old and had thick, curly hair and muscular legs that were usually clad in shorts. She radiated energy. Tella was a person who lived by the rules, and some of the girls were afraid of her at times. But Eva was like an older sister, someone you immediately felt you could confide in.

A few of the girls knew Eva from Brno. She belonged to a circle of young Zionists who had met regularly on Friday evenings in a room at the Jewish community center, among them Fredy Hirsch, Franta Maier, and Felix Strassmann. Until her deportation in April 1942, Eva had spent many hours with children and teenagers at the Maccabi Athletic Field in Pisárky, a suburb of Brno, leading them in gymnastics and dancing, playing dodgeball and other games. She continued to do this in Theresienstadt, in the Children's Homes or on the Bastei, a special area on the south ramparts of the ghetto that was set aside for young people. "I used my entire arsenal to distract the children from their problems," Eva Weiss

113

says, describing her activities. "I used athletics and games, dancing and singing, whatever was possible."

On Purim the year before, some of the boys in the Boys' Home L 318 put on a play based on the Purim story, called *Esther.* It had been arranged by Flaška's brother, Michael Flach, who was one of the counselors there.[11] This year it was the girls' turn to perform the play, and Eva Weiss supervised the rehearsals. Fiška assumed the role of Esther, Flaška was cast as Esther's cousin Mordecai, Eva Stern was the evil Haman, and beautiful Eva Landa, wrapped in a bathrobe and with a crown atop her head, transformed herself into the Persian king Achashverosh.

Helga chronicled the events of the day in her diary. "At two o'clock we went down into the garden for a costume party. I was a girl sailor. In the garden we were given a package of toiletries (soap powder, toothpaste, stationery, a shoehorn, and a notebook), a package of sweets (sugar and cookies), and a bun. Then I went to see Papa, where I ate everything I'd been given. Then I went back home where I ate my bread and sausage, and afterward we played dodgeball in the garden. At a quarter to seven we began our program. We put on a

Eva Weiss, born in Brno on June 14, 1923, now lives in England. "She brought a bit of warmth into our lives and instilled in us an appreciation for the arts and a sense of humor, which sometimes helped us not to take things so seriously," says Eva Landa.

play — *Esther.*"

After the play, the children put together what they called a *žranice* — a "blowout" banquet, although it was certainly a far cry from the feast customarily held on the holiday. There were no hamentashen — the traditional triangular Purim pastries filled with poppy seeds or prune butter. All they could bring to the table were a few slices of bread that had been saved for the occasion and a bit of margarine that was spread on the bread, which was then toasted on the hot stove until the margarine melted. Over this they sprinkled a pinch of sugar or paprika. Sometimes Ela could add something to such feasts — a tomato, a carrot, or a piece of red bell pepper that had been secretly taken, at considerable risk, by her mother, who worked in the fields. These colorful little extras were not much more than decorations, however. To "organize" or "clean up" fruits or vegetables while working in the fields was considered theft by the SS. A "thief" could be severely punished, so great care had to be taken, and only tiny pieces of vegetables would end up on the girls' bread. "But just to see it!" Helga recalls. "I still remember how impressed I was by it. Even though everyone got just one or two little pieces. But for me it was a feast for the eyes — it was done with such love!"

This, too, was primarily the work of the imaginative Eva Weiss. She was constantly coming up with variations on the *žranice.* Sometimes sugar and margarine were combined in a pan and set on the stove to make "candy," gooey little roasted bonbons that were passed around as "sweet nothings." Or a potato was sliced, sprinkled with paprika, and roasted. Sometimes flour and yeast were formed into a dough that was filled with a piece of onion or a little mustard. Or a "cake" would be magically created from painstakingly saved bits of buns, with an icing that looked like chocolate but was actually ersatz coffee powder. These buns — simple yeast pastries baked in the shape of rolls — were sometimes so doughy that, despite their rather bland taste, at least one could chew on them for quite a while.

A *žranice* was always a great event for the girls; that Purim was no exception. As they usually did on such occasions, the girls joined hands and shouted their cheer made up of nonsense syllables: *"Aba cucka funde muka funde kave kave cuka, ab cuk, funde muk — funde kave kave cuk."* Then they dug in. "We each had two slices of bread with curds and half a slice with mincemeat,"

Helga recalls. "After that came something sweet with coffee cream and sweetened sour milk. After the *žranice* we exchanged presents. I got a little purse, a brooch, and a heart on a stickpin."

Tuesday, March 23, 1943
Put everything in order! We were finished by eleven. At three we went to the theater. The play was about Ahasver [*sic*], not the way it's taught in Jewish history, but rather as a comedy, because Purim is a happy, not a sad feast. Everyone laughed. But not me. I don't know why?! . . .

I've become more serious here somehow. Yesterday Mimi gave me a necklace with a pendant as a belated Purim present. Lea was doing better, she hadn't had a fever for six days, but she's worse again. She's got a new infection, this time in the left lung. . . .

When I was still at home I never paid any attention to nature. But I do here in Theresienstadt. Our windows look to the west, and we cannot see the sun rise. But at six o'clock I always go to the toilet in the hall, which has windows facing east. What beautiful mornings! I've been watching now for several days: budding trees, blue sky, and a red, rising sun. I completely

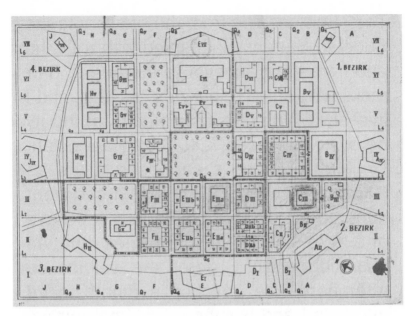

The layout of Theresienstadt, from Vera Nath's album

forgot that I've been here now for two months.

In her diary, Helga described the layout of Theresienstadt:

The town consists of eleven barracks. Only men are housed in the Sudeten Barracks, only women in the Hamburg Barracks. The Hohenelbe Barracks is a hospital. Instead of police we have the Ghetto Guard, which is quartered in what was once the German House on the other side of the barricades. You see Aryan people moving about there, too. The streets leading to it are closed to us by barricades.

The street leading from the brewery to the Sudeten Barracks is marked with a Q; the one from the Hannover to the Aussig Barracks with an L. Papa lives at L 231 and I live at L 410. There's a health authority here, whose head is a young physician, Dr. Munk. There is supposed to be an infirmary in every building with over four hundred people, but only a very few have one. We have two infirmaries and an outpatient clinic. Children are well looked after here. We go once a month to be measured and weighed. For fresh air we go to the ramparts, which is not open to adults. It's open three days a week. There are public showers, and also a few stores where if you have a special pass you can buy things with ghetto money. There are two shoe stores, two for women's clothes, two for men's clothes, one children's store, one for luggage, one for fancy goods, two for linens, a drugstore, a glass shop, and a general store. You're given permission to buy a certain amount of linens, clothes, and shoes each year. You can get herbal tea and ground pepper, paprika and caraway at the general store.*

* What Helga could not possibly have known at the time was that a large portion of the items sold

Almost without realizing it, Helga became caught up in the daily life of Room 28. She no longer felt like a stranger. Her shyness had gone, giving way to feelings of friendship and solidarity. Helga became increasingly aware that none of the girls had freely chosen to live in Room 28. Deep in their hearts all of them hoped for the day when they would once again be free. But Helga sometimes felt that some of her roommates had become more accustomed to this difficult situation than others, possibly because they realized that there was no alternative but to transform this forced community into some sort of congenial home until the war's end. Pavla Seiner, Lenka Lindt, Eva Landa, Handa Pollak, and Eva Winkler were among those girls. They tried hard to make a true community out of Room 28. Flaška did, too.

Helga admired the devoted way Flaška looked after the other girls and tried to console them when things got bad. She seemed to manage her daily chores with a

---

in these stores had been confiscated by the SS from the deported Jews upon their arrival at the Theresienstadt checkpoint, the so-called sluice. Some also came from the possessions of those who had died, or from prisoners who had been sent on to the death camps.

light touch. In the morning, as the girls were making their beds, Flaška could often be heard calling to Ela, who shared a bed with her: "Elinéz, Šmelinéz, Rolinéz, Malinéz, Roliz" — it was one of her nonsense rhymes that always got the girls giggling.

Flaška, Lenka, Ela, Zajíček, Maria, Handa, and Fiška — this was the group of girls to which Helga was becoming increasingly attracted with each passing day. Vivacious Ela, Flaška with her lively imagination, and beautiful, dark-eyed Maria — Helga liked them all. Tella encouraged her wards' musical talent and was delighted when these three, her best singers, formed a trio. Sometimes they rehearsed in L 410's cellar, where an old harmonium stood on rickety legs.

By this time the cellar in L 410 had become an all-purpose social hall. Sometimes it was used for little stage productions, like the one put on by Walter Freund with his puppet theater. Sometimes there were art exhibitions, lectures, or discussions. Once or twice it was used for a Passover seder. But mostly it was a rehearsal space, where the girls worked on their plays and Tella rehearsed her girls' choir.

The choir, which was made up of sopranos, second sopranos, altos, and soloists, had a fine sound, and it was Tella's pride and joy. The repertoire ranged from Czech and German folk songs to classical music and Hebrew melodies. Girls who didn't measure up to Tella's musical standards weren't allowed to participate, much to the disappointment of some. One of them, Eva Landa, would sometimes just sit there and listen to the beautiful music that carried out into the street, where passersby would stop for a moment to enjoy it.

"The best part," Ela recalls, "was when the room had turned dark and we would sing these wonderful Hebrew songs. Even when we didn't understand every word of what we were singing, our soloists, our choir, they just sounded so lovely! We really believed we were very good singers."

In the spring of 1943 Kamilla Rosenbaum, a dancer and choreographer from Prague, began rehearsals in the basement of L 410 with the younger children for *Broučci* (*Firefly*), a dance poem based on the children's book by Pastor Jan Karafiats. A collaboration with other committed artists, it soon became an ambitious theater project. Vlasta Schönová, a young actress who had studied directing in Prague, set to work adapting the story for the stage; the artist Friedl Dicker-Brandeis designed colorful, imaginative costumes together with the children; Adolf Aussenberg and Franta Pick created the set; and Karel Švenk, a cabaret artist from Prague, arranged the music based on Czech folk songs.

Eva Weiss, an enthusiastic dancer, assisted Kamilla and helped the children learn Slavic and Czech dances. She also had a role in the production. "I still recall the first song exactly. I leaped onto the stage and we danced to a wonderful medley."

A special attraction in the cellar were the puppet plays put on by Walter Freund, a lawyer from Moravia and the chief elder at the Girls' Home. In Theresienstadt he had thrown himself into his great passion, puppet theater, devoting every free minute to it. His handmade marionettes were masterly works of art that enhanced the children's enjoyment of his productions. Among his best-known plays was *A Girl Travels to the Promised Land,* for which the renowned former designer made the sets and Friedl Dicker-Brandeis created the costumes. But other plays also remained in the girls' memories, such as *A Camel Went Through the Eye of a Needle* by František Langer and *The Enchanted Violin.*

In these sorts of productions the old harmonium usually played a lead role. Although it was out of tune and several of its keys were always sticking, it was one of the most prized instruments in the Girls' Home. Sometimes it was even brought up to the top floor, to Room 28, as we learn from an essay Handa Pollak wrote in October 1943:

Before the premiere of *The Bartered Bride,* Tella, along with a few of the girls, brought the harmonium up to our room and played the opera for us. She explained everything, so that we would know the story and could concentrate on the music. The next day we went to the gym at L 417, which was full when we arrived. I found a spot close to the piano. I'd heard *The Bartered Bride* three times in Prague, but it was never as beautiful as it was there. What Rafael Schächter, the conductor, was able to accomplish was a real miracle. Back at the Home, the talk revolved around the food, the "sluices," passes for getting in and out, and work in the fields. I felt like someone who is caught up in dreams of beautiful things and is suddenly torn out of her dreams and wakes up — and everything is as gray and ordinary as ever. I just kept thinking about *The Bartered Bride,* and even as I dozed off I could hear "Our True Love."

Gideon Klein was a fascinating and strikingly handsome young man. He often accompanied Brundibár *rehearsals on the piano. "He was a friend of Tella's," Ela Stein recalls, "and once he even composed a song for our choir, which we then rehearsed with Tella. It went, 'Kushiba, Kushiba — a black man comes from Africa.'"*

Sometimes, toward evening, the Girls' Home became unusually quiet as lovely voices came from the old vaulted cellar. Everyone knew that Rafael Schächter, the celebrated and multifaceted musician — conductor, pianist, composer, and great inspiration to Czech musical life — was rehearsing with his choir and preparing for a new performance.

Schächter's legendary Theresienstadt productions — Bedřich Smetana's *The Bartered Bride* and *The Kiss,* Mozart's *The Marriage of Figaro* and *The Magic Flute* — all had their genesis in the cellar of L 410. "After work I often slipped down to the cellar," Eva Weiss recalls. "I would squeeze into a corner and stay very quiet, and so I was allowed to listen. There stood the old rickety harmonium that Tella often played. And it was there that I heard Mozart's *The Marriage of Figaro* for the first time, and *The Bartered Bride,* too. And of course the *Requiem*! I heard the *Requiem* so often that even today I can still sing most of it in Latin in my mind."

Verdi's *Requiem* — a funeral mass about dying, redemption, consolation, and resurrection — performed in Theresienstadt by Jewish prisoners in death's waiting room! It was one of the ghetto's most stirring and unforgettable concerts. As the music critic

Kurt Singer wrote at the time — despite his own objections to the choice of this work — it was "the greatest artistic accomplishment born and presented thus far in Theresienstadt, an achievement that also demanded the most meticulous preparation . . . a triumphant success for Rafael Schächter and his choir . . . a masterpiece."[12] And although it was meant for adults, it impressed a great many children as well.

"I heard only the rehearsals. I don't think that I ever attended a performance," Helga says. "And yet — it made such a deep impression on me that years later in England, when I was asked what I wanted to see on my twenty-first birthday, I said Verdi's *Requiem*."

Magically drawn by the music, many of the girls would slip down to gather outside the cellar door. If it wasn't Rafael Schächter or Gideon Klein sitting at the old harmonium, then it was Tella, who accompanied the rehearsals, with Handa sitting beside her.[13] "I was the one who turned pages of the score. Because of that I was allowed to be present at rehearsals," Handa says. "Those rehearsals — they left a very, very strong impression. Even today I can still hear the voices of the chorus: *'Dies irae, dies illa, solvet saeclum in favilla, teste David cum*

Rafael Schächter (d. 1945)

Sibylla . . . Lacrymosa dies illa, qua resurget ex favilla judicandus homo reus . . . Agnus Dei, qui tollis pecatta mundi, dona eis requiem.' Or the final prayer: *'Libera me, Domine, de morte aeterna, in die illa tremenda, quando coeli movendi sunt et terra.'* ('Free me, O Lord, from eternal death on that dreadful day when heaven and earth shall be moved.') For me, that work — and music in general in Theresienstadt — was an extraordinary experience. It was as if angels were singing in hell."

Flaška also occasionally tiptoed down to the cellar to be closer to these musical events. Music was — and still is — the elixir of her life. Once she even had the chance to audition for the role of Bastienne, alongside Piňťa Mühlstein, who was to play Bastien, and his sister Maria, who had the role of Kolas the magician. "But it wasn't easy for us," Flaška recalls. "It was hard to live up to Rafael Schächter's expectations. He set the highest standards. We rehearsed the Mozart opera for maybe two weeks. Then he decided to present it in concert form with adult singers."

But this decision did not spell the end of Flaška's musical career. She continued to sing in the girls' choir. She especially loved singing in the trio, which had taken on an unusual assignment. Flaška, Ela, and Maria would occasionally go to the quarters where the elderly people lived, to serenade them but also to offer them practical help. The girls did not do this for fun; it was hard work, a task given to them by an organization called Yad Tomechet ("Helping Hand" in Hebrew). Yad Tomechet was a youth organization founded in Theresienstadt in the late summer of 1942 by leading members of the Hechalutz movement and the Youth Welfare Office. They had agreed that something had to be done to try to alleviate the misery of the elderly inmates of Theresienstadt, however hopeless this seemed to be.

Beginning in the summer of 1942, elderly men and women arrived in Theresienstadt by the thousands, primarily from Germany and Austria. Many of them presented some piece of paper with the name of what they believed to be a hotel or a boardinghouse, claiming that they had reservations there. Some of the Jews from Germany had even signed a so-called *Heimeinkaufsvertrag* ("home purchase agreement"), for which they had been induced to hand over their remaining assets. The Germans had assured them that in return they were going to be given fine homes "in the spa town of Theresienstadt," where they would spend their later years in peace. And now these people, some from once well-to-do families, found themselves locked up in a sealed ghetto. They were crammed into military barracks, often in wretched attics or cellars, amid dirt, noise, and foul odors, with nothing to sleep on but straw-filled mattresses or just the bare floor. Many of them could not get to the toilets and washrooms, because these were too far from where they slept and were impossible to reach without assistance. They never had enough water or food, and what food they could get was practically inedible. The elderly quickly lost hope and the will to live. The number of suicides rose rapidly.

What could be done for these people? Perhaps the youngsters could be encouraged to help them. And so, at the suggestion of Hebrew teacher Ben-Zion Weiss, Yad Tomechet was founded. Over time, a large number of boys and girls joined in and helped to care for the elderly. The young people brought them their meager meals from the kitchen, accompanied them to the toilet, bathed them, cleaned their dismal sleeping quarters, and helped them pack when their names came up for transport to the East.

The girls in Room 28 also tried to think of ways to help. At first they set up a schedule of greeting new arrivals and helping the elderly with their heavy baggage. But that didn't work, because the new arrivals, thinking they were coming to a spa, were so horrified at their surroundings that they were initially incapable of comprehending their situation. Some did not trust the girls, especially those who did not speak German. Thinking that the girls were trying to steal their baggage, they brusquely waved aside those who sought to help them.

So the girls looked for other ways to be useful. Soon they were going straight to the quarters of the elderly. "If someone had a birthday, for example," recalls Flaška, "we just went over, wished the person a happy birthday, and helped out a little — beating mattresses, cleaning up for them. And then those of us in the trio would sing a little something. We had practiced a lot of songs with Tella just for that purpose. And sometimes we sang our own words to the tune of Schumann's *Träumerei*."

"Once we even sang a Dutch song especially for people from Holland," Ela recalls. "It was called 'Wade blanke.' To this day I don't know what it means, but the melody still runs through my head."

Sometimes the girls gave the elderly little gifts, usually handkerchiefs that the Youth Welfare Office had provided. The old people would then rummage helplessly through their paltry possessions, hoping to find something for the children. But there were no cookies, no chocolates, no bonbons. They had nothing to offer, and the children knew it, and at such moments they would quickly take their leave.

One of Flaška's outstanding qualities is her desire to help people. She may have inher-

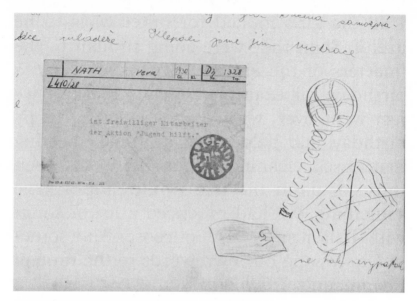

A Yad Tomechet membership card

ited this from her mother, for whom the education of her children in the spirit of enlightened humanism was paramount. Elisabeth Flach even wrote a book titled *The Most Important Question in Life.* No less than Tomáš G. Masaryk, the revered president of Czechoslovakia, had a copy in his library, for which he had sent a thank-you letter to Elisabeth Flach. For many years this letter was among her most treasured possessions.

Her mother's influence only partly explains Flaška's compassionate nature. She had also been sensitized to suffering by the bitter experiences shared by this whole generation of Jewish children during the years leading up to their deportation. Some may have hoped that life in the Theresienstadt ghetto in the company of others in the same circumstances would be an improvement over the nightmare they had just left. They were sadly mistaken. But the miserable conditions in Theresienstadt did help forge a sense of community and solidarity — even for an eleven-year-old girl. When Flaška was finally released from a long stay in the hospital, where she had wound up shortly after her arrival, she hurried off to see her father and brother in the Hohenelbe Barracks. And she was determined not to arrive empty-handed. "I was so happy I could bring them a gift, a piece of bread that I saved especially for them."

That was what happiness looked like in Theresienstadt. Unhappiness bore a different face. In February 1942 Flaška's grandmother Ottilie died. The elderly had the poorest chance of survival. They suffered the torments of starvation or died of disease. Thousands of elderly people perished in Theresienstadt.

Thursday, March 25, 1943
I'm getting along with the other girls now. We're holding meetings without the presence of counselors. We're trying to set up

a connection with the "Niners," the boys of Home 9 at L 417. We'd like to see some changes in our Home. Things are very bad at the moment, not very friendly. We're working on a kind of uniform — white shirts with a badge, blue pleated skirts and blue or black Pullman caps. We go to the ramparts every day now, where we play dodgeball and have other competitions. We return home single-file, singing, one behind the other, the little ones in front. — Lea's health is unchanged. It's very serious. When I came to the Girls' Home I weighed 113 1/2 lbs. Now I weigh 101 lbs. Papa has lost over 15 lbs.

Monday, March 29, 1943

Nothing out of the ordinary has happened over the last few days. The weather is very bad. We play the game of City, Country, River and sing. We have a new English teacher. She's very likeable. I have already managed to get a white shirt for our uniform.

Tuesday, March 30, 1943

It is the first day that the children's kitchen is open again. It was closed for about a month because of typhoid. The food is much better. For lunch today, there was potato soup with bread and noodles, and supper was a bun with half an ounce of margarine and black coffee. It was good, but too little of it. Papa had lentil soup and potatoes, and soup again in the evening. Am I ever stupid!!! I just keep on writing about the food.

A little while ago we celebrated Maria Mühlstein's birthday. Her mother cooks porridge for sick children and gives the children in the Homes extra food when they need it.

Now I'll describe the birthday party. For Theresienstadt it was very nice. Maria received a lot of presents, colored pencils from me. Frau Mühlstein had baked an oatmeal cake with coffee icing and marmalade filling. We drank cocoa with it. Imagine that — cocoa for forty people!

Wednesday, March 31, 1943

It's been four years since Mama left for England, and four and a half years since I saw her last. It will probably be a long time before we see each other again. For now we have only one hope that each day brings us closer to the end of the war.

Besides pneumonia, Lea has now developed pleurisy. She gets drained every day. The doctors have given up hope. I believe and hope in God, who cannot let such a little innocent creature die.

The counselors in the Girls' Home had set themselves an almost impossible task. How does one go about easing the unhappiness that each girl bore within her? How should one react to their fears, answer their questions? How could one help them live a semblance of a normal life together — a community of twenty-five to thirty girls crammed into an area that should accommodate no more than one-third their number?

Very few of the girls managed to come to terms with such conditions. On top of their personal suffering, the girls had plenty of reason to be upset by the problems they faced every day — bad air, not enough room, not enough food, too much noise. The smallest thing could set a girl off — someone in an upper bunk putting a foot on her bed as she climbed down, for example. And the constant disorder, wherever one looked! But was it even possible to keep order with so many children in such close quarters? Tella, at any rate, demanded it. And at times there were severe punishments if the rules were broken.

"One day Tella discovered a comb full of hair, a pair of dirty panties, and a toothbrush in Lenka's food bowl," Judith recalls. "She was so angry that she punished the whole room. Our punishment was that we weren't allowed to leave the Home that evening and could not visit anyone, not even our parents."

Such measures were not very effective. Nothing was going to hold Judith back from seeing her mother and father. She simply would not accept the idea of Tella punishing everyone just because Lenka wasn't tidy. Lenka was even less inclined to be impressed by such punishment. She was an extremely intelligent girl with a stubborn, rebellious streak. She was determined to form her own opinions and to see things from all angles. As a result, she often stood firm when asked to toe the line regarding matters she considered outmoded and obsolete, such as Tella's implacable passion for order. Lenka was by far the least tidy girl in Room 28. And yet Lenka was truly treasured by them all, even by Tella. "She was very clever and mature for her age and had a lively imagination — what a personality, one of a kind," her comrades said about her. "We admired her, and we all liked her. She radiated energy."

Lenka was not the only girl who had trouble with their strict counselor. Even today Marianne Deutsch has nightmares when she thinks of Tella. Marianne came from a prosperous family in Olomouc, in northern Moravia. For the first ten years of her life, her world had been a pleasant and agreeable one. "I had everything I needed," she would say later. Above all, she had "Memme," Emma Fischer, her governess, whom she adored, and who stayed with the family until their deportation in June 1942. "Memme would have preferred to convert to Judaism and accompany us to Theresienstadt. She cursed Hitler something awful and almost got herself arrested because of it." Saying goodbye to Memme was very hard on Marianne. "It was worse than being separated from my parents. When I had to leave her, I shed the first truly bitter tears of my life."

Marianne missed her governess. Despite her joy over every package that arrived from Memme — and Memme sent as many as she possibly could — each one rekindled Marianne's agonizing longing to see her. It was especially at such moments that Marianne railed against her fate. She simply wasn't able to adjust to the community of Room 28, and Tella's iron hand just exacerbated the problem.

"If there had been no Tella, I'm sure I

would have liked it better," Marianne comments. "The other counselors were very nice. What wonderful evenings we had when they spent the night in our room. But Tella spoiled every minute for me. Either you take me as I am, or just leave me alone." Tella evidently did the latter.

Things were different with Handa — even though she was a match for Lenka when it came to the matter of messiness. Her little portion of the shelving along one wall, the only place where a girl could put a few personal items, was usually such a mess that even Handa's neighbor, Eva Landa, fussed about it. But to no avail. Orderliness was not Handa's strong suit, and in her eyes Tella, at least in this matter, was more or less crazed. "Our clothes had to be hung up neatly behind the curtain, and our shoes had to stand in dress ranks like soldiers. We had a place for shoes under the window, but it was always one big jumble. And every evening our slippers had to stand in pairs under our own bunks."

And then one day it happened. A single, forlorn slipper was found under a bunk. The slipper was old and terribly tattered, and its partner was simply nowhere to be found, no matter how hard the girls searched and how thoroughly Tella interrogated them all.

It remained lost — much to Tella's annoyance.

For Handa and her friend Fiška, however, it became a great inspiration. They wrote a little play, *Trikena,* in which the main character was a single, tattered slipper:

One day a single slipper showed up beneath a bunk — Trikena. And all the other shoes, the good shoes, made fun of Trikena because she was so alone and so shabby that no one could wear her anymore. Finally Trikena died — weary, old, and abandoned.

Suddenly everyone felt sorry for her, and all the other shoes sorely regretted having treated Trikena so deplorably. They wondered: What can we do to bring her back to life? It was so mean of us to make fun of her, to humiliate her. They heaved many sighs of woe — and sounded like the chorus from an ancient Greek tragedy.

The girls laughed heartily at this little cabaret, which Handa and Fiška performed for them with slipper puppets, and which can be read today in Handa's little notebook. Handa had been given this notebook by Piňt'a Mühlstein on November 4, 1942, for her eleventh birthday, and she called it *Všechno* (*Miscellany*). In it she jotted down all sorts of things: classroom notes, mathematical formulas, poems, sketches for stories and plays, drawings, doodles.

Performances of dramas such as *Trikena,* or of a comedy about two old maids, *Amalka and Posinka,* which Flaška and Lenka wrote and presented, were the sort of creations that even someone as strict as Tella appreciated. What better way could her girls be diverted, for a little while at least, from the gravity and misery of their imprisonment?

Counselors had to walk a fine line between strictness and sympathy, punishment and indulgence. Some counselors, such as Tella, were strict enforcers of the rules. Others — among them Eva Weiss, Laura Šimko, Lilly Gross, Rita Böhm, and Eva Eckstein — relied upon compassion and creativity. But they were all united in one goal. As Rosa Engländer, the director of the Girls' Home, put it, they wanted "to create a foundation of harmony and balance for each child. This foundation is the source of the energy that enables a child to meet the demands of the outside world, a world that is tough and volatile and will continue to be so for our Jewish children."[14]

Eva Weiss contributed to the achievement

of this goal in her own special way. She loved aphorisms and adages, and she used them to create art with a pedagogical bent. If she heard a clever saying or came across a wise adage, she would jot it down on a piece of paper, quickly paint a picture to accompany it, and then hang it on the wall. Eva's pictures already adorned the walls of Room 104 in the Hamburg Barracks, and now they enhanced Room 28 as well.

One read: *Quidquid agis, prudenter agas et respice finem* ("Whatever you do, do it cautiously and with an eye to the end"), while another cautioned: *O si tacuisses, philosophus mansisses!* ("Had you kept silent, you would have remained a philosopher!"). Rudyard Kipling was also represented: "If you've been knocked down a hundred times and get up a hundred times and keep on fighting, then 'Hero of Life' will be inscribed on your coat of arms."

In the beginning, they were all-purpose adages. Then Eva came up with the idea of having each girl select a saying of her own. Soon little mottos with accompanying pictures were hanging from all the bunks. Eva Landa's image had a laughing face and beside it the words: "No matter what, be cheerful, always be cheerful." Flaška and Zajíček joined forces — they painted a little house and beside it wrote the unusual phrase *Vlajici taška* ("Flying purse"). It was an anagram of their names — an innovation that was characteristic of Flaška, who had a fondness for whimsical amusements. Ela Stein's page was decorated with a painter's palette and Helga's with a lighthouse. Helga's saying was "Always be prepared."

"The lighthouse," Helga wrote in her diary, "could be hope, so the girls say. But I picture us here as being caught up in a storm, the raging sea all around us — war."

Eva's breezy, cordial ways were an ideal counterbalance to the strict discipline that was so important to Tella. Because they worked so well in tandem, they were able to live up to the standards that Gonda Redlich, the head of Theresienstadt's Youth Welfare Office, set for his colleagues. "More than ever, what is needed here are real love and enthusiasm, which are far more important and more difficult to instill under such hard living conditions than they would be in normal life. More than ever, it is crucial not to let a counselor's creative spark be extinguished by a stultifying set of regulations. Even in those instances where counselors find it necessary to employ discipline, they must always present the best model for both children and adults, and be in a position to win the children's trust."[15]

Friday, April 2, 1943

This is a day full of joy. The Germans are suffering one loss after another. This afternoon I moved to a different bunk, beside Ela Stein. I'm so happy, because I had an unpleasant neighbor who would constantly scold me if I moved just an inch or two onto her space. Ela's uncle and mother come from Kyjov, and her uncle's bed is next to Papa's.

Yesterday we had for the first time a meeting in our blue and white outfits. Because things in our room are sometimes so terrible, we've decided to start afresh, as if we had only just arrived. We're going to have a parliament, so to speak. Our counselors are the ministers, then come the members of parliament, in two classes. The second class is like a lower house, and the first class is like an upper house, which is called Ma'agal. The girls who are obliging and friendly and hardworking are in Ma'agal — and so can serve as examples to the others. The rest are ordinary people. Whoever has fifteen points or is voted in is part of the second class. We vote once a month. Whoever is voted in twice advances to the first class. Ma'agal

146

makes its decisions in consultation with the counselors. Our motto is: *Věřiš mi — věřim ti. Viš a vím, bud' jak bud'. Nezradiš — nezradím.* ["You believe me — I believe you. You know what I know. Come what may happen, you won't betray me, and I won't betray you."]

The idea for Ma'agal was one of those inspirations that catch on right from the start and develop an unexpected dynamic of their own, almost as though Ma'agal had set free a latent potential within the girls and given them a structure and direction. The atmosphere in Room 28 changed from one day to the next — as if a bud had burst into blossom overnight.

Ma'agal is Hebrew for "circle" and, in a more metaphorical sense, for "perfection." The girls wanted to strive for perfection. They resolved to be helpful and considerate at all times. Ma'agal became the symbol for this spirit of cooperation, and a great many hopes were bound up in its founding. The counselors saw it as a golden opportunity to improve both the discipline and the atmosphere in Room 28. Some of the girls might have seen in it a means of enhancing both their room and their own standing, and others were convinced that Ma'agal would

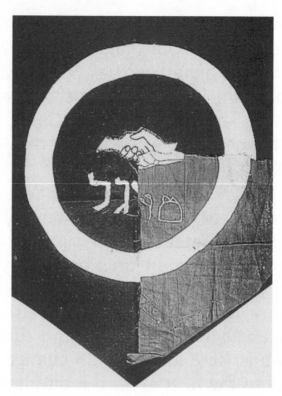

*The Ma'agal emblem on the flag
created by the girls in Room 28*

reinforce an awareness of community and
solidarity among all the girls — just as had
happened in Boys' Room 1, about which
they were learning some surprising things.

The boys in Room 1, in Boys' Home L
417, had come up with an extraordinary
idea. They had proclaimed their room the
"Republic of Shkid" and conferred upon
themselves the status of an autonomous
democracy. They also published a newspaper that they read aloud among them-

selves every Friday evening, providing information and sometimes amusement to those involved. The newspaper was called *Vedem (We Lead)*.[16]

Room 1, headed by Walter Eisinger, contained some exceptionally talented boys, especially Petr Ginz, the editor of *Vedem*. More than half a century later, on January 16, 2003, the Israeli astronaut Ilan Ramon would take Petr Ginz's drawing *Moon Landscape* with him on his flight aboard the American space shuttle *Columbia*. "I feel," Ramon said at the time, "that my journey fulfills the dream of Petr Ginz fifty-eight years ago. A dream that is ultimate proof of the greatness of the soul of a boy imprisoned within the ghetto walls, the walls of which could not surrender his spirit." Ilan Ramon did not return from his flight into space — he died on February 1, 2003, along with the six other astronauts on board *Columbia* when it exploded as it approached Earth on its flight back home.

Another resident of Room 1 was Piňťa Mühlstein, Maria Mühlstein's brother and a good friend of Handa Pollak. It was from him that the girls would hear about the latest achievements of the writers and journalists who contributed to *Vedem*. They spoke in particular about Hanuš Hachenburg's

Moon Landscape, *by Petr Ginz (1928–1944), pencil on paper. According to Petr's sister, Eva Ginz, the picture was drawn in Prague before his deportation in October 1942. Numerous other documents from within the pages of* Vedem *are evidence of the range of Petr's talent, which matured within the walls of Theresienstadt. They also document his unbending spirit. Ilan Ramon quite rightly called Petr Ginz "a symbol of the talent lost in the Holocaust."*

talents as a lyric poet — he was *Vedem*'s most admired writer. His poems are among the most moving documents left behind by the children of the ghetto.

My Land

I bear my land within my heart
For me and me alone!
It's spun from threads of beauty,
The only dream I've known.

I can caress you now, that's all,
And feel you as my guide.
My land is not upon this earth,
It is within and yet so wide.

My land is set among the stars,
It is the bird named space.
I long for it and weep sometimes
And feel it everyplace.

And yet one day I'll fly away,
Freed from my body's chains,
And soar toward freedom where I'll see
My land of endless plains.

For now it's still a little land
And found in dreams alone.
It holds me soft in its embrace,
Here in this awful zone.

One day I shall go to my land

And be forever free,
For in that space my longing found
There is no "I," no agony.
                Hanuš Hachenburg (1929–1944)

Similar talents were displayed by the boys
in Room 9. These boys, among them Honza
Gelbkopf and Kurt Drechsler, were the
same age as the girls in Room 28. Sometimes the boys and girls did gymnastics and
played games together on the ramparts. It
was there that friendships developed, sometimes accompanied by the first stirrings of
romantic feelings. What could be more
natural than the desire to ensure a certain
regularity to these meetings, especially since
the girls' artistic ambitions were just as
powerful as the boys'?

"We shall give it a try," said one of the
boys' counselors, the beautiful Licka Maut-
ner, during a visit to Room 28 on the
evening of March 26, 1943. She agreed that
the boys and girls could meet daily on the
ramparts for gymnastics, games, and con-
tests, and that they could visit each other's
rooms on occasion. For some of the girls it
was a dream come true. Others did not take
to the idea and were in fact skeptical. Helga
noted in her diary: "Licka was just telling
us about how wonderful it is in Room 9,

how they've formed a club, are writing a newspaper, and what a fine community they've formed — and right away the girls started arguing. Licka left at a quarter to eight. I'm sure she was thinking: *These girls can only ruin her lads.*"

This much was clear — things had to change in Room 28. No more arguments, no groups of girls taking sides against other groups of girls. What could encourage this effort better than the Ma'agal? The transformation triggered by this idea was already apparent after just one week. The first formal meeting took place on April 1. All the girls wore their new blue and white outfits. The letters VVBN were embroidered on each blouse. This was the acronym for the Ma'agal's motto: *"Věřiš mi — věřim ti. Viš a vím, bud' jak bud'. Nezradiš — nezradím."*

From this point on, these words were the motto of the girls of Room 28. And the girls created a symbol to go with it: a dark blue linen flag bearing the emblem of Ma'agal — a white circle around two clasped hands. On April 1, this flag was displayed in their room for the first time. And the first two members were elected to the Ma'agal, the "circle of perfection" — Pavla Seiner and Eva Landa.

"Pavla Seiner was the first girl who went to great lengths to turn our Home into a good home," Handa recalls. "She always tried to include girls who weren't at the center of our community — such as Zajíček, Olilie, and Marta Kende. Even when we played dodgeball — Pavla was very athletic — she looked out for those girls because she didn't want them to feel like outsiders."

Eva Landa was also given special recognition for her exemplary behavior. She was tidy and diligent, and she paid attention to the counselors' instructions — in part because Eva sincerely liked living in the Girls' Home. For her, life in a "collective" — a word that Eva heard for the first time in Theresienstadt — had a dash of adventure about it. At the very least, she preferred it to being under the influence of parents who were beleaguered by their own worries. In this regard she was an exception to the other girls. Eva was optimistic about her fate; at times she even felt as if she had ended up "in the Girl Scouts."

Eva must have felt this way on the evening that she and Pavla were inducted into the Ma'agal. As a solemn conclusion to their meeting, the girls sang for the first time the anthem of Room 28, which they had written themselves and set to the melody of a

Czech folk song — "Ach padá, padá ro-
sička" ("The Dew Is Falling").

> We want to be united,
> To stand together, to like each other.
> We have come here, but our hope,
> A hope that shall come true,
> Is to return home again.
>
> We shall do battle with evil
> And forge the path to the good.
> We shall drive every evil away
> And won't go home until we have.
> And then we shall sing:
>
> Ma'agal must triumph
> And bring us on the path to good.
> We clasp each other's hands
> And sing
> This anthem of our home.

A few months later, in October 1943,
Lenka Lindt alluded to this event in her essay written to answer the question "What
has made the deepest impression on you
since you have been living in the Girls'
Home?":

I never want to leave our Home, not for
anything in the world. We have many

155

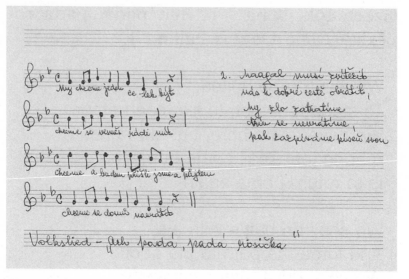

The Ma'agal anthem. The musical notation was done by Flaška.

things in our Home that I cannot write about, because that might betray our Home. We have many celebrations with little banquets. Everyone likes being here. Our Home impresses me very much. Our Home is my life. I don't know what I'll do when I return home and have to live alone with my mother in an apartment. Brrrr — . . . I shall go to some sort of Home even when I have returned home. And I shall think about our Twenty-Eight Home and of the girls who lived there.

When you read this, Frau Professor, you will say, "Lindt, you were supposed to write about what has impressed you the most about the Girls' Home, and you are writing nonsense like this . . ."

And so I shall tell you that my most impressive experience was when we wore our uniforms — and nothing more should interest you! Please don't hold my being so fresh against me.[17]

At moments like these, the room came under the spell of the magic word *naděje* ("hope"). When darkness had fallen and the girls were lying in their bunks, this word would brighten their conversations, like a star shining in a nighttime sky. At first, those sharing a bed would whisper to each other, then those sharing a bunk, and finally — all it took was one word to ignite it — voices were coming from every corner, and what had begun as a murmur evolved into a lively conversation.

"When I go back home . . . When the war is over . . ." That was how many of their sentences began, circling in ever-varying patterns around the magical concept of hope like variations on a musical leitmotif. "When the Germans are defeated, when we are free again . . ." Helga would join her mother in England. Eva Winkler would visit her old hometown of Miroslav. Judith

157

Lenka Lindt and her mother

Schwarzbart would return to her parents' house with its large garden in Brno-Jundrov. Marianne Deutsch would go back to Olomouc and her governess, Memme. Eva Landa, Lenka Lindt, and Pavla Seiner imagined returning to their beloved Prague; Ruth Schächter and Eva Heller would see their parents again in Eretz Yisrael, the Promised Land. Each had her fantasies, her dreams, her longings. "Yes, yes, yes," they sometimes heard Flaška and Helga chant. It sounded like a battle cry: "Yes, yes, yes, *Konzervatoř!*" ("We'll attend the conservatory!"), and it would continue until the counselor urged them for the last time to be quiet. Their thoughts would circle around what they had experienced and heard until they finally drifted off to sleep.

A new phase of Helga's life in Room 28 began with the formation of Ma'agal and her move to a bunk next to Ela Stein. Helga liked this girl with dark eyes and black hair. There was something fascinating about Ela, who was so different from Helga. Ela was vivacious, enterprising, talkative, and always surrounded by friends. And she was quick to join in whenever there was singing, painting, or dancing — or when the conversation turned to boys.

Helga and Ela sat next to each other more often now, in class and during their free time, when they had to stay indoors because it was raining. Sometimes they would join the others for a game or prepare their lessons.

"Tella has just announced our grades," she wrote on April 11, 1943. "I've got the best grades of anyone. If that's true, and I'm only just starting to believe it, then I've undergone a fundamental change. I'm not the same person I was in Kyjov. Cleanliness: very good. Tidiness: very good. Conduct: good. Interest in learning: very good."

Daily lessons were a fundamental part of

life in Room 28. Officially they were called "activity time," because while the SS had forbidden formal classroom instruction, they permitted "activities" such as singing, painting, handicrafts, dancing, sports, and games. In the eyes of the Nazis, these pursuits were harmless. But an education in history, literature, and languages was dangerous. "It is enough if they can count up to 100," an official in Rosenberg's ministry had said, summarizing Hitler's views on the differences between the Master Race and what he deemed the inferior races. "Every educated person is a future enemy. Religion we leave to them as a means of diversion. As for food, they won't get any more than is absolutely necessary. We are the masters. We come first."[18]

This kind of thinking lay behind the Nazis' determination to restrict education in every country they occupied. The Jewish leaders in Theresienstadt had to find ways to circumvent this control if they were to ensure that the children received a proper education. Their guiding principle was that no effort be spared in imparting the knowledge and experience of the adults to the children. One of their primary goals was to transmit Jewish culture and tradition; their method was to disguise the teaching as playing. The leading figures in Theresienstadt — Jakob Edelstein, Otto Zucker, Leo Jannowitz, Gonda Redlich, Fredy Hirsch, Milos Salus, and Viktor Ullmann, to name just a few — were all united in this cause: to protect and preserve intellectual freedom.

The unique situation in Theresienstadt gave rise to a sophisticated system of child welfare and education. Willy Groag, a Zionist youth leader who became head of the Girls' Home in late autumn 1943, described it as follows: "The majority of the teachers were members of Zionist and, in some cases, Communist organizations. But because we did not want to shortchange the children's development and their specific talents and interests in any way, we brought people who were independent of these associations into the pedagogical program as well, so new arrivals in the ghetto who appeared qualified to teach or supervise the children were asked by administrators to submit their résumés to the Youth Welfare Office. On the basis of their professional qualifications and pedagogical experience, they were assigned either to the administration of the Youth Welfare Department or to one of the children's Homes as counselors or teachers — sometimes as both. It was in this way that the Youth Welfare Office was able to enlist not only devoted Zionists and Communists, but also extraordinary people from all walks of life — teachers, professors, scientists, and artists."[19]

To some extent, the children of Theresienstadt had the opportunity to learn more than children of the same age in Prague or Brno. For one thing, the artists and professors teaching the children in Theresienstadt would rarely be found in ordinary schools in normal times. Moreover, outside Theresienstadt, Czech schools suffered under Nazi rule, their curricula distorted by Nazi ideology. Although the children of Theresienstadt had to learn in secret, their education included subjects that were forbidden by the Germans.

"Our room was divided into three groups — A, B, and C — on the basis of our knowledge and interests," Handa Pollak recalls, as she explains the educational system. "We had classes every morning. But it was a bit strange, because so many transports were arriving and departing. And the same was true of our teachers — they came and went. For example, if an English teacher arrived, we were taught English. But it wasn't long before he had to leave on a transport. Then another teacher came to replace him, but maybe what he knew

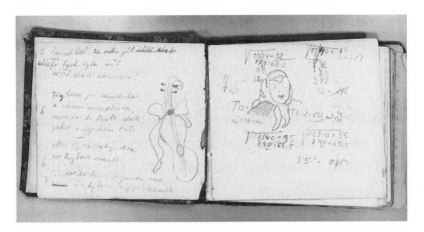

Classroom notes and doodles from Všechno, *Handa Pollak's notebook*

wasn't English but mathematics. And so we were taught mathematics. That's how we learned. We could never keep to a fixed curriculum. Everything was uncertain. And pupils came and went as well."

Magda and Edith Weiss taught Latin and Czech; Kurt Haček (whom the girls nicknamed Kartáček, Czech for "little brush") taught modern Hebrew. For a brief time the girls had an English teacher who introduced herself as Mrs. Idis and whom the girls called Missisipidis. They called another Hebrew teacher Shemihl Springer, because the first words he had spoken to the girls by way of introduction were *"Sh'mee* Springer," which is Hebrew for "My name is Springer."

For a while the girls were taught mathematics, which was not exactly Handa's favorite subject, as is evident from her notebook. Alongside the mathematical formulas and calculations are all sorts of doodles — of people, landscapes, animals. She was much fonder of Czech literature, German, drawing, history, and geography.

Three subjects are linked in the girls' memories with unforgettable individuals: drawing with Friedl Dicker-Brandeis, and geography and history with Zdenka Brumliková.

"I loved Professor Brumliková most of all," Handa recalls. "I remember the way she told us stories from Greek and Roman mythology. We sat there spellbound, following every word of her account. She was wonderful! She had such a grand way of telling things. For example, the life of Prometheus. How he wanted to bring the gift of fire to humankind, holy fire from divine Olympus, how he secretly stole it. But the gods noticed, of course, and meted out an awful punishment. They bound him to a rock with strong chains and sent savage birds to eat his liver. But each time his liver would grow back after the birds had eaten it, and the birds kept returning. I still remember her telling us about that."

The girls hung on her every word. Frau

Brumliková was small and slender, with freckles and short salt-and-pepper hair. She kept the memory of a free Czechoslovakia alive for them, recounting the old legends of Bohemia and Moravia and drawing a map of their Czech homeland — its prewar borders; its mountain ranges, rivers, and cities; each landscape with its distinctive characteristics. The hours with Frau Brumliková simply flew by.

Although there were such lighthearted moments, everyone was constantly aware of the lurking danger. "We were always afraid because we knew that all of it was forbidden — and punishable. One girl would stand watch outside the door." Under no circumstances were the girls to be caught at their lessons by the SS. This would have had serious consequences, especially for the adults involved, who might be taken to the Little Fortress. which was the name for the Gestapo prison outside the ghetto walls. The mere mention of it filled everyone at Theresienstadt with fear and trembling.

The children knew just what to do if the SS showed up unexpectedly. "When we got the sign that the Germans were approaching our Home, we quickly gathered up all the papers and pencils and hid them under our blankets or in the attic." When the alarm did sound, those standing watch would warn: "The Germans are coming!" or "SS inspection!" The girls would quickly hide the evidence of their intellectual activity — notebooks, test papers, books — and return to the activities that were allowed. In Room 28 that was usually singing. So it was that while SS officers were on the ground floor questioning the leaders of the Girls' Home and peering into one or another of the rooms, girls' voices were coming from upstairs, at first softly, then gradually swelling, singing a favorite round to fight off their fear. *"Bejvávalo, bejvávalo, bejvávalo dobře . . ."* ("Life was once, was once, was once good, when we were young and the world was like a flower — life was once, was once, was once good . . .").

On only one occasion did the SS come really close. They were searching for an illegal radio receiver, first in the Boys' Home, then in the Girls'. They combed through everything. They even crept into the sewer down in the courtyard of the Girls' Home. Then they tromped up the stone staircase in their black boots, the deserted stairwell echoing with the sound. On the top floor, in Room 28, the girls sat on their bunks, terrified by what might happen next. They heard voices, footsteps, doors banging. "The door was flung open, we saw the brief glow of a flashlight, and then the door quickly closed. They didn't enter the room."

Tuesday, April 6, 1943

The daily routine in our day in our Home is unvarying, but the days still pass quickly. It's hard to imagine that I've been here three months now.

Günther, the top SS man, is coming tomorrow. No children are allowed on the streets tomorrow. Papa doesn't know about this yet, but I'm going to die of hunger in the evening. He got word that he's received a package, and I won't be able to pick it up for him today. Papa can't really carry anything.

Wednesday, April 7, 1943

I was missing my father a little, but I got over my longing to see him, since the other girls can't visit their parents either. I know that Papa will surely come here to me. It's not as though I was bored. This morning we sang and a counselor read to us from *Microbe Hunters.* After our noonday meal I washed up and then read a fantastic book: *Gold Rush* by F. Lloyd-Owen. I liked it a lot. It is about a 12-year-old boy who ran away from home and traveled west.

Saturday, April 10, 1943

The barracks are all under lockdown. No one is allowed on the street without special permission, and children don't get special permission. This can last for days, or even months. I thought I wouldn't see Papa for a long time. But he came twice, and Mimi came and brought me something to eat. I feel like a bird trapped in a cage with other birds. We're not even allowed outside the building. Not even allowed to see our parents. And all because two people, a brother and sister, escaped.

A new girl has joined us, Emma Taub. They call her Muška — little fly. She arrived yesterday from Prague, from an orphanage where she stayed for two weeks. She is from Telč in southern Moravia. She's a very likeable girl and has splendid thick braids.

Sunday, April 11, 1943

At times I think it's better that Mama isn't here with us. I start wishing she were here with me, and then I feel very selfish. I'm getting quite annoyed at having to hang around in the same one room all the time. To hell with this barracks lockdown.

A "big shot" was expected to visit on April 7, 1943: SS *Sturmbannführer* Hans Günther, the head of the Prague Central Office for Jewish Emigration. As even the girls of Room 28 knew, this did not bode well. Usually he marched through town escorted by a squad of SS men and flanked by the camp commandant, Siegfried Seidl, and Adolf Eichmann, the man behind all deportations, the man from the Reich Security Main Office in Berlin and Himmler's "head of the department for Jewish affairs." "Every time he came, problems were sure to follow," Eva Weiss, the children's counselor, recalls. "Usually it was followed by transports to the East. And there was always a barracks lockdown, and we weren't allowed out on the streets."

The "Eichmann men" never came without a reason. The Council of Elders, the involuntary middlemen between the Germans and the ghetto's inmates, were painfully aware that Eichmann always acted according to plan, but they had no way of knowing what that plan might be. When transports to the East were ordered, the purpose of their visit became evident to everyone, of course. But many of the Nazis' objectives were unveiled only over time. Or too late.

Eichmann was frequently in Theresienstadt. At his trial in Israel in 1961, he explained that he always made a stop there, whether or not he had a specific purpose in mind. "We were passing through," he said. "It's the route you take by car when you're . . ."[20] He did not finish the sentence. He would presumably have revealed more than he intended if he had named all his assignments, all the camps and places that he inspected and contacted as special deputy and secret ambassador in charge of the "final solution to the Jewish question" — Lublin, Chelmno, Lodz, Auschwitz, Treblinka, Minsk, Lemberg, Warsaw. . . .

And so once again, in April 1943, there was a flurry of *bonkes,* the prisoners' slang for rumors — a muddle of any scrap of news that could be picked up somewhere, would then become latched onto the prisoners' own hopes and fears, and then make the rounds of the ghetto in every conceivable variation.

Sources of news were sparse, but they did exist: a quick peek in the central office at reports from the front prepared by the High Command of the Wehrmacht and printed in *The Black Corps,* the newspaper of the SS; an official German broadcast overheard while cleaning the Germans' offices; listening in secret to broadcasts from London or Moscow on radio receivers smuggled into the camp or rigged up illegally by the prisoners; a brief conversation with a kindly Czech policeman.

Most rumors sprang from the conviction that the Germans would soon lose the war and that the liberation was only a matter of time. These rumors were fueled by reports of the Allied landing in North Africa in November 1942 and the devastating defeat of the German Sixth Army at Stalingrad in February 1943. The relative peace and quiet that had reigned in the ghetto over the last two months gave additional impetus to the hope that it would be possible to survive the war in Theresienstadt. The last transport from the ghetto had left Theresienstadt on February 1, 1943, and since then there had been nothing to indicate that more would follow. Was this because the Germans knew that their defeat was imminent?

But what was the significance of the visit from the "big shot"? And of this lockdown that went on for several days? "I saw Eichmann from the window," Eva Weiss recalls. "We all had to stay inside. We were terrified. Why was he coming here? Is that good for us? Is it bad for us?"

The boys in Home A in the Children's Home at Q 609 came up with their own explanation. In early April there had been a big to-do, about which they reported a few months later, on November 26, 1943, in the fifth edition of the newspaper the children produced on their own, called *Kamarád:* "Five of our boys escaped from the ghetto, three of whom returned on their own. Müller was caught, but Belov escaped with his sister. Then the local police came . . . and the criminal division, and turned everything upside down, but found no incriminating evidence. But as punishment the entire ghetto was placed under a total lockdown and lights-out for two months, which also meant we were prohibited from visiting our parents."[21]

Was the escape of these five youngsters the reason that leading officers of the SS had come to Theresienstadt? Those inside the ghetto could only speculate. They could not know what the Nazis were really up to — could not know what was happening in the East, what awaited them there. Nor did they have any way of learning about the directive Heinrich Himmler gave his staff on April 19, 1943:

"The most important thing for me continues to be deporting as many Jews as possible to the East. All I want to read in the brief monthly reports of the security police is, if at all possible, the number of monthly deportations and how many Jews are still left."[22]

Sunday, April 11, 1943
My dream job would be a medical doctor; it's been my dream for three years now. How splendid it is to heal people. Ever since we read *Microbe Hunters* I haven't wanted anything else. My role model is Robert Koch.

Monday, April 12, 1943
If I ever should become a doctor, I'd like to have a practice in a quiet little town and a little villa at the edge of the woods, where I could have my laboratory and where I could spend my free time. But enough of that!!! What a lively imagination I have! I still have such naïve ideas about the future. I can't think about my future until the war is over and I'm out of this hated Theresienstadt. I hope Mama will have saved enough money to make it possible for me to go to college. Only then can longings become reality. I've been going crazy thinking about medicine, I think about it constantly, but today I will stop, otherwise I'll end up in the madhouse in the Hohenelbe Barracks.

I guarded the door from six to six-thirty

173

today to prevent any children from running outside.

Friday, April 16, 1943
I've been in bed for three days now with a very bad cold.

Sunday, April 18, 1943
It's been three months now since I lined up for transport to the ghetto in the Hungarian town of Brod. I received a package yesterday. Today is my first day out of bed. Mimi has been visiting me every day. Yesterday she brought me two crepes. Hurrah! We have fourteen days vacation. There will be no lessons, and instead we can play and dance or just keep busy for fourteen days. The only stupid part is that we still have a barracks lockdown and can't go to the ramparts.

What was the SS plotting? The children had no idea, but they sensed the trembling uncertainty in the camp, and that the adults, too, were groping in the dark. How could anyone know what was going on beyond the hermetically sealed ghetto walls of Theresienstadt? How could anyone know that reports about Nazi genocide were increasing in the foreign press, that the Germans were worried that this publicity would rob them of their ability to carry out their plans and would force them to resort to tricks to camouflage their murderous deeds? Or that Theresienstadt, of all places, was to play a crucial role in the next stage of the propaganda game?

They could not know about these developments, any more than they could get wind of anything about the tireless inquiries and interventions on the part of Gerhard M. Riegner, head of the Geneva Bureau of the Jewish World Congress, Richard Lichtheim and Fritz Ullmann of the Jewish Agency, or Saly Mayer of the American Jewish Joint Distribution Committee. These men were doing everything in their power to inform the Western world, especially President Roosevelt and Prime Minister Churchill, about Nazi atrocities, to shake them up and move them to take immediate and effective action against genocide.

They were equally persistent in their repeated demands that the International Committee of the Red Cross (ICRC) send representatives to the concentration camps in Poland and especially to Theresienstadt — demands to which the International Red Cross responded only slowly and hesitantly. The reason for this was partly, as Gerhard M. Riegner would later write, that under the direction of the Swiss jurist Max Huber, the ICRC proceeded "incredibly cautiously and legalistically."[23] But it was also true that their German colleagues were anything but allies. The German Red Cross had long since been made part of the Nazi machinery; its organization was run by Nazi bigwigs and permeated with Nazi ideology. The more critical the situation became in 1941 and 1942, the more the German Red Cross refused to cooperate with its international partners.[24]

No one in Theresienstadt knew much about the activities of the resistance group in Geneva, which included the work of Jaromir Kapocky, a member of the Czech government in exile that was based in London and led by Jan Masaryk. The inmates of Theresienstadt might speculate that the SS visit could in some way be connected to such efforts, but this was simply wishful thinking, as was the belief that transports had been ended because the Germans were expecting defeat.

In reality, the leading National Socialists had no intention of stopping the transports. Their machinery of death was running in high gear. No matter how great their military losses, and no matter what reports might appear in the foreign press about

German crimes, they were not about to veer from their course. Quite the opposite was the case. Failures and the threat of impending defeat only fanned the fanatic zeal of the SS to employ all its energies in completing the "final solution" before the war came to an end.

Paradoxically, the urgent appeals to the Allies, in particular those coming from Geneva, gave the Nazis greater latitude for their actions. The information sent by telegram in March 1942 to London and Washington was so monstrous that it exceeded the ability of its recipients to comprehend it, and so the credibility of the messages was undermined — which suited the Germans just fine. It was easy for them to publicly brand such reports horror stories invented by their enemies and to turn to an old but effective instrument of their own: counterpropaganda.

What shape such counterpropaganda might take had long been decided, as is clear from a document issued by the Reich Security Main Office. When its head, Ernst Kaltenbrunner, suggested to his superior, Heinrich Himmler, that there be a "dispersal of those in Theresienstadt over sixty years of age," and requested permission to begin transporting five thousand Jews over the age of sixty, Heinrich Himmler had his secretary reply on February 16: "The Reich Führer SS does not wish these Jews to be transported from Theresienstadt, since this action might disrupt the general tendency for Jews to die quietly in the old folks ghetto of Theresienstadt."[25]

Thursday, April 22, 1943

I had a horrible earache and cried all night. I saw the ear doctor this morning — ear infection. I have to stop writing because it hurts too much.

Friday, April 23, 1943

I'm lying in sick bay. This morning they punctured my eardrum, and it hurt a lot. There are four of us in one room. I have my bed and my peace and quiet. Papa has a bad cold and won't be coming to see me for two or three days.

Thursday, April 29, 1943

I'm still in sick bay, there's a lot of seepage from the ear, but my fever is no longer so high. I'm reading a book of fairy tales that Auntie borrowed for me. I play with the doll that I borrowed from Trude. But most of the time I sleep. My other ear hurts a little, too.

Tuesday, May 4, 1943

I'm doing quite well today. They drew some blood from a vein yesterday, and twice from my finger. And again today. Dr. Stern has found something to indicate that I might have typhoid. Results will be back in a week. But I'm told that if I do have typhoid, it's almost over, since my fever has gone down.

Papa received a package, but sad to say there was no fruit in it. I have such a craving for lemons and oranges. I haven't eaten an orange for a year, or a lemon in two months. I lie here while it's so beautiful outside. Everything is in bloom. The girls are still on vacation for Pesach, and Frau Prof. Brumliková has been reading Victor Hugo's *Les Misérables* to them. They're going to draw more blood, and I will scream with pure anger.

I hope that the war is over in a year. People here come up with rumors that are so optimistic, and they make everybody happy. When they learn the truth, they are crushed. And in Theresienstadt that sort of news spreads like wildfire.

While Helga was in sick bay, several girls in Room 28 were making presents for Mother's Day. Ela carved the emblem of

Theresienstadt out of a piece of wood. Judith would lay aside small bits of her scant daily rations, especially from the buns, in order to create a "cake" from them. Others painted a picture or designed Mother's Day cards.

Little Zajíček — Ruth Schächter — stood sadly on the sidelines and watched her friends' activities. She had no one in Theresienstadt except her brother, Alex, who was two years older. Her parents had fled to Palestine, leaving both children behind in the Jewish orphanage in Brno — and her case was not unique. Many Jewish children ended up in orphanages even though their parents were still alive. Often the only choice adults had was to flee abroad illegally, but it was far too dangerous to take children along. And so many parents made the heartrending decision to place their children in the care of a Jewish orphanage and hope that the children would be able to follow them as soon as possible with what was called a "youth certificate." This hope was rarely realized. Zajíček had just turned twelve. She felt very much alone. Like all girls her age, she was at a crucial point in her development, when a mother figure is indispensable.

"Although Tella was very strict," Helga

recalls today, "I did everything I could to gain her attention. I had a passionate need for a mother's affection. I missed my mother very much." Her longing for her mother comes up again and again throughout her diary. On June 9, 1943, she wrote:

For several days now I've been tormented by thoughts that keep circling around Mama and the question of why she divorced Papa. I plucked up my courage this evening and asked Papa. He told me that he would rather not reveal the reason for their divorce just yet. But, as I already knew, they had not separated in anger. He even bought her an apartment after the divorce, and furnished it, and bought her an entire wardrobe when she left Vienna. And they still correspond regularly. He also told me that Mama was very worried about me (but not like Papa — very few people worry the way he does).

People who don't know why Mama left for England think she simply left me with Papa. I know it was Mama who wanted me to go to Auntie in Kyjov, and Papa agreed that this was better for me. Back then, Hitler wasn't in Czechoslovakia yet. Mama was to go to England first and get herself established there. Then I was supposed to follow. But war broke out in the meantime.

I started sobbing yesterday, without meaning to, and Papa began to cry as well. When we calmed down, he said: After the war you'll join your Mama, and things will get better for you. You'll learn how a young lady behaves.

Utopian dreams give strength, as do memories of enjoyable moments — such as the time when Lenka's mother had bought an old guitar for herself. Perhaps this was the last time that Lenka had seen her mother carefree and cheerful. Why else would she have written, with the help of her friend Handa, the following poem for her mother, which Handa had copied down in her notebook.

Once when times were very good
You bought for fun, in music mood,
An old guitar

At first the urge to strum was strong
And you practiced very long
On your old guitar

Less and less you played by choice,

Weaker got the guitar's voice
Sometimes in and sometimes off

Time flew past, you did not play,
Not even touch it every day.
"I will tomorrow," you did say

Alas, tomorrow never came
Abandoned the guitar became
You never ever played again

Two years have passed,
Fast and fleet
Since your guitar fell asleep

Will you with this gift remember
All the beauty of its song
All the days when your desire
To play it well was very strong
Translated by Eva Gross, née Weiss

Lenka clung to her mother; Handa and Helga leaned on their fathers. Just knowing that they had a parent nearby gave them a vital feeling of security. Girls like Zajíček and Muška lacked that feeling of security; they lived in Theresienstadt without their parents. Eva Landa can still picture Muška — with those thick braids that made her look like an angel — on her thirteenth

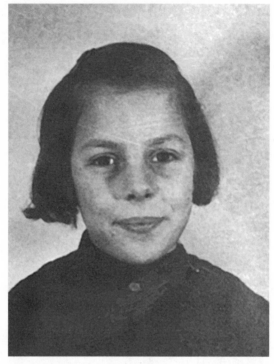

Zajíček ("Bunny") — Ruth Schächter

birthday, on April 30, 1943. A relative came to see her with a bouquet. Muška clasped the bouquet and wept.

Zajíček and Muška looked on wistfully as their friends prepared for Mother's Day. And then Zajíček came to a decision, which she described later that year, in October 1943, in her essay answering the question "What has made the deepest impression on you since you have been living in the Girls' Home?"

It was Mother's Day. The girls were all busy making presents for their mothers. I felt so dreadfully out of place. I thought maybe I should give a present to someone I felt about the way I feel about my mother. And that someone — my substitute mother — is really two people: Frau Mühlstein and Tella! They've looked after me for a year and a half like a mother. Why shouldn't I thank them for that? I'd like to grow up to be like them.

I made little gifts. When I saw Frau Mühlstein sitting at the table, I was filled with emotion. I slowly went over to her, and eventually gave her my present and a big kiss. Then I ran away. I could see how surprised and happy Frau Mühlstein was. But my joy was a hundred times greater than hers.

Then I went to Tella. I was shaking all over. I wished her a happy Mother's Day and began to cry. Suddenly I felt very good. — For as long as I live I shall never forget Mother's Day in Theresienstadt.

Home 28
Ruth Schächter (Zajíček)
My parents live in Palestine.

185

Helga's diary continues:

Thursday, May 6, 1943

It is horrible here in Theresienstadt, a regular Babylon: Germans, Austrians, Czechs, Dutch, a few Danes, French; I even know a Finnish girl. There are baptized Jews and so-called *Mischlinge [children of mixed religious heritage]*. A girl named Antonia, who bunked next to me, has had a very tough time. She arrived three weeks ago from Brno. Her father is Aryan, her mother Jewish. She's fourteen and was baptized in 1939, but her baptism is not recognized. She is here all alone and has few belongings. She feels uncomfortable in a Jewish environment. She longs to go home so terribly that she cries almost all day. Her father accompanied her as far as Prague, where they said their heartrending goodbyes. Now she lies in the bunk beside me.

Monday, May 10, 1943

I'm almost well again and have another reason to be happy today, too. Lea is finally healthy!! She has started to walk and she is smiling from ear to ear. She calls Papa Uncle Otto. She still drags one foot, but just one.

I weigh ninety pounds. There are only

two of us in sick bay. I hope I can see Lea soon. They drew blood from me two more times. Frau Professor Brumliková came to see me twice, although she has an inflamed foot. She brought me *Les Misérables* to read. Such a valuable book is a rarity here in Theresienstadt. In a couple of days our girls will be sent to work in the garden. I'm looking forward to it very much. I hope I'm all better soon.

Thursday, May 27, 1943

I've been out of sick bay for a week now, and my ear infection is gone. For five days now I've been working in Josef's garden, but not with our girls. They work only half a day. I'm with another girl from my room. I like it quite a lot, but it's a little too much for me all the same. The nerves in my face hurt.

Friday, May 28, 1943

Today is my thirteenth birthday. We celebrated at Mimi Sander's. I broke down in tears, I don't know why. They prepared a little table for me with presents. Papa gave me a necklace with a silver pendant — the Theresienstadt coat of arms with a silver lion. Mimi made me a cake and gave me a bouquet of wildflowers. And from Maria I got a lovely package with birthday greetings, and thirteen little packages inside.

Saturday, May 29, 1943
I'm lying in bed again, sick, and don't know what's wrong.

It was May, and spring was in full bloom when the barracks lockdown was finally lifted. For Helga, nothing really changed. She was still sick, as were many others. Judith Schwarzbart, for example, her roommate from Brno, was also on the mend from a serious illness, and was living in her father's shed in the backyard of the Girls' Home.

Before setting up a place to live in this shed, Julius Schwarzbart had slept in a little hut on the ramparts of the fortified walls that encircled the town. In the wide ditches between the ramparts he tended a large vegetable garden for the SS. It was the first garden in which young people were put to work, an arrangement that was the result of Julius Schwarzbart's initiative. In the ghetto, young people under the age of sixteen were not officially required to do their part, but in reality, many children were put to work at age fourteen, sometimes even earlier. Julius Schwarzbart had gone to great lengths to have them employed on farms wherever possible. That way, even though they were strictly supervised and could not lag behind, they could at least get a few hours of the fresh air they so badly needed.

That May of 1943 was not the first time Judith had spent recuperating with her father, who, along with her mother, took care of her and did all he could to restore his daughter to health. Her parents fretted that their previously spirited and healthy child kept falling seriously ill. Judith will never forget how she frightened her mother at one point by saying, "Do you know what I'd really love to eat, Mama? Pumpkin soup." Amazing! As a child Judith had hated this soup, which her mother regarded as a delicacy. Judith recalls her mother's reaction: "And then she fell silent. I still remember it. Today I understand that my desire for pumpkin soup must have shocked my mother. She realized at that moment how undernourished I was, how terribly hungry I must be if I was demanding, of all things, pumpkin soup."

HANDA POLLAK

Handa Pollak was born in Prague on November 4, 1931. She spent her childhood in Olbramovice, a small village about thirty-five miles south of Prague, where her father

owned a large farm. Her parents divorced when she was four. Handa's mother, Alice Pollak, was not meant for country life. She loved to travel and preferred life in the city. She enjoyed plays and concerts, especially when her cousin Karel Ančerl, a well-known conductor of radio and theater orchestras in Prague, wielded the baton.

Handa grew up in the care of her father, assisted by a Jewish governess named Jitka. Jewish traditions were not observed in her family of assimilated Jews, who considered themselves Czech first and foremost. It was not until she started school that Handa learned of her religious affiliation. On her first report card, under "religion," the word "Mosaic" appeared. "I still remember how hard I cried, and I remember asking my father why my report card had something entirely different from the report cards of all the other kids. 'Yes, we are Jews,' he answered. 'But that's not so important. We're Czechs like everyone else. This just means we are of a different religion.'"

The events that were building up to a catastrophe in Germany after Hitler took power had little resonance in Olbramovice at this time, apart from rumors, wild stories, and crazy theories, all of which were easy to dismiss.

That changed when the Germans occupied the Czech lands on March 15, 1939. A seemingly endless train filled with German soldiers rode through Olbramovice toward Prague. Restrictions of human rights for all Czechs ensued, especially for Jewish Czechs. The entrance gate to the Pollak farm now bore a sign announcing in large letters: ŽIDI VEN — JEWS GET OUT!

What followed was an odyssey with a recurrent pattern: Karel Pollak sought refuge with relatives in Prague. Handa lived with her father's sister for a while, then with a brother. In 1940 she stayed with her mother in Prague-Dějvice. Eventually Handa returned to her father, who was staying with his sister Hanička in the Smichov section of Prague.

In the autumn of 1941 Karel Pollak was assigned to Theresienstadt as part of the "construction commando." This first transport arrived on November 24. It consisted of 342 young men, craftsmen and laborers, whose task was to build up the ghetto. "They told us that the men could return home every weekend," Handa recalls. "But that was a lie. No sooner were they there than the gates were locked behind them. We could write only an occasional special postcard, which was then censored — thirty words in German and in capital letters."

Handa was without her father for about six months. "I missed him terribly, and longed to follow him to Theresienstadt. In July of 1942 I finally arrived there, along with my aunt Hanička."

ANNA FLACH

Anna Flach ("Flaška") was born on November 26, 1930, the youngest child of Leo and Elisabeth Flach, née Kober, in the Polish-Czech border town of Polsky Tešin (now Cieszyn). When she was a year old the family moved to Český Tešin; shortly thereafter they moved on to Ostrava.

In February 1937 the family resettled in Brno, on Adler Gasse 13, where Flaška's father opened a wholesale zipper business. Flaška had her first piano lessons in Brno, and along with her sister Alice attended the renowned ballet school of Ivo Váňa-Psota. In 1939 she began her first singing lessons with the great master of voice, Professor Sigmund Auspitzer, who had trained Maria Jeritza, a world-famous opera star from Brno.

Shortly after the Germans marched into Brno, Leo Flach's business was placed under the supervision of two "Aryan trustees." "My father worked while the Germans kept watch on him and pocketed a lot of money doing it. We had to put up with them in our house every day. And from that point on the hostility grew worse."

In August 1940 Flaška's sister Irena, assisted by the Youth Aliyah, managed to board a ship illegally transporting Jews to Palestine. "I shall be waiting for you to arrive soon, safe and sound." These were the parting words that Irena wrote in her sister's poetry album. "But for now — best wishes. Above all, practice your singing, because your voice is your sole possession."[26]

But Flaška was less and less in the mood to sing. One disheartening event followed another. Once, during the period when she had to wear a yellow star, a woman stopped in front of her, pointed to the new white felt boots that her mother had just gotten for her, and screamed, "You Jewish pig, give me those boots. Somebody like you shouldn't even own boots like that!"

"It was horrible. I still remember exactly how

it felt. After that I was always afraid to wear those boots. But then it turned cold and I didn't have any others." Another time two Germans in uniform walked past her. "What a beautiful girl," she heard one of them say, pointing at her. "Pity she's a Jew." That came as a great shock to Flaška. "What's so bad about being a Jew? I still have the same strong, bitter feeling inside me when I think back to that. Or when I hear anti-Semitic remarks. It hurts me deeply. More than hunger and the other restrictions and prohibitions, it was the hate hurled at us, the unjustified humiliation that we were subjected to. That stays with you your whole life."

The Jewish New Year had arrived, but people barely risked going to the synagogue. The admonition to the congregation after worship to "behave with calm, restraint, and dignity, and not to create a stir" only added to the anxiety and fear during that September of 1941. If the Jewish community had been able to do so, it would have made itself invisible altogether.

On November 26, 1941, Flaška's eleventh birthday, came the directive to "join the ranks for transport." "That was my birthday present! I can still see my father bursting into tears. It was the first time I'd ever seen him cry." Three days later the family set out for the assembly

GEBETORDNUNG.

	Ponavka-gasse	Leopolds-hof	Allee-gasse
Rosch - Haschanah.			
Sonntag 21. 9. 1941 abend (Erev)	17.45	18.30	17.45
Montag 22. 9. 1941 früh (Schacharit)	7.00	7.00	7.00
nachmittag (Minchah)		16.30	
abend (Maariv)	17.45	18.45	17.45
Dienstag 23. 9. 1941 früh (Schacharit)	7.00	7.00	7.00
nachmittag (Minchah)	17.00	17.00	—
Jom Kipur.			
Dienstag 30. 9. 1941 nachmittag	—	14.00	—
abend (Kol nidre)	17.15	17.30	17.15
Mittwoch 1. 10. 1941 früh (Schacharit)	7.30	7.30	7.30
Maskir	11.00	11.00	11.00

AN DIE SYNAGOGENBESUCHER!

Wir bitten Sie dringend, unter Berufung auf den Ernst der Zeit und auf die Schwere der Verantwortung, die auf jedem von uns ruht, überall, besonders aber in der Umgebung der Synagoge bei sich und bei Anderen auf ein ruhiges, zurückhaltendes und würdiges Verhalten zu achten. Ganz besonders bitten wir Sie aber um folgendes:

Auf dem Wege von und zur Synagoge bleiben Sie nicht vor der Synagoge, auch nicht in der Umgebung der Synagoge oder an der nächsten Ecke stehen. Gruppenbildungen sind zu vermeiden. Lassen Sie Angehörige nicht auf sich warten. Sorgen Sie mit uns dafür, daß alle Andächtigen ohne großes Aufsehen die Synagoge verlassen und sich auf dem kürzesten Wege entfernen.

Wir bitten Sie alles zu unterlassen, was öffentliches Aufsehen erregen könnte.

Diese Zettel sollen n i c h t weggeworfen werden.

Jüdische Kultusgemeinde Brünn.

Order of Worship, Rosh Hashanah, September 1941

point. From there they were put on the first family transport from Brno, which arrived in

Theresienstadt on December 2, 1941. Flaška was among the first children in the ghetto.

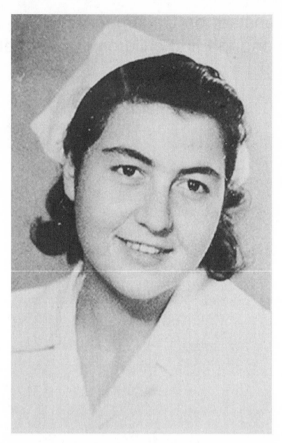

This photograph was taken in Israel in 1948.

JUDITH SCHWARZBART

Judith Schwarzbart was born in Brno on March 2, 1930, and was a year old when she moved to Mrštíkova 13 in Jundrov, on the outskirts of Brno, with her parents, Julius and Charlotte Schwarzbart, her sister, Ester, and her brother, Gideon. It was a large house with a garden that bordered on the woods. She loved it with all her heart, and even now has fond memories of it: "There were so many trees in our garden, with all sorts of fruit: white, black, yellow, and pink cherries, apricots, and two kinds of plums. There was also a fruit that I've never found anywhere else in the world. My father called it *mischpulle,* which was some sort of medlar. It was a brown, round fruit with one or two pits, not very large. The flesh tasted wonderful — a little like honey. Then there were currants — white, red, black. All kinds of apples. It was a garden of Eden — marvelous!"

For Judith's father, the large lot was a dream come true, and also the ideal spot to pursue his interests. He was an inventive man, a passionate do-it-yourselfer. One of his inventions, insulated bricks, guaranteed the family a steady income for several years. Judith's parents were Zionists, but they were not religious in any strict sense.

" 'You don't need to go to a synagogue to pray,' my father used to say. 'If God exists, he is everywhere.' " Still, Jewish holidays were always celebrated, because Julius and Charlotte Schwarzbart believed strongly in making their children familiar with Jewish culture and tradition. Judith's mother, who was born in Vienna, saw to it that a holiday atmosphere prevailed and always served the most delicious foods. "She was a wonderful cook — an artist. Her food was a dream come true!"

In those days, a lovely old clock stood in a glass case in the living room, and engraved on it were these words in Hebrew: "May this hour be a blessed hour in this home." That clock and a beautiful Pesach plate are all that remain of her parents' possessions. Today they symbolize everything Judith had lost — childhood, parents, happiness, and the dreams of the first nine years of her life. Then the expulsion from paradise began. "It started when someone at the Sokol Athletic Club[27] said to me, 'You can't come here anymore.' Then my best friend, Teresa, came to me and said, 'My father won't let me play with you anymore. We're not allowed to speak to each other.' She came from a very pious Christian family, and we had often visited each other. Everything changed from one day to the next. I cried all the way home, asking myself, why? Why is this happening all of a sudden?"

School grew more difficult for Judith with each passing day. She was the only Jew in her class, and the animosity of her fellow students became increasingly blatant. Before the occupation, she had occasionally attended Catholic religious instruction, since the class was held between other classes. "One day our religion teacher, a priest, said that Jews

The Schwarzbart family home in Jundrov

kill their firstborn sons to make matzos with. I stood up and said, 'That's not true. We have never killed a boy and we eat matzos every year!' But the other children believed the teacher, not me."

In 1939–40, after Jews were excluded from public schools, Judith attended the Jewish high school in Brno — an hour's walk each way. Home did not ease her sadness; her parents' anxieties were inescapable. How were they supposed to live? Julius

201

Schwarzbart had his business license revoked and his car confiscated. Hoping for better times, he tinkered with his inventions and developed a shoe-polishing machine. But no one showed any interest in it.

Judith's happy childhood was turning dismal. Nature, which had once buoyed her youthful exuberance and dreams, became a refuge from her hurt and disappointment, and a place of increasing isolation. The only thing still holding her fragile soul together was her love for her sister and brother and for her parents, especially her father. "I idolized my father. He was a calm, quiet man — he spoke only when he had something to say. When he saw people chatting for hours about silly things, he would say, 'They're just flapping their jaws!' "

One day neighbors denounced Julius Schwarzbart to the Germans, claiming that he was making brandy and doing other forbidden things. "Men in uniforms and clanking boots came to our house three times, turning everything upside down — they didn't find a thing. Once my father showed them his medal from the war and the Germans just laughed at him. I can still picture them laughing. It was horrible. Nothing happened at that point. But our fear just kept growing."

In May 1942 the Schwarzbarts ended up on a transport. "I still recall it exactly. I was glad

to leave. The atmosphere was so charged —
like dynamite. We were living on a powder
keg. When we received our deportation orders, I told myself that now at least there
would be peace and quiet."

Chapter Four:
Island in a Raging Sea

"Helga has chosen a lighthouse as her symbol for her Home," Otto Pollak wrote in his calendar diary on July 5, 1943. "She says it represents her life. The lighthouse is meant to light the way amid the stormy waves of life and lead her out of the darkness and into the light. I surprised my girl today with a drawing done by my comrade Bauer, the engineer, at the Home for the Invalids, showing the silhouette of a sailboat approaching a lighthouse. Helga was overjoyed, hugged me, and told me that I understand her so well. This new emblem will adorn the wall beside her bed."

This expressive drawing of Helga's personal emblem came at the right moment. The "stormy waves of life" had churned up a worldwide typhoon of death and destruction and hurled Europe into darkness. In Warsaw and in Bialystok (Poland), in Kolomyja, Ternopol, and Lvov (Ukraine), in

Skopje (Macedonia), in Lemberg (eastern Galicia), in Novogrudok (Belorussia) — wherever their war of conquest brought them, the Germans engaged in horribly bloody massacres. On May 16, 1943, after several weeks of battle, the Warsaw Ghetto uprising was put down. The factories of death were running in high gear — Auschwitz-Birkenau, Chelmno, Belzec, Sobibór, Treblinka.

On the Russian front, near Kursk, the largest tank battle of the war had begun; the British and American armies were about to land in Sicily, while Allied bombardments of German cities began to intensify after May 30, 1942, when the English flew their first thousand-bomb attack on Cologne. Events were coming to a climax, and the tremendous tension that hung in the air was palpable even in Room 28.

Tella chastised her wards at a meeting of Ma'agal on July 9, 1943, for the lack of discipline in their room. "If you don't pull together soon, there will be a catastrophe, and we shall have to introduce more severe punishments. Each of you in Ma'agal has slipped back by several points. You are inconsiderate and uncooperative, and some of you are egotistical as well. Be more tolerant and gentle with each other, but stricter with yourselves!"

Helga had crept back into her shell: "Somehow I've become a bit of a loner here in Theresienstadt," she brooded. "I know that I've become careless, that I must improve. Am I weak? Ela is at her singing lesson now. It's already ten o'clock and she'll be back any minute. I'm going to say to her: I need a friend. Maybe it could be you! Do you want to be? I'll see how that goes."

The very next day brought disappointment. "Ela doesn't want to. I can sense it. She's trying to back away a little. It's probably my fault."

The truth was that Ela simply had other things on her mind. She had a crush on Honza Gelbkopf from Home 9 — a state that brought on a whirl of emotions and questions that Helga tended to shrug off. Lenka, Flaška, and Eva Landa showed far more understanding and compassion for these sorts of issues, since they had boyfriends of their own. Ela was gratified by their response.

And there was something else, too. On July 7, 1943, the last transport of children from the Prague orphanage had arrived in Theresienstadt. With it came Ota Freudenfeld, the legendary head of the orphanage, and his son, Rudolf. The arrival of this transport drew everyone's attention, especially that of the children who had lived in the orphanage on Belgicka Street prior to their own deportation. Decades later, Rudolf Freudenfeld would recall their arrival:

As news spread through town that the head of the orphanage had arrived, the streets near the "sluice" were lined with children. My father passed through the crowd, happy to be among his children again. And they welcomed him the way you greet someone you hold most dear — with childlike love amidst all that misery.

That evening, Rafik [Rafael Schächter] arranged for a concert performance in our honor, in one of the attics, of *The Bartered Bride,* with a piano instead of an orchestra. After the performance, I proudly pulled out the score for *Brundibár,* and we decided then and there that I should begin rehearsing with the children.[1]

The news spread through the ghetto like wildfire, and it wasn't long before Tella sent her best musical talents to the attic of Boys' Home 417, where Rafael Schächter and Rudolf Freudenfeld were holding tryouts and making their choices among the many candidates for the various roles in the opera.

"There were three of us from our room — Flaška, Maria Mühlstein, and me. And we had to stand in a row and each had to sing up and down the scale, la la la." Ela Stein has vivid memories of the casting of *Brundibár.* "When my turn came I shook with fright at the thought that I wouldn't sing well enough. But then Rudi Freuden-feld said to me, 'You know what? You'll play a cat.' — A cat in a children's opera? That was something extraordinary!"

Gushing with joy, Ela brought the sensa-tional news to her mother and uncle. " 'A children's opera?' they said in amazement. They couldn't imagine what that might be. But they were so happy that I'd got the role."

Maria Mühlstein had reason to be happy as well. She was chosen for the role of the sparrow; her brother Piňt'a got the male lead role of little Pepíček. The female lead, Aninka, Pepíček's sister, went to Greta Hofmeister from the Girls' Home, Room 25; she had already sung in Smetana's *Bartered Bride* and Verdi's *Requiem.* Zdeněk Ohrenstein from Room 1, L 417, was cast as the dog.

The other roles were assigned as well: a baker, a milkman, an ice-cream vendor, and a policeman.[2] There were children who would play the people at the market and others who formed the chorus of schoolchildren. Among these were several girls from Room 28: Flaška, Handa, Zajíček, and Ruth Gutmann.

The title role of the evil organ-grinder Brundibár was given to Honza Treichlinger, an orphan from Plzeň. Rudolf Freudenfeld later recalled the manner in which this casting took place: "He had virtually begged for the role. We became acquainted in the washroom. He came up beside me, pretending to wash his hands, and casually remarked, 'I've heard that you're looking for children for your opera. Can I come, too?' "

Later, when the time came to cast the role of Brundibár, Honza came up to Rudolf Freudenfeld again and asked him in his special way, "Could I give it a try?" From that moment on there was only one Brundibár — Honza Treichlinger.

A second and third cast of understudies were chosen for all the main roles. Stephan Sommer, the son of the Prague pianist Alice Herz-Sommer, enthusiastically practiced the role of the sparrow. Piňt'a Mühlstein's brother Eli likewise studied the role of Pepíček, and his sister, Maria, rehearsed as first understudy for the role of Aninka. "She had a beautiful velvety voice," Flaška recalls. "She was so natural. A very different type from Greta Hofmeister, who was a little older than we were."

In the days that followed, boys and girls came streaming from all corners to gather in the hot, sultry attic of Boys' Home L 417 — Danka, Daša, Raja, Hanka, Sonja, Ruth, Eva, Lilian, Lisa, Hana, Drixi, Renate, Zdenka, Marta, Jiři, František, Hanuš, Petr, Pavel, Rudi, Karel, and Zdeněk. For some of these children, the world suddenly seemed to revolve around nothing but rehearsals — and around Baštík, their nickname for Rudolf Freudenfeld, who often arrived at rehearsals exhausted and bathed in sweat after a hard day's work in a stone quarry in nearby Litoměřice. Still, nothing could keep him from dedicating his evenings to *Brundibár* — although it certainly was not all that easy, as Rudolf Laub wrote in the newspaper *Vedem:*

Have any of you ever been a director and had to deal with fifty strapping boys and charming girls who are convinced that the more noise and fun during the rehearsals, the better? No, it's not easy,

and I take my hat off to Rudi Freudenfeld, because throughout the rehearsals
he got angry only a few times, and then
calmed down again immediately. I would
not have had that patience, and I doubt
whether anybody else would have either.

But some sort of aura held us together,
the feeling that "when it's finished, it'll
be super." We made progress, we got a
better rehearsal room, and interest grew.
Everybody began to look forward to
rehearsals, and would tell his acquain-
tances with a certain pride, "We're
rehearsing a children's opera."[3]

Of course the people who had taken on
these young actors were themselves outstanding personalities who lent a special
luster to the enterprise. Along with Baštík,
Rafik, and Gideon Klein, there were the
play's set designer and artistic director,
František Zelenka, and *Brundibár*'s composer, Hans Krása. The two of them kept a
close eye on the rehearsals of the children's
opera, and while Hans Krása set to work
reorchestrating the music according to the
instruments and musicians available in
Theresienstadt, František Zelenka prepared
a modest set design and a poster announc-
ing the upcoming premiere.

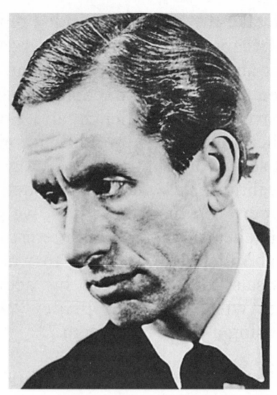

Hans Krása. "His creative process seems effortless, somewhere between check and checkmate, but the result displays uncanny sureness." These were the words Viktor Ullmann chose to praise the composer in 1928.

The rehearsals for *Brundibár* generated considerable excitement — and disappointment as well. "I remember feeling very hurt," Eva Landa says, "because I didn't get the role of the schoolgirl who throws her book in the air. I wanted so much to play it.

But another girl, Hana Vohrysková, was chosen."

Eva was not the only girl who was feeling out of sorts in those days. Helga was crushed when out of the blue Rita Böhm, their new counselor, scolded her, saying, "You are one of the first girls that I shall think badly of if you don't settle down at once." All Helga had done was chuckle while Rita was talking about England. In reality she was hardly in the mood for laughter — Rita's descriptions of England had awakened a dreadful longing for her mother.

"Should I tell her?" she asked in her diary. "I've got to explain it somehow. I really do like Rita an awful lot, and that's why this hurts even more." Helga made herself talk it over with Rita. "A quarter to eleven in the evening: Rita is no longer angry at me."

Others were experiencing some of these same feelings, these emotional ups and downs. Friendships formed, encountered their first snag, broke apart, and were then renewed. Jealousy played no small part in this carousel of friendship. No sooner had a girl shown another more attention than her old friend felt rejected, no longer loved. Misunderstandings, taunts, and defiance followed. Then came attempts at renewing the relationship and reconciliation. Friendship was everything for these girls — life, love, the future. A girl's own visions, dreams, and hopes were reflected in the eyes of her friend. They both drew energy from their relationship, took heart from it.

Flaška and Lenka were quite fond of each other. Flaška found in Lenka a friend whom she admired greatly, with whom she could laugh and discuss many things. They did not always see eye to eye, and sometimes they fell out, for Lenka was the epitome of a critical spirit. But Flaška always brought them back together. She had a definite need for harmony, and worked very hard to be friendly and fair with everyone.

But the two friends eventually had a row. For Flaška this was no great problem, since she was convinced that the quarrel would soon be forgotten. For Lenka, however, it was a minor catastrophe. She withdrew inside herself — what choice did she have? It was impossible for them to stay out of each other's way, to keep the distance that would allow them to move closer together when they were ready to do so. The only retreat possible was an inward one.

And so Lenka wrote a poem.

Reaction to a Quarrel with Flaška

I wanted to be good
And have tried very hard,
But in just the shortest time
The girls have
Disappointed me.
They didn't respect my effort,
And I have tried
To deal with that.

And they asked me
Why I was not able
To get rid of the bad in me.
But I am trying!
And I will keep on trying
And will prove to Flaška
That I have reached my goal.
I will, I must —
In the shortest time.
And the next time
They accuse me of the same thing again,
I will not get angry.
I will quietly move toward my goal.
And come closer to it with each day.

Until I can say to Eva
I have arrived at my goal
And I shall keep going on
Until I am in Ma'agal,

Alongside Eva,
And then higher still.
And Flaška will no longer be able to say
That I am not trying.
Just the opposite,
She will stand aside and wonder
How I could reach the heavens,
Because I shall be as high as the sky.

A few days later, Flaška and Lenka renewed their friendship and confirmed it in blood. They pricked their fingertips and with drops of blood wrote on a piece of paper: "We, Flaška and Lenka, pledge our eternal loyalty and friendship." They buried the paper on the grounds of the ramparts.

Meanwhile, Helga was taking a good hard look at herself. Was she also uncooperative, egoistic, intolerant, as Tella was constantly upbraiding others for being? She confided her crisis of confidence to her diary: "I have to speak with Tella again. What happened was: I was just starting to get used to life in the Home when Ela disappointed me. I didn't want to begin another friendship all over again for fear of further disappointment. But I forgot one thing, and Tella is truly right about this: Be strict with yourself, but more tolerant and gentle with others. I need to follow that rule."

These were tense times, and everyone was on edge. The temperature had been high for days. Life was barely endurable under the roof of the Girls' Home. No wonder their Sabbath service just wouldn't go right. "Frau Mühlstein prayed and lit the candles. Normally we play games afterward. This time someone read aloud, but many girls were already on their bunks, some had even fallen asleep. Of twenty-seven girls there were seven at the table. What an impossible Sabbath. Ruth, who had made the arrangements for the evening, was so disappointed that she cried."

Even Ma'agal was not as successful as it had been earlier. During this period not one new member was chosen for the "circle of perfection." But those who were already in Ma'agal decided to divide it into three classes. No one made it into the first class; in the second were Handa and Muška, with Irena, Pavla, Eva Landa, and Eva Heller in the third.

Helga was a bit hurt that she had been excluded from this select circle. "I will try hard to be the way the girls would like me to be. I would like to be better than I have been until now. I want to reach a higher level. I have to get into Ma'agal," she wrote in her diary while standing at the window, shortly before midnight. Then she spent a long time gazing out into the night. "What a lovely sight! Everyone asleep. The whole town wrapped in darkness, and oppressive heat brooding over the entire region. There is a deep serenity, with only a bird chirping here or there. Some lights are on in the factory, where you can hear the regular thumping of the hammer. It reminds me of something, though I don't know what."

The counselors joined forces to try to relieve the tension in Room 28. On July 16 they celebrated the birthday of Karel Pollak, Handa's father, whom everyone called Strejda (Uncle). The girls put on a little play entitled *Twenty-five Years Later,* which focused on Fiška and her problems, with Eva Stern as an absentminded doctor carrying a scalpel in her shoes, storing a hypodermic in a wastebasket, and the like. Then the counselors presented the surprise the girls had been anticipating for days. "It was very amusing. They had written a funny rhyme to sing about each of us. They were unrecognizable in their costumes. Tella had braids done up in red nets, a very short dirndl skirt, with underwear that reached below her knees. Instead of stockings she had painted red stripes on her legs. And her cheeks were red, too. Laura was wearing a man's formal coat, a top hat, and a genuine mustache made of curls. Eva Weiss wore a long skirt like those worn in the nineteenth century, a black hat with feathers, and a velvet cape that was cut to look like a fur. Her eyebrows were painted red. No one would have recognized her."

Eva Weiss gave each girl a sketch with an appropriate verse. Helga's picture showed a girl just leaving sick bay, with the words: "A girl named Helga / was a long time ill / she's back again now / thanks to God's good will." After each stanza was the refrain: "Yes, yes, yes / it's as clear as day / Yes, yes, yes / it's true in its way."

On July 25 the Youth Welfare Office put on a program in one of the barracks to honor the memory of Theodor Herzl. There was a speech by Gonda Redlich, a performance by Tella's girls' choir from L 410, a poem recited by an actress, and a ballet that depicted the story of the slaves in ancient Egypt. "I forgot to join in the singing, because I was dreaming," Helga jotted in her diary that evening. "I was standing at a window in the attic, gazing out on a picture come to life — a tree-lined road near Litoměřice. I could even see as far as the clock and, at some distance, little villages in the valley and on the hill, surrounded by splendid golden fields framed with woods and mountains."

Was liberation near? Helga's "picture come to life" was followed three days later by news that spread like the wind and set every heart in Theresienstadt aflutter. "And now for something very new," Helga wrote on July 28. "Mussolini abdicated yesterday, and I've been almost crazy ever since. I have this strange feeling, like the one I had when Papa moved to Kyjov to join us for good. Three days ago I said, the war is coming to an end. But I didn't feel anything. It seemed so unreal, faraway, but now I sense it is very close. I would like to dance, if I only could, and sing. I'm going to go crazy."

At the end of July, Theresienstadt was still baking under a merciless dome of heat. The temperature had reached ninety-five degrees in the shade. Days went by without a drop of rain. Unwelcome denizens of the town crept out of their hideaways and began to multiply out of control: bedbugs, lice, fleas. Above all, bedbugs. Suddenly the little black beasts could be seen, smelled, and heard tap, tap, tapping everywhere — on mattresses, beams, floors, and walls, in suitcases and shoes.

"Bedbugs. Bedbugs. The dreadful word

sent a wave of horror throughout Theresien-stadt," Hana Lissau wrote when she described the plague in an essay she composed six weeks later. "One day one of the girls in Room 28 found this horrible animal boring its way into her wooden bunk. She went into hysterics. When she had regained control of herself, she joined several other girls in banging against the wood of various planks, and then came the real horror — bedbugs, bedbugs everywhere, a sea of bedbugs! Bedbugs wherever you looked, nothing but bedbugs. We murdered whole families of bedbugs that day. They died wherever their enemy, human beings, appeared. It was simply impossible to stay in bed. We slept on the floor and in the hall, and the girls who remained in their bunks were covered all over with little red spots. Only gas can destroy these vermin — that was the word on everyone's lips, because gas was the only, the ultimate salvation. People kept coming into the room to inspect the bizarre situation."

"I can still recall," Judith Schwarzbart says, "how we dragged our mattresses and bedclothes outside, cleaned and beat and aired them in the garden — they were full of bedbugs. It was a terrible plague."

"It was worst between the wooden

planks," Eva Weiss adds. "The cracks were black, black with bedbugs. Battalions of bedbugs! They had to spray the rooms. And at the entrance there was a sign, black print on yellow: GAS. BEWARE. MAY BE LETHAL. With a skull at the top."

"We slept in the hall a second night because of the bedbugs. Seven girls slept outside. We are all covered with bites," Helga reported on July 31. "We have permission to sleep in the garden, because you can't really sleep in the hall, since many Homes get up at five and raise a ruckus. Spraying didn't help at all. I caught six fleas and three bedbugs last night. Now wasn't that a successful hunt! And I didn't even need a gun. Something fell into my shoe. Walter, one of our Home's elders, killed whatever it was. Now I'm going to join Ela and Jiřinka to make a 'tent' for tonight."

It was not until the night of August 4 that the first real thunderstorm arrived. Some girls went to the window to watch the jagged lightning bolts cut across the nighttime sky. Others climbed onto their neighbors' bunks for a better look at the spectacle. The storm was directly overhead for a good while. Each bolt was instantly followed by a clap of thunder — loud and eerie. Gradually the tension ebbed, as the girls fell into a deep sleep.

But there was still something in the air, an unidentifiable sense of unease that the thunderstorm had not swept away. "I'd like to know what the Germans have up their sleeves. They've emptied out the Sudeten Barracks and the armory," Helga jotted in her diary on July 31. "The entire Sudeten Barracks has to be completely evacuated within forty-eight hours. I saw a whole crowd of people moving their things. It's how I picture a retreat during war. And Papa told me that I was right about that."

Otto Pollak observed: "July 31, 1943. Evacuation of the Sudeten Barracks. Forty-five hundred people to be resettled. A whole city breaking camp. People packing, moving what little they have, all in a great commotion. Two-wheeled carts, hearse wagons — those are the modes of transportation. Waves of people, unlike any I've seen. The square in front of the barracks is like some lively, colorful harbor scene."[4]

More disturbing changes were carefully noted. "The Germans are having even more Homes vacated. Every street has been given a name. Some are called lanes, some streets." Otto listed them in his diary: "New street names: L1 = See Strasse. L 1A = Kurze Strasse, L 2 = Bahnhof Strasse. L 3

= Lange Strasse. L 4 = Haupt Strasse. L 5 = Park Strasse, L 6 = Wall Strasse, the road to Bohušovice = Süd Strasse and what was Kopitzer Strasse = West Strasse . . ."

SS *Obersturmführer* Anton Burger had begun his work. He was the new camp commandant, having taken over from Siegfried Seidl on July 5, 1943. Because he was already privy to "Secret Reich Matters," Section IV B in Berlin considered him the ideal candidate for the post, especially since he had worked in close cooperation with Eichmann in the Central Office for Jewish Emigration in Vienna, Prague, and Brno, where his fanatical hatred of all things Czech and Jewish had already been put to the test. Above all it was his scheming in Brno, where he headed the Evacuation Fund for Bohemia and Moravia until his transfer to Berlin, that had established his reputation as one of the most brutal and unscrupulous Nazis.

Anton Burger's arrival as the new camp commandant of Theresienstadt was a bad omen. Of course, no one could know precisely what he and his henchmen actually had in mind. When interrogated after the war, he claimed that he had taken on the work as Seidl's successor in order to achieve a smooth implementation of the imminent deportations ordered by Eichmann, but especially in order to make the ghetto "a jewel box, ready for representatives of the press and the Red Cross."[5]

Vermin continued to have the run of Theresienstadt. There was stench and filth everywhere, and there were forty-six thousand sleep-deprived, edgy, badly bitten human beings in close quarters. The hospitals and sick bays were overflowing. On August 11 the girls had to vacate their room, pack their few belongings, and sleep in the garden again. More radical measures had to be employed to deal with the bedbug plague. Helga did not find it easy to leave her diary behind. "I'll say goodbye to you, my dear friend. No one is to be allowed into the building until Saturday. It is being gassed."

On one of those sweltering summer evenings, Giuseppe Verdi's *Requiem* was given its first public performance, under the direction of Rafael Schächter, in a room in the old town hall on the main square. "It was a brilliant premiere. The mixed choir was up on the podium — a hundred and fifty strong. The soloists stood in front of the choir: Marion Podolier, Heda Aronson-Lindt, David Grünfeld, and myself," Karel

Berman wrote in his memoirs.[6] For the first time, the Latin mass for the dead unleashed its immense power in the ghetto. The effect on the audience was overwhelming. The girls listened from the evening stillness of their garden as the singing, like a gentle earthquake, rolled toward them.

"At last the day came when the gas had taken care of the vermin," Hana Lissau described the end of the plague in her essay. "Three days later, we returned to Room 28. And what did we see? Dead bedbugs everywhere. We heaved a sigh of relief. And then our life went on as before. Thank God, without bedbugs."

"The news, or rather, *bonkes,* is moving through Theresienstadt, that a transport of 5,000 people is being put together," Ruth Gutmann wrote in her essay. "A tense atmosphere has descended over the streets, barracks, and Homes. Here and there people are saying 'I'm telling you, if a transport is leaving, I'll be on it.' 'Don't say that, you are protected here. And I'm only a simple worker.' Sad to say — this time it's not just *bonkes.* Now it is the sad truth. Last night 5,000 people were ordered to be on the transport."

Thursday, August 26, 1943

Things are terrible here. There's an awful tension among the adults and in the girls' Homes. Transports are being prepared, off to a new ghetto, into the unknown. The first transport is to be made up of people who were convicted by the ghetto court, usually for minor offenses, plus sixty people from the AK transport. It looks like Pavla will be on it, too, since her father was in jail for three months. One of Papa's neighbors will be on it as well.

And something else: 1,500 children are to arrive tonight. Word is that they're from Poland. We're making toys and little sewing bags for them. They will be in quarantine for a month, so that they don't bring in any disease with them. — I have infectious diarrhea. Of twenty-seven girls, sixteen are already confined to bed, and three more are also sick.

The next day there was a barracks lockdown — it was forbidden to leave any building without permission. That evening Eva Winkler watched from the window in the hallway on the third floor as a procession of little children marched down the street. "I can still see it before me. There were maybe fifty, sixty little children. It left a horrible

The children from Bialystok; drawing by Helga Weiss, Room 24

impression on me."

Other girls cautiously crowded around the closed window. It was forbidden to open windows, and the girls didn't dare let the Germans see them gazing with curiosity at the street below where the children were straggling past. They were dressed in rags, many of them in shoes far too big for them, some in wooden clogs, some barefoot, the larger children holding tight to the hands of the smaller ones.

Otto Pollak watched the same spectacle from a different perspective that evening. "At 5:30, I was crossing the deserted Q3, Badhaus Gasse, and saw a sad procession of children, maybe twenty-five in all, coming from the bathhouse where they had been 'disinsectified' [disinfected]. Led by a few female counselors, they moved slowly in the direction of Bohušovice/Süd Strasse."

There they were assigned to quarters in the West Barracks, outside the city walls — some twelve hundred children from the Polish ghetto in Bialystok. Any contact with them was forbidden. "But we did learn a few things about them all the same," Helga Weiss wrote in her diary. "None of the children can speak Czech, we don't even know whether they are Polish or Jewish children. From the ramparts we can catch glimpses of them. This morning they were marched to the Receiving Office. They look awful. You can't even guess at their ages. They all have old faces and very thin little bodies. They aren't wearing stockings, and only a few of them even have shoes. They came out of the Receiving Office with shaved heads, which means they have lice. Their eyes are full of fear."[7]

To take care of these children, fifty-three doctors and counselors were specially selected — among them Franz Kafka's youngest sister, Ottla David-Kafka, who worked in the ghetto as a children's counselor. They were housed in the West Barracks and were not allowed back into the ghetto. The adults were sworn to complete silence about anything they heard or saw there. And everyone else was forbidden under threat of punishment to have any contact with the children.

People in Theresienstadt were puzzled by something very unusual about these children. Why had they held back and screamed so loudly when they were sent to the showers, they asked themselves? Why had they acted so strangely? It was incomprehensible to the residents of Theresienstadt, for whom a shower in the bathhouse was the ultimate luxury. The whole affair was veiled in secrecy. Rumor, *bonkes,* had it that they were to be sent to Palestine or Switzerland; some sort of exchange, some deal was being planned. But no one knew anything specific about it.[8]

Uneasiness and anxiety had held sway over the ghetto since the announcement of the imminent transports, especially after August 24, when all residents of the Hamburg Barracks between the ages of sixty and eighty had to register.

The first and second transports, Dl and Dm, were to be made up of twenty-five hundred persons each, plus eight hundred others on a reserve list — all of them primarily from the Protectorate. Who would receive the dreaded slip of paper this time? Fear was growing throughout the ghetto.

Ruth Gutmann wrote in her essay:

A few girls in our Home knew they would be on the transport. Among them was Pavla, my best friend. My first thought was that I could not live without her.

There was no order to assemble for transport that night, or the next morning either. We were so agitated that we couldn't remain inside the Home. There was still no news at noon.

That afternoon our Kuče (Zdenka Löwy) received her summons. We thought she would cry. But Kuče was brave. That evening the summons came for Pavla and Olile. Olile's parents didn't want to tell her. We decided we would all stay awake. But we all fell asleep after a while, as if someone had dropped us into deep water.

The next morning the reserve list was posted, and Poppi's and Helena's names were on it. Now began a great flurry of packing. They were supposed to report at three that afternoon. It's hard to fathom how much fright one morning can contain! Zdenka's father came and wanted to help her pack. She offered him three tomatoes. But he refused them and said, "Keep them, Zdenka. I'm so hungry I could eat all three at once." And then he began to cry, and it became clear to us that he hadn't eaten anything and that the whole family didn't have even a piece of bread. When we heard that, we all began to cry too, and each of us looked for something to eat. That day was the third time I had ever seen a grown man cry.

Zdenka gave us all a kiss, happy that her suitcase was being stuffed fuller and fuller. We told her, "Don't forget, we are in this together, we all help each other. It's the most natural thing in the world." Olile didn't have anything to wear either. We gave her what we could. Then at three o'clock they left.

Helga's diary continues:

Saturday, September 4, 1943
People are to board the transport tomorrow morning. For the time being, Zdenka is the only one of us on it. But the summons will come in several batches. Zdenka is being brave. Everything's in a terrible

commotion here. Lilly's parents and her sister are leaving, which is why she volunteered to join them. It will be a total of 5,000 people, only Czech Jews. Frau Stein is leaving with her husband, Uncle Max, and Aunt Paula. They are supposed to stay at the building where they live, and get together with their families only at their assembly point. There are so many assembly points. Zdenka is going to the Hamburg Barracks, where she will stay in quarantine with 500 other people.

From Otto Pollak's diary:

Sunday, September 5, 1943
A dark day despite the sunshine. The 5,000 to be transported are quartered in barracks, awaiting transport. Twenty-nine people from our Home have been summoned for transport. Assembly at nine o'clock at Hamburg Barracks. Four people from my room are among them.

It's a beautiful day, so people can do their packing outside. Both courtyards look like an oriental bazaar. Everywhere tables are piled high with things. I'm working hard in the main office.

Helga is all churned up inside, since six of her best friends are leaving. She has a little goodbye gift for each one. Helga doesn't want to spend time with me in the garden tonight because it reminds her too much of her comrades, who had to line up to be counted there — about seventy in all. It is an awful evening. Saying our goodbyes, perhaps forever, is cutting us to the quick.

Helga's diary continues:

Sunday, September 5, 1943
What a day! But it's all over now. They are all in the "sluice." Pavla, Helena, Zdenka, Olile, and Poppinka are the ones from our group to be going. Poppinka and Helena are in the reserves, and there is a possibility that they will be left out. Each of us gave Zdenka something. She is so poor. I gave her a half ration of bread, a tin of liverwurst, some linden blossom tea, and sugar. Her father came to help her pack, and Zdenka gave him bread, sugar, and tomatoes. He didn't want any of it for himself. We girls forced him to take it and promised to give Zdenka more things. He began to cry and thanked us children and the counselors for taking such good care of his daughter. We were so touched that by now we were all crying. Strejda gave him a whole loaf of bread. We managed to furnish them with a little bag of food in

a very short time.

At six o'clock in the evening they reported for assembly, each to a different place. The goodbyes were hard, but we were all very brave, except for Helena, whom I saw really breaking down in tears for the first time today. At eight o'clock I went looking for Zdenka. She was with her entire family, all sitting on their luggage, and she was so happy to see me that she wept and laughed at the same time. Although I did sleep last night, I had terrible dreams, and when I woke up I had black circles under my eyes.

Monday, September 6, 1943

I got up at six o'clock to see Zdenka one last time. When I got to the Hamburg Barracks, people were just coming out the back gate on their way to board the transport. Everything was blocked by wooden planks, so that you couldn't see them and they couldn't get away. I climbed over the fence and ran toward the last people at the end of the line as they were leaving through the barracks gate. When I got to the gate I watched the cattle car pull up that Zdenka left on. I blew her kisses.

Helena has been removed from the transport. For our friends who were still in the "sluice," we went to the barricade and brought bread and marmalade as breakfast. There was not much left for us to eat, but somebody did find a couple of old crusts, so each of us at least had a bite.

I didn't see any of our girls who had to line up for the transport other than Poppinka, as she marched past our Home this afternoon on the way to the train. We went out to say a last goodbye and brought her four buns from our evening meal. Her mother was so touched that she cried. Eva Weiss brought her a couple of apples and Frau Mühlstein had two little sacks with gingerbread and cookies; one was for her seven-year-old brother. Poppinka cried; her courage was at an end. Zajíček and Flaška stood on either side of her and led her along because she couldn't see anything through her tears. I'm lying in bed now, and maybe they have all arrived by now — somewhere.

"That evening, as we all lay in bed," Ruth Gutmann wrote at the end of her essay, "we were constantly aware of someone missing: the girls who had left. Then we told one another that never again will there be a real Room 28."

The trauma ran deep. The two September

transports were the first ones to the East in six months. More than 5,000 people left the ghetto on them: 4,769 Czech, 124 German, 83 Austrian, and 11 Dutch Jews. There were 327 children under the age of fifteen. The selection had not been random; the SS made sure of that. Many of the members of the Ghetto Guard, which had been disbanded a short time before, were among them, likewise men with families — young, strong men in particular, who had had some connection with the Czech underground organization. Evidently the point was to weaken Theresienstadt's potential for resistance in order to prevent any events like those that had taken place in the Warsaw Ghetto a few months earlier. That the transports also served another nefarious purpose did not become clear until later.

In Room 28 the bunks of Pavla Seiner, Zdenka Löwy, Olilie Löwy, and Ruth Popper were now empty. "Suddenly something was missing," Handa says of the changed situation. "It wasn't just the girls that we especially liked, but the others, too. Our community was really like a little clock, with each girl a gear, whether larger or smaller. Each had added her own spice. But at the time for me the particular shock was that, of all people, it was Pavla who had to leave. I liked her very much. And I think she was a girl everyone treasured. She was a focal point in our little community. I know that the empty bunk where she had slept made me very sad."

Tuesday, September 7, 1943
Milka has moved in with us. She sleeps in Elinka's spot. I've taken over Zdenka's place, with Ela beside me. We have made our space quite attractive. On one wall we have shelving for clothes and under-clothes, with a curtain in front, across the top a board that we are decorating. My two pictures are hanging on the wall. I have to get all my things in order, because there could always be another transport leaving for somewhere. Everyone, or no one, could be forced to depart. You never know what scheme they are hatching for us, these Germans.

The bond linking the girls had grown stronger. Proofs of friendship multiplied. Each girl wanted to bring some joy to another, to solidify the friendship. "I must admit that I like Ela more than I used to," Helga remarked. "We want to exchange friendship rings."

The room was put in order and some

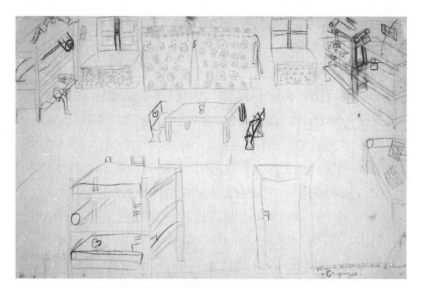

Room 28, drawn by Maria Mühlstein

things were rearranged. Helga put the photograph of her mother on a little shelf on the wall, and she decorated her bunk with her little colorful pillow, which she called "Dopey," after the smallest dwarf in Walt Disney's adaptation of *Snow White and the Seven Dwarfs.*

Life went on. Each girl had her own way of counteracting the fear — even if it was only a matter of clinging more tightly than before to the daily routine, which despite its difficulties was easier to bear than to be caught in the terrible transports that swept you away into the unknown.

Thursday, September 9, 1943
I would like to describe what it looks like

here and how a typical day goes. We have three wooden frames for triple bunks, a double bunk, a single, and a sixer. Opposite the door is a closet for our coats. Our clothes are to one side of the door, and the corner has hooks for our towels and little bags of toiletries. The cupboard for dishes is there, too, and two shelves for the large bowls that we fetch our meals in. In the middle of the room is a table with two benches and two old chairs. Under the window is a shelf for shoes.

No sooner are we awake than we begin airing our beds. "Get out of bed!" someone says, while someone else calls out, "Today's my turn to use the window!" A third girl chimes in with: "What do you mean; you're supposed to use the table today!" — "Then I'll wait until Lissau's done, and use the window!" — "But I called dibs on that!"

Almost everyone dresses very slowly. "Zajíček, get up, it's seven o'clock already!" — "Fiška, get dressed, the others have already washed up." They are all back from the washroom. "First group, take everything in and make your beds!" — "Who's on *toranoot* today?" — "Didi, you haven't done it for a long time!" — "I'm not allowed to carry anything."

It takes a good while until someone is chosen to fetch food for us all. The cleaning brigade tidies up the room, while the rest sit on their beds, talking or putting their things in order. Some, still sitting on their bunks, quickly shove some food in their mouths, although that isn't allowed. If a counselor catches us at it, we're put under house arrest. At nine o'clock we sit around the table and eat breakfast. We're not having any lessons this week. We're allowed a half hour for breakfast. Tella: "Clear the table! Go outside for a while now, so we can sweep up. Afterward I'll tell you what we're going to do."

We're supposed to take work with us to the garden. It takes a while until at least a few girls comply and go outside, but most stay in the room. "I'm not going anywhere. I'm cold!" — "I'm not going to cart all this downstairs!" — "I've got nothing to wear!" One after the other they find an excuse for not going down to the garden. But the main reason, which no one says, is that we're all lazybones and want only to loll around on our beds. But if boys were involved, almost all of them would fly downstairs as if somebody had fired a gun in the room — except for a couple of us, including me.

Of twenty-two girls, ten go down to the garden. There we sit on school benches without a table. In each corner of the garden are benches of some sort. We put them in a little square and sit huddled together, to keep from being cold, while we chat or darn our underwear and stockings, knit, play cards, or whatever. Two hours pass like this — it seems like half an hour to us — until a counselor sticks her head out the window: "Time for lunch! Who's on *toranoot?*" — "Where's Eva Stern gone again?" — "A couple of you need to go fetch the food right now, otherwise we'll get nothing to eat. Eva Winkler, you're one of them!" — "I'm not allowed to carry anything!" And Rutka: "But you can do handstands on the ramparts, can't you!"

The voice of the counselor can be heard again, calling each girl by name, but they all find some excuse. Now it's Helena's turn, who pretends she doesn't hear, while the girls call out in saccharine voices: "Leave poor little Helena alone, she's doing her history homework. It would break her heart to tear herself away from it." The mood is edgy. We have to get hold of ourselves. I like it when Helena flies into a rage and starts her river of sobs, until she finally sounds like a howling hyena. Then come a few caustic remarks, and we hear Helena's pretty voice: "Well, how would you all feel?" After all her shouts and curses, Helena goes to fetch our midday meal anyway. A quarter-hour later we're called upstairs. After lunch, those on *toranoot* clean up, and the others go to visit their parents. We have to be back in the Home by three o'clock. If the weather's nice, we go to the ramparts — once again, reluctantly of course. "I don't like to walk!" — "My shoes pinch!" — "That's no fun!" — the same sort of excuses we've heard all day. But once we're on the ramparts, no one wants to go home. By the time evening rolls around, some of us are back with our parents. But by a quarter to nine, we have to have washed up and be in the Home, or at a quarter after eight if we've not washed yet. If there is an evening program, we have to be in the Home by eight, and we go to bed right away, but that rarely happens. If there is no program, we don't hurry, just talk — no one even thinks of undressing. That's the job of the counselors. "Off to bed with you! Lights out in five minutes! Whether you have your pajamas on or not."

Now it gets hectic, and within fifteen minutes the room is dark. Here and there you can hear suppressed laughs and whispered words that were too loud all the same. After a few minutes there's not another word — only the regular breathing of girls asleep.

Along with Milka — her real name was Bohumila Poláček — two other girls had come to Room 28: Vera Nath and Hana Wertheimer, who was nicknamed Hanka. The three had known one another in Prague, where they had been stranded after their flights from their hometowns. Hanka was originally from Znojmo, Vera from Opava. Both towns were in the Sudetenland, the border region of the Czech Republic that contained a German majority. The Sudetenland had been under German rule since the autumn of 1938. Milka came from Chrastany, a small town in southern Bohemia.

The new roommates awakened old memories in those who knew them from Prague — above all memories of their time together at Hagibor, the Jewish athletic field. Pavla Seiner and Hanka Wertheimer — both tall, athletic girls — had been among the best dodgeball players there. Everyone wanted Hanka in particular on their team, for not only could she run fast and catch a hard-thrown ball, but she could also throw with

Bohumila ("Milka") Poláček (far right) *in the garden of her house in Chrastany. With her are* (left to right) *her cousin Hanus Lederer; her father, Vojteč Poláček; her brother, Jiri Poláček; and her cousin Hanna Lederer.*

real power.

Hagibor. For every Holocaust survivor who had spent time on the Jewish athletic field in Prague-Strašnice between 1940 and 1942, the very word evoked hope and confidence. In the midst of hatred, prohibitions, persecution, and fear, that place was like an island, where the word "future" was infused with life and where Jewish children's self-confidence, which had been so badly undermined, could be rebuilt and restored. "When I think of Hagibor, I think of happy times," Hanka recalls enthusiastically. "Hagibor was a very long way from our apartment, and I often walked the whole distance. Sometimes if I couldn't find a friend to go with me, I hid my yellow star and went by streetcar. To avoid arousing suspicion I would go one stop farther and then walk back. But of course I was always afraid."

But once they were there, the fear was forgotten for a little while. Through athletics, games, and songs, the pressure on a group of psychologically battered children fell away for a few hours. "We were almost happy at Hagibor," Eva Landa recalls. "There was something resembling normal life for us on the athletic field. There were track-and-field events, gymnastics, acrobatics; we could ice-skate in winter. It often felt like the Spartacus Games. There were various competitions and team games. We danced and sang — especially Zionist songs."

Fredy Hirsch at Hagibor, the Jewish athletic field in Prague

Ela adds, "Toward evening potato soup would be cooked over an open fire. For me, that was always the best part. I can still taste that potato soup."

There was a special atmosphere at Hagibor, which is Hebrew for "the strong man." It was not just about being athletically active, as the very colors of the uniforms indicated. They were blue and white, the colors of the Zionist movement.

Most important was to instill in the children hope and the courage to face life, and to prepare them to live in Eretz Yisrael, the Land of Israel. They learned Morse code, practiced tying knots, and sometimes military commands in Hebrew rang out — *"Smolah pnei, yeminah pnei, kadimah, tza'ad"* ("Left, right, forward march, halt!") — as children followed the orders of their group leaders, among them Nita Petschau and Dita Sachs, who were in charge of the ten-to-twelve-year-old girls.

Sometimes, however, the three to four hundred children would come together in rank and file and Fredy Hirsch, the legendary leader of Hagibor and of the Zionist youth organization Hechalutz, would take over, whistle in hand. Whenever Fredy appeared, everything seemed more welcoming. The children loved this young man with his well-trained body and wavy black hair. He always had a smile and an encouraging word for them. The fact that this émigré from Aachen in Germany spoke broken Czech did not detract in the slightest from the enchantment he radiated.

"If a young Jew decides to live for his people, he has to go to Hachsharah [Zionist training camp], become a worker in Eretz Yisrael, and conquer the soil. But first and foremost, he must overcome his own fear and lethargy, get involved in sports, do gymnastics, steel his body, and make good use of his competitive drive."[9] These were the words that kept echoing across the Jewish athletic field. Fredy Hirsch was a charismatic speaker, and he inspired many children to become passionate Zionists. To meet him was to remember him forever.

"Fredy was almost like a god to us," Eva Landa recalls. "We even sang a song about him, with the melody taken from the Czech folk song 'Two Wanderers Stood on an Ant Hill.' It went, 'Life would be gray without Fredy's whistle / He whistles so hard we turn pale.' We sang that song over and over with great enthusiasm."

Vera Nath adds: "The person I shall always remember, the person I took to my heart — that was Fredy Hirsch. He did so much for us! He made it possible for us to have a beautiful summer back then in Prague."

In the early 1940s nearly all the Jewish children in Prague encountered one another at some point, and many friendships that had begun there were later renewed in Theresienstadt. When Hanka, Milka, and Vera were assigned to Room 28, they saw familiar faces, and so they did not find it too difficult to join in the life of the community.

Vera Nath had arrived in Theresienstadt on July 8, 1943, and she was glad to be placed in Room 28. She was still in shock: as if by a miracle, she and her family had escaped the September transport. They had already passed through the "sluice" and their baggage had been loaded. Just as they were approaching the train, a young man who could not bear to see his mother go by herself pushed his way forward. The moment he boarded, the quota of twenty-five hundred people was met, and the doors closed. Without a moment's hesitation, the Nath family turned around.

Vera was a strikingly pretty girl with gentle, dark eyes. She was dainty and very reserved. It is hard to say if that trait was inborn or the result of her childhood experiences. "I stopped trying to make friends early on," she says today. "All my friends kept disappearing. I had a close girlfriend in Prague, Suse Pick from Žatec. She and her family were deported to Lodz. Then I was in another group with two boys my age, Rus and Jerry. Their father was a soccer player. We often played together in the Old Jewish Cemetery. They were born in America, which made them American citizens, so they didn't have to wear a star. Sometimes they brought me ice cream from the grocery store, which had been forbidden to me for some time. But they disappeared, too, from one day to the next. What a horrible thing it is, when friends that you've just come to know simply vanish and you don't know where they went. You simply never hear from them again."

It became second nature for Vera not to get too close to anyone, to consciously avoid seeking out friendships. In Theresienstadt she had her parents and her sister — that was the main thing. She became open to friendships much later, after she had begun a new life in Israel and could provide her children with what she had so painfully missed in her own childhood. "Once I had my own children, I made sure that they never had to switch classes or schools. I did not want them torn from familiar surroundings. I didn't want them to keep losing friends and having to look for new ones."

Hanka Wertheimer's upbringing and attitude were very different. Hanka was a tall, athletic, sociable girl with a winning and hearty laugh. She was accepted into Room 28 from the first, even by girls who did not know her. Hanka had a delightful personality. And as young as she was, she knew what she wanted: She wanted to go to Palestine.

In her parents' home, the ideas of Theodor Herzl had been the dominant topic of conversation, and so it was no surprise that she had joined the Zionist youth organization Tekhelet-Lavan (Blue-White) at the age of six. The events of the next few years only intensified Hanka's longing for Palestine. In Prague, where her parents had fled from Znojmo in the autumn of 1938, Hanka had quickly formed a circle of close friends whose hopes and ideas were bound up with the Zionist cause.

Hanka met most of these friends again in Theresienstadt, and soon a regular meeting was arranged, every Friday evening, in the little shed in the courtyard of Boys' Home L 417, which housed an electrical workshop. The group called itself Dror, which is Hebrew for "bird" and a symbol of freedom. They spoke about Palestine, learned Hebrew, expanded their knowledge of agriculture, and discussed the Zionist books they read together. Occasionally they would share a piece of bread or a bun. "And once," Hanka recalls, "we made cheese out of sour milk and devoured it with gusto."

Hanka's friends Resinka Schwarz and Miriam Rosenzweig were part of the group, as well as a few boys from Home 5 — Jiřka Broll, Micha Honigwachs, Yehuda Bacon, and Hanka's first boyfriend and first love, Yehuda Huppert, who was nicknamed Polda.

Whenever Hanka took a walk with Polda around the block of Building L 410, she could count on being followed by curious eyes gazing from the upstairs windows. "As soon as we saw one of our girls taking a walk with a boy outside the Home, it was instantly the talk of the room, and soon everyone was at the window to see what they were doing," Handa recalls. "Are they holding hands? Are they walking close together or apart? Are they kissing? What are they up to? Where are they going? There really wasn't much to see. These couples were very young and shy. Usually they walked half a mile apart. But all the same — it was always very exciting for the rest of us."

Especially when Eva Landa and Harry Kraus walked past. "They were a very famous couple in our minds, because they really were going together and met often. And Eva was a beauty," Handa recalls. She can also remember "Eva knitting a cap for Harry, with long braids attached, which was all the rage at the time. And he always wore it, summer and winter — that's how much he loved her."

Eva and Harry had first become acquainted in Prague, at the Jewish School on Jáchymová Street, where both were in the fourth grade during the 1940–41 school year. At first Eva had felt flattered by Harry's obvious interest in her, but she had not taken his feelings seriously and had definitely not returned his attentions. She was only eleven years old and Harry was the first boy to fall in love with her. He was short and athletic, sometimes very funny and witty, if not as ambitious in school as Eva, who was always among the top students. Since they shared the same route to school, they often met before and after classes and occasionally went for a walk in the Jewish cemetery, one of the few places besides Hagibor that was still open to Jewish children.

This was a time when children grew up a lot more quickly than nature had intended. The pressure of events broke through the wall that normally separates the adult world from the children's world. The curiosity, playfulness, and simple joy that usually drew children to one another were now replaced by a shared fear of a world of deprivation and humiliation.

Eva had been the first to be put on a transport. As Harry said his goodbyes, he pressed a letter in her hand. She was so distraught that she locked herself in the bathroom and wept.

Nine months later, as Eva looked down from an attic window of the Hamburg Barracks, she spotted Harry among the new arrivals. "I was so excited that I came down with a fever. And our friendship continued. I liked him more and more."

Eva has not forgotten those moments. But she did forget the dedication that Harry wrote in her poetry album in Theresienstadt. If her friend Handa had not recalled it, Eva would not know it today, because her album vanished a few months later, when she arrived at Auschwitz. "Life flows like water," Harry had written, "what a shame to lose a single minute. Your loving Harry."

For some of the girls, the evening promenade with their boyfriends was the highlight of the day. This was also true of Ela, who often went to bed with her head whirling and so full of questions that she could not fall asleep. What had Honza meant by this or that word? By this or that gesture? Was he really in love with her? A thousand questions, the ones that fill the heads of so many young girls her age. But Helga was in no mood to keep up with her friends in this regard — there were, after all, far more important things going on in the world.

Monday, September 13, 1943
Italy has surrendered and abandoned Hitler! Tra la la! He's all by himself in the stew! Mussolini quarreled with the king and handed the government over to others. Mussolini is in jail! — Learning is so wonderful! I'm in group A. It's the best group and the equivalent of the third year in gymnasium. We might have Latin, too. Of fifty-seven children, I scored third best on the math test.

A wave of hope swept over Theresienstadt. Mussolini's fall from power appeared to foreshadow a quick end to the war. The news "broadcast" via word of mouth sounded more and more promising. The reports spurred a whole series of programs: lectures, concerts, theatrical performances, and cabarets.

Monday, September 20, 1943
What a splendid day. I still haven't recovered. Papa and I attended a play about François Villon — a fifteenth-century French poet. People thought he was a beggar and a bad man. He hated the rich.

The text was compiled from selections of his ballads, interspersed with ballet. The scenery was splendidly painted. Villon was played by a mime, but I can't describe it and know that I didn't really understand it. It's a lyrical, yet also political work. It is called *The Beggar's Ballad.*

VERA NATH

Vera Nath was born near the Czech-Polish border in Opava, the capital of the Moravian Silesian region, on March 25, 1930, four years after her sister, Hana. Her father, Hermann Nath, was of Russian heritage and dealt in textiles and carpets. Her mother, Elisabeth Nath, née Kolb, came from Sopron in Hungary.

Like most people in Opava, her family spoke German. But in 1936 Vera was sent to a Czech school, in response to the obvious change in the political climate caused by Germany's policy of expansion and as an expression of allegiance to the Czech Republic. The next two years were peaceful ones for Vera, apart from the language problems she faced at school. The family still spent vacations in Hungary or Yugoslavia, or at Spindler-mühle in the Giant Mountains.

Then came March 1938 and the annexation of Austria. "We had just returned from a vacation in Yugoslavia, when my Papa suddenly

Vera Nath . . .

came home very upset and said, 'We must
go to Slovakia at once. There might be a
plebiscite. It would be better for us not to be
here.' I still recall that moment very clearly. I
was terribly sad, because I had brought a
turtle back from Yugoslavia and had to leave

. . . and her transport tag, which she was wearing around her neck when she arrived in Theresienstadt

it behind."

Six months later, the Sudetenland was occupied and the Naths fled — first to Trenčin, then to Brno, and finally to Ostrava in Moravia. There Vera was enrolled in a Jewish school. "People spoke a different Czech from the one I had learned, which was something I didn't like at all. I was very unhappy. I was in the third grade. But I had not even finished the year when the Germans marched in and burned down seven houses of worship, and we fled to Prague."

Trapped in Prague, the Nath family met the fate typical of Czech Jews in the years that followed. Although Hermann Nath had a considerable fortune, the Nazis' policy of Aryanization of Jewish property barred him from any access to it. By the time the family finally managed to obtain a visa and tickets for passage to Chile, the borders were closed. They were lucky, however, not to have set sail on the ship on which they had booked — the *Goral* — which ran into a mine and exploded. There were no survivors. Eventually the Naths, along with four other families, wound up in cramped quarters at Karová 13 in the Old City. They arrived in Theresienstadt on July 8, 1943, on one of the last transports from Prague.

HANKA WERTHEIMER

Hanka Wertheimer was born on December 12, 1929, in Znojmo, an industrial town in southern Moravia, where her grandparents owned a canning factory that was steeped in tradition and famous for its Znaimer pickles and sauerkraut. It was a family business that was run by Hanka's father, Fritz, and several of his siblings.

Hanka's mother, Lily Wertheimer, née Reich, came from Nový Bydzov in Moravia and had studied philology and philosophy at the Sorbonne. She was a progressive, cosmopolitan woman who loved to travel. She was one of the first women in Czechoslovakia to own an automobile and to drive it herself.

Hanka had a close relationship with her

governess, Mařka, who was like a second mother to her and who stayed with the family even as the times grew difficult. After the Wertheimers fled from Znojmo to Prague, their living space became smaller. Hanka's sister, Miriam, managed to emigrate to Palestine in 1939, but her father was seized by the Gestapo in 1940.

From 1941 on, Hanka, her mother, and Mařka lived in a little apartment at Žitná 38, near Wenceslas Square. Mařka had rented it in her own name. Although she was a Christian and although the family could no longer afford to pay her, she stayed with them.

During this period, Hanka attended the Jewish School at Jáchymová 3 and spent most of her weekends at Hagibor, the Jewish athletic field. Life for her became increasingly defined by fear.

Then, in May 1942, came the assassination of Heydrich and the German reprisals. Prague was put under curfew, with no one allowed on the streets after eight in the evening. The Gestapo began their sweep. Zitná 38 was not spared. "Two SS men with a big dog entered our apartment. Each of us had to show our papers. My mother couldn't find hers. Because my mother spoke very good German, the SS man asked, 'Are you German?' And my mother responded, 'No.' — 'Are you Czech?' — 'No.' — 'Well then, what are you?' And my mother said, 'I'm Jewish.' And the SS man said, 'Quick, quick, your papers!' While my mother looked for her papers — I knew the whole time where they were but didn't know whether she intentionally wasn't finding them or simply couldn't locate them — the building's caretaker told the SS, who were actually looking for men, 'There are no men living here. Only three women.' He was on our side — which was very lucky for us. Once I realized that my mother really couldn't find her papers, I told her where they were. She showed the documents, and the SS left. But the fear remained."

The order for transport to Theresienstadt came in March 1943. Hanka experienced an odd sense of comfort when it did, because she knew that there she would meet many of her friends and relatives again. She owed her assignment to Room 28 to Rita Böhm, a counselor who was a cousin of her mother's and who told her, "Put her in Room 28. It's the best-run Home."

Chapter Five:
Light in the Darkness:
BRUNDIBÁR

Wednesday, September 22, 1943

Ela and I are like sisters. We share everything, from cottage cheese to pepper. I'd love to have an answer: What is nothing? Nothing doesn't even exist! But there's no such thing as total emptiness either; everything contains something. And then I'd love to know: How can a person imagine infinity — for example, an infinite line or the infinite universe?

Lights out in fifteen minutes, so I'll have to stop writing soon. — The lights won't be turned off after all. Eva has promised to leave a light on if we're very quiet. That's fair. I can go on writing and won't have to start in all over again tomorrow morning.

Why is there life on Earth? Did nature do it, or is there really a higher power? Who can answer that for me, and whom can I believe? No one knows for sure. I don't believe that our Earth is the only planet where there's life. In infinite space we're just a tiny island, so why would it be the only one with life on it???

I wish humanity's dream of living in peace comes true. If two people live on a little island they become closer and grow fond of each other. And we on Earth are but a little island in infinite space. We're constantly waging war for more *lebensraum* — and if we could we would declare war on other planets. Maybe we'll be wiser someday. Maybe someday we'll realize that by constantly waging war on each other we shed blood for nothing.

Eva said today that I would be a scientist someday. I don't think so. We won't have enough money after the war. But if I ever have the chance, these are the things I will study.

On September 22, 1943, the premiere of *Brundibár* was just one day away — and so was the twenty-second birthday of its musical director, Rudi Freudenfeld. The children's excitement during rehearsals had been growing by leaps and bounds over the last few days.

Down in the basement of L 410, Kamilla Rosenbaum, the choreographer from

Rudolf Freudenfeld, the musical director of the Theresienstadt production of Brundibár

Prague, was rehearsing the waltz steps with the young people for the umpteenth time. Tella was at the piano, playing the magical *Valse lente cantabile* that comes from Brundibár's barrel organ. "One, two, three — girls, left foot forward, right foot to the side and draw the left foot across. The boys just the opposite, always keep the three-quarter time, one, two, three, and stand up straight, don't let your head droop, keep your arms at the level of your eyes and right foot back and left foot to the side and turn, turn in waltz time. Keep an eye on your feet, otherwise you'll be stepping on each other." The children danced and danced, they whirled in circles. The world was whirling with them.

"I was so happy," Ela says, as if this all happened only yesterday. "I ran to my mother, and my mother was an excellent dancer. And I said, 'Mama, now you can dance the waltz with me, the English waltz.' And she looked at me in astonishment and asked, 'Where did you learn that?' And I began to sing, and she threw her shoes to one side and said, 'Let's dance, Elinka!' She loved dancing with me."

As Markéta Stein danced across the room in three-quarter time with her daughter and gazed into Ela's radiant eyes, reality was forgotten for a moment or two, and the room was filled with the conviction that everything would soon be all right again. How very much Markéta wished for a better life for her daughter! That Ela is taking part in a children's opera — even playing the pretty role of the cat, that she had learned to dance — all this in the ghetto! Weren't these good omens?

Perhaps the prophecy of her brother, Dr. Otto Altenstein, with whom she shared the little room, would soon come true. "When the plums are ripe," he would say, "we'll be going back home."

Quite possibly Dr. Altenstein patted his niece on the head that day as he said those words. And even though the plum trees would soon be dropping their fruit for the second time since they arrived, he clung resolutely to this idea. One day he and his sister and her daughters Ela and Ilona would return to Prague and begin a new life there. And the children would gradually get over all they had experienced in their younger years.

Late in the afternoon of September 23, 1943, throngs of people, young and old, streamed into the attic room of the Magdeburg Barracks. The hundred or so chairs were not nearly enough for an audience of at least three times that number. The doors were thrown open and there were more people crowding outside. They all wanted to be part of the extraordinary event that the children had been talking about for weeks: the premiere of *Brundibár,* an opera performed by children, for children.

In a little side room opening onto the

An original poster for the Theresienstadt production of Brundibár

improvised stage, the young actors, tense with stage fright, prepare to make their entrances. They go over their lines again and again, encouraging one another and humming their songs. With some dabs of makeup they are transformed into their characters. Ela, all in black in her sister's ski pants and her mother's black sweater, is electrified when, with a few strokes of chalk, František Zelenka, the stage designer and artistic director of the play, gives her face its feline expression. Then he quickly smears bootblack over her naked feet, and the metamorphosis is complete. She feels as if she is on a "real big stage."

Excitement is running high, both backstage and out in front. The musicians take their places. The composer, Hans Krása, is present, as is the choreographer, Kamilla Rosenbaum. Baštík takes a peek at the audience and spots his father, Ota Freudenfeld, sitting in a place of honor. It was on Ota's fiftieth birthday, in July 1941, that Rafael Schächter mentioned *Brundibár* for the first time, and on that very evening the decision was made to rehearse the opera with the children of the Boys' Orphanage in Prague. Hans Krása followed the rehearsals of his opera with great interest. But he never got to attend the premiere. On August 10, 1942, a few days before the opera was performed — clandestinely, in the dining hall of the orphanage — he was on a transport to Theresienstadt.

Now, a year later, nearly all of them were together again — the young actors from that first performance and many of the friends who had met in the orphanage on Belgicka 25. And within a very short time, *Brundibár,* Krása's children's opera, was displaying its remarkable powers.

Forty children have gathered behind the plank wall. A few lamps cast a dim light. Then the first few notes sound, by genuine masters of chamber music: Karel Fröhlich, Romouald Süssmann, the Kohn brothers, Fritzek Weiss, and Gideon Klein.

The children keep repeating their opening lines in their minds. Their eyes move back and forth, from the audience to Baštík, who greets their glances with a smile. They do not even notice how hot it is in the room. All they can feel is the tension, the expectation in the air. Then Baštík steps before the orchestra and raises his baton.

The spirited opening measures have begun, and now the children are singing: *"Tohle je malý Pepíček, zemřel mu dávno tatíček za ruku vede Aninku, mají nemocnou maminku. . . ."* ("That is little Pepíček. His father is dead. He's holding Aninka's hand. Their mother is sick. . . .") Aninka and Pepíček come onstage, and Piňťa Mühlstein

271

A scene from the children's opera Brundibár, *sketched by Ruth Gutmann*

sings: *"Jà se jmenuju Pepíček, dávna mu zemřel tatíček. . . ."* ("My name is Pepíček. My father died a long time ago. . . .")

"Actually we conceived of the opera as a kind of Brechtian didactic play," the librettist Adolf Hoffmeister, who managed to escape to England, would explain after the war. "The plot is very simple. The mother is ill, her two children, Pepíček and Aninka, go to fetch milk, but they have no money. They notice that passersby are giving money to the organ-grinder. So they stand at a street corner and begin to sing. But their voices are too weak. Then the animals of the town come and advise them to form a children's choir to make their voices stronger. And the animals invite schoolchildren to join in, which they do, and their voices get strong enough to defeat the organ-grinder. The children's solidarity allowed them to triumph over the organ-grinder Brundibár because they were undaunted by the task."[1]

"The most difficult problem in planning this children's opera was, needless to say, the libretto," Hans Krása revealed in a brief retrospect in his 1943 report, written just a few days before the last children from the orphanage arrived in Theresienstadt on July 7, 1943. "The usual dramatic, human conflicts — erotic, political, and such — could not be used, of course. Neither the librettist nor I was partial to fairy tales. But all the same the author managed to create a text that has a childlike (but not childish) gaiety about it and that dramatizes a real-life occurrence, in which the effectiveness of collective strength in the struggle against evil is compellingly presented. In the case of this children's opera it is a singing contest that pits all the children against the organ-grinder.

"The special charm for me as a composer

lay in writing music that is absolutely sing-able for children, but that sounds modern to audience members of all ages and does not resort to the clichés of children's songs. Despite the fact that music for children should not have a range greater than the fifth, I did not want to do violence to my natural temperament as a composer."[2]

Hans Krása and Adolf Hoffmeister had created the opera in 1938, inspired by an announcement in *Rythmus,* a monthly magazine for contemporary music. "The As-sociation for Musical Education is announc-ing a competition and offering 5,000 crowns for a children's opera," the text read. "The rules are that the opera run no longer than sixty minutes and be written in such a way that it can be performed entirely by chil-dren. Any piece that was written or per-formed before this competition will be ineligible. The plays must be offered anony-mously, in the form of piano music. The deadline is September 16, 1938. Address: SHU, Prague IV, Toskan Palace, where entrants can receive additional informa-tion."

It was not the first time that these two friends had participated in a joint effort. Hans Krása had written the music for a theater piece titled *Mládí ve hře (Youth at*

Hans Krása (left) *and Adolf Hoffmeister in 1938*

Play), Adolf Hoffmeister's comedy produced in 1936 by the avant-garde theater director E. F. Burian. Krása's *Song for Anna* became a popular hit when it appeared in a German version by Friedrich Torberg under the title *Anna Says No.*

Hoffmeister and Krása seized the opportunity offered by the competition and set to work. The danger from Germany was advancing relentlessly and the future appeared increasingly gloomy. What would become of the next generation?

Although their motivation for this final joint artistic effort was the competion, their underlying desire was to resist the political turmoil with the only weapon they had — art. Above all, they wanted to arm the children with the courage to face a perilous future. They could never have imagined what the fate of this generation of Jewish children — indeed, of their own families — would be, or the circumstances that would land one of these two friends in Theresienstadt.

On their small improvised stage, the children perform with growing ease. Excitement and fear yield to an awareness of being part of something important. The actors merge with the opera's plot, with their roles, with the songs and music. Reality is forgotten. The play is reality. Reality is life. They are performing for their lives. They sing, play, dance, spin in three-quarter time; ultimately they defeat and chase away the organ-grinder Brundibár. *"Brundibár poražen"* ("We have defeated Brundibár") resounds triumphantly in every throat. They sing it one more time, and the voices of the audience blend with the voices onstage. Everyone is singing now, singing at the top of their lungs this hymn of victory over the evil Brundibár. Both the performers and the audience are caught up in the enthusiasm of a momentary certainty from which no one wants to awaken: *"Brundibár poražen."*

"The applause was incredible," recalls Ela, describing the elated response to the performance. "Whenever we sang the finale at the end, *'Brundibár poražen,'* there was a storm of applause, and the audience wanted to hear the song again and again, until they almost had to throw us all out. We made the most of this moment of freedom." Whenever Ela remembers this moment, it is as if the scene is coming back to life. "And there was something else, too," she adds. "We didn't have to wear the yellow stars. Even in Theresienstadt we always had to wear the yellow star — but not when we were performing *Brundibár*. It was the only exception. For those moments we were not branded with the yellow star, which meant that for this brief precious time, we were free."

From then on *Brundibár* was performed once a week. Every performance was a sellout. Tickets, which were given out by the Freizeitgestaltung (recreation office), disappeared in a flash. This little piece mesmerized both audience and performers. "It was a light in the darkness for the children, and even for the adults," said Leopold Lowy, who had also seen the production at the orphanage in Prague.

Suddenly there were young stars in Theresienstadt. "There goes Aninka," the children called out when they saw Greta Hofmeister. "Hello, Pepíček," they said when they ran into Piňt'a Mühlstein. Zdeněk Ohrenstein now answered to the name of Dog. Ela was Cat or Kitty, and Maria Mühlstein was Sparrow. And little Stephan Sommer, the youngest member of the ensemble, who shared the role of the sparrow with Maria Mühlstein and hopped about the stage so charmingly, often heard people say, "Here he is, our sweet little sparrow."

But most popular of all was Brundibár himself, the organ-grinder, played by Honza Treichlinger. Rudolf Freudenfeld composed an unforgettable memorial to him: "He truly joined the ranks of the famous. He was renowned and revered. Wherever he went, the cry went up, 'Brundibár, Brundibár.' Honza instinctively portrayed the figure of Brundibár with such humanity that, although he played the role of the villain, he was not just the children's favorite, but the audience's as well. He learned to wiggle his pasted-on mustache, wiggle it so brilliantly and at just the perfect moment that all tension in the audience vanished and we could actually hear the children heave a sigh of relief. From the moment he first created the character he played every performance without a stand-in. No one could have replaced him."[3]

Everyone was thrilled by Honza Treichlinger. "We loved him," the girls of Room 28 say, "although he was playing Brundibár, the villain and the enemy of us children. But he did it so comically and with such wit — we loved Honza in that role. He was one of a kind — simply wonderful."

Greta Klingsberg, née Hofmeister, lived in Room 25 of Girls' Home L 410. She played the role of Aninka. "It was incredibly beautiful," she says of the production. "It was out of this world. The opera's message was, of course, very important to us: Those who love justice and stand by us can play with us. Most important of all: Good will triumph because we stick together."

Handa Pollak sang in the choir and on one occasion played the role of the dog. "The opera's strength was in the idea of solidarity, of holding together," she says. "We saw Brundibár as Hitler, and the baker who does not want to give bread to the children and the milkman who does not want to give them milk as the SS. With every performance we triumphed over them. It was something like our small underground war against Hitler and the Nazis."

Eva Herrmann lived in Room 24 of Girls' Home L 414. She sang in the children's choir. "We just belted the finale out," she recalls. "At that moment, we felt free. Somehow we sensed that this was not just a play. Suddenly we were able to identify with an idea that embraced all our hopes: that good would triumph over evil."

Jiří Kotouč lived in Room 1 of Boys' Home L 417. "Most of the children who acted in *Brundibár* did not survive. So it must be said that for them, *Brundibár* was the last source of great joy in their lives."

Eva Landa tried to get tickets for as many performances of *Brundibár* as she possibly could. Although she was still sorry that she had not been chosen to play one of the schoolchildren, and although she envied her close friends — especially Ela, Maria, Flaška, and Handa — because they were part of the ensemble, she was still happy just to sit in the audience in the Magdeburg Barracks alongside one of her girlfriends or her boyfriend, Harry.

By now she knew every scene and every song, as well as many of the actors and musicians. The moment the first measures of the opening song rang out, the boundaries between her and the brother and sister on the stage fell away, and Eva lost herself in the performance as if in a wonderful, recurring dream. She eagerly awaited the lullaby, which sounded as if it was being sung by angels. *"Maminka kolíbá, dětátko houpy, hou, myslí si co bude, až děti vyrostou."* ("Mama rocks the cradle and thinks, my, my, what will become of the children when they are grown?") It always grew very quiet in the audience, everyone holding their breath in expectation. *"Každý kos ze hnízda jedenkrát vylétá."* ("Every bird will one day fly from the nest. Must leave, not knowing why, and fly out into the world.")

"For me it's one of the most beautiful songs," Eva says today. "It's about saying goodbye to childhood — and that had a very deep meaning for us back then. We were twelve, thirteen years old, and our childhood was coming to an end. We were facing the adult world, the world of bakers, ice-cream vendors, policemen, and

Brundibárs. And the better world, the world of the children, defeated the adults and Brundibár, who underestimated us. During the time that we were caught up in the opera, we firmly believed in our victory."

Why should what was happening in the real world be any different from what was happening onstage, where a dramatic example of the united strength of children and animals — a dog, a cat, and a sparrow — was played out before their very eyes? Why shouldn't everything turn out all right? *"Panta rhei"* ("Everything flows"), Eva Weiss had written on one of the motto cards she hung on the wall of Room 28, and now the choir of schoolchildren was singing the lullaby's refrain: *"Roste strom, teče proud, plyne cas mraky jdou."* ("The tree grows, the river flows, time flows, clouds pass. Year after year, step by step.")

On the stage, the visitors to the market are tossing coin after coin into Pepíček's cap. He happily shows them to his sister, Aninka. Then suddenly Brundibár appears, snatches the cap from the boy's hand, and runs away — along with all the money! "Children, children, catch the thief!" Pepíček cries, and the entire chorus of schoolchildren chases after Brundibár.

The hunt begins. Because Brundibár

represents the evil that has brought misery into the lives of the children, because they see him as Hitler, as his Nazis, and as all the hangers-on and supporters of his dictatorial regime, they pursue him with furious determination. The wellspring of sudden energy that fuels their common cause against Brundibár seems inexhaustible. It is an energy that flows from all sides — from the audience, from the musicians in the orchestra, from the very streets and barracks of Theresienstadt, and, of course, from the hearts of the performing children. All these energies are united to strike a single blow against the evil organ-grinder. The children finally catch up with Brundibár, who flings the cap away and flees. *"Brundibár poražen!"* ("We have defeated Brundibár!") cry one and all. He is defeated by the children and their friends — the dog, the cat, and the sparrow. Good has triumphed over evil.

It was like a fairy tale, yet for the moment this was reality. It was a vision of the future transported to the stage, borne up by the principle of hope and belief in the victory over Hitler. "When at the end we all sang *'Brundibár poražen,'* we firmly believed in ourselves and in our victory," Eva says. "At that moment we looked optimistically into the future."

Tuesday, September 28, 1943

Ela is going with Honza (from Home 9, he used to go with Lenka). Every evening she tells me about their rendezvous. My last thoughts here in Theresienstadt are about boys. At home they had been my first thoughts — for the simple reason that after 1941 I was no longer able to attend school and I had little opportunity to find a girlfriend. And so I made friends with boys. I had a lot of free time and was bored. Here, things are different. Every noon and every evening I go visit Papa for a while, and I have to spend the rest of my time in the Home, even when there are no classes. When we have a free day I use the time for drawing. When would I go out with boys?

Soon it will be Rosh Hashanah. We're going to have a celebration.

Rosh Hashanah, the two-day observance of the Jewish New Year, was approaching, and the counselors made every effort to create an atmosphere of contemplation and introspection appropriate to the holiday. According to Jewish tradition, it is time when the books containing the deeds of all humanity are opened and the fate of each person is determined for the coming year.

This is why people place special emphasis on the wishes and dreams they hope will be fulfilled. "May you be inscribed for a good year," or simply *"Shanah tovah"* ("A good year"), was the greeting on everyone's lips.

Of course, it was impossible to celebrate Rosh Hashanah in Theresienstadt in the traditional fashion. There were neither apples nor honey to dip them in. There was no fish, whose head meat is customarily eaten (the literal translation of *rosh* is "head"), because just as we are directed by our heads, we pray that the good fate set down for us on Rosh Hashanah will direct our actions for the entire year. And there was no "new fruit" over which to say the traditional blessing of thankfulness for having been kept alive and healthy so that we can celebrate the holiday.

Yet most of the girls did not miss these rituals. Until now they had never known them. Like Helga, Ela, and Handa, they came from assimilated families. It was not unusual for their homes to be decorated with Christmas trees in December. Handa recalls just such a moment — it was right after their flight from Olbramovice. She was living with her aunt in Prague. Christmas Eve was drawing ever closer, and there was still no Christmas tree in the house. Finally she grew very nervous and asked her aunt about it. "My aunt pointed to the Hanukkah candles and said, 'That is our Christmas tree.' And I was very disappointed. I didn't even know that there was such a holiday."

In 1943 Professor Israel Kestenberg wrote about the goals of the Youth Welfare Office at Theresienstadt, pointing out that it was everyone's duty to familiarize himself or herself with Jewish traditions and customs. "This is a prerequisite for any connection with a Jewish community. To celebrate the Sabbath and the High Holy Days, to behave in synagogue in traditional fashion, is a basic requirement for Jewish communal life. It is especially important to learn about our people's past. Only in this way can our young people learn to value our nation, which has always been prepared to sacrifice like no other."[4]

Flaška and Lenka did their part in helping to prepare for the feast in Room 28. They wrote a comedy about two old maids titled *Amalka and Posinka* and presented it as a prelude to Rosh Hashanah. The performance was a great success. They subsequently presented *Amalka and Posinka* with new variations and sequels, sometimes in other rooms of the Girls' Home.

AMALKA AND POSINKA

Two old maids are sitting on a bench fast asleep. They are dressed in very funny clothes. One has a stocking on her head.

Posinka (suddenly wakes up): Amalka!

Amalka: What is it, Posinka?

Posinka: It will soon be Rosh Hashanah. Shouldn't we buy something good to eat?

Amalka: A goose?

Posinka: That's too expensive!

Amalka: A pig?

Posinka: That's not kosher!

Amalka and Posinka together: Let's buy a turkey!

Amalka and Posinka go off to buy a turkey and soon return with one. They tug it in by the wings and pluck all its feathers. Suddenly the turkey comes to life — but alas, without feathers! And since it's so cold, the turkey starts to shiver. So Amalka and Posinka decide to knit it a sweater. They knit and knit, and keep trying the sweater on the turkey, and finally pull it down over it.

All of a sudden, someone comes bounding in and calls out:

"All Jews have to hand over their warm

winter clothes!"

(There was, as Eva Landa recalls, always applause and laughter at this point.)

Amalka and Posinka take the turkey with them to the Council of Elders and ask for permission to let the turkey keep its warm sweater. They negotiate with the chief elder. Finally Amalka says to him: "You have hair on your body. But our turkey doesn't have a single feather!" And the chief elder takes pity on the turkey and allows the two women to keep the sweater.

Very happy now, Amalka and Posinka return home, pulling the turkey by the wings and shouting: Long live Poppi — our turkey!

In another version, Amalka has false teeth that she keeps in a glass of water overnight. One night she wakes up thirsty and drinks the water, and her false teeth with it. This gives her a terrible tummy ache, and she goes to the doctor (played by Zajíček), who prescribes a laxative for her and says, "Take Darmol now; you'll soon feel — wow!" Amalka takes the medicine and suddenly her false teeth drop into her chamber pot. Still half asleep, she picks them out, puts them in her mouth, and scrunches her face into a grimace.

At this point everyone laughed again, as did Amalka, who shook so hard that her false teeth fell out again.

Helga's diary continues:

Thursday, September 30, 1943

Yesterday evening was so beautiful! I'll never forget it as long as I live. We had the most beautifully decorated room. Since we don't have a chandelier, we wove a wreath of green leaves, red berries, and colored ribbons around the lamp. Our flag, which we hung on the closet, was decorated with wildflowers, and the large table was covered with a tablecloth, and was then set with wonderfully prepared food. We had three sandwiches, each one different, and after that a pudding with a delightful topping. There were candles in the middle of the table. We all wore white blouses and dark blue skirts. First we sang, then Tella spoke about the past year, about all the good things we experienced, and the sad things, too. But the happy moments outweighed the sad, and as a way of promising that we will never forget the good things or our ideals, we sang our hymn. Frau Mühlstein lit the candles and said the *brachah.* And then we had our blow-out banquet.

I thought: I really should hug Tella. She was so beautiful and winning, and far more radiant than usual. But it wasn't that I was surprised by Tella — she was simply happy to see what she had made of us.

On today of all days, we had to learn that Walter Deutsch had escaped from Theresienstadt two weeks earlier, only to be caught and sent to a concentration camp. What was that crazy boy thinking? It's not so awful here. His parents are in Poland, and he's twenty-three. But even worse is that we learned from a postcard sent by Frau Korschil that Walter Pollak and his wife died on January 27, 1943. Our whole family figures it happened like this: Walter left Theresienstadt along with Uncle Karl on January 26, 1943. On the 27th they were still en route, or might just have arrived at their destination. It definitely wasn't suicide. That's just not like them. So we think that maybe they were too old to do hard labor and so were murdered. We have no news from Uncle Karl, and we're afraid he has met the same fate as the Pollaks.

The escapee Walter Deutsch was a distant relative of Helga's, the son of Gustav Deutsch from Prostejov, who was her father's cousin. Why had he risked fleeing? What was happening to him now in the concentration camp? And why had Walter Pollak and his wife died under such mysterious circumstances as soon as they had left Theresienstadt?

Hardly a day passed that was not darkened by such questions, by upsetting news and events. As always, the counselors tried to shield their wards from such daily horrors. But too much was happening, and they had reached the limits of their ability to cope with it all; they were often at their wit's end.

This atmosphere also affected relations among the counselors. Especially in the Girls' Home, the antagonism between Communist and Zionist counselors became heated. Moreover, the building itself was in a desolate state. The plaster was peeling from the walls and ceiling. The beds were falling apart, the toilets were often clogged, and the doors and windows no longer closed properly.

These poor conditions had to be tackled, and the leadership of the Girls' Home reinforced. Gonda Redlich, the head of the Youth Welfare Office, decided that an energetic and prudent man should share the leadership role with Rosa Engländer. He gave the position to Willy Groag and entrusted him with the task of "bringing a breath of fresh air to the Girls' Home."

Willy Groag, a handsome young man, was born in Olomouc on August 7, 1914, to assimilated Jews who were passionate monarchists, a sentiment that couldn't help but creep onto their son's birth certificate: Wilhelm Franz Mordechai Groag. "Wilhelm, in honor of Kaiser Wilhelm," he liked to emphasize, "Franz, in honor of Kaiser Franz Josef, and, just so that something of the Jewish tradition remained, Mordechai, in honor of my grandfather Markus Mordechai Groag."

Willy Groag had a doctorate in chemistry, and ever since 1938, when Gonda Redlich had recommended he read Heinrich Graetz's eleven-volume *History of the Jews from the Earliest Period to the Present,* he had been a committed Zionist and educator for Hachsharah. From 1939 to 1942 he had been the head of the Prague branch of Maccabi Hatza'ir, a Zionist youth organization, and had taught chemistry, physics, mathematics, and drawing at the Youth Aliyah School, the Jewish middle school. Many of the children already knew this pleasant blue-eyed young man from their days in Prague.

Once appointed to his new position in the Girls' Home, Willy Groag lost no time in ordering remedial measures. Craftsmen were organized and the worst damages repaired. The young woman who was in charge of bread rations in the Provisions Office was relieved of her post on grounds of having "provided for her own stomach," and was replaced by another woman. Several counselors, and even several children, changed Homes.

But otherwise everything remained as it had been. Frau Roubiček, who was in charge of the registry lists, continued on in her office in L 410, right next to the main entrance, keeping a meticulous record in a large thick book of the daily count of residents of the Girls' Home. In the infirmary, pediatricians Dr. Stern and Dr. Fischer worked alongside social worker Margit Mühlstein and nurses Eliska Klein and Ilse Landa to take care of the sick children. And Frau Salus, who was in charge of toilets, was still sitting outside the washroom, her basin of Lysol and a fine-tooth comb always handy, keeping a constant watchful eye on the girls' hair in order to make sure that she didn't miss a single louse. She also tried her hand at writing poetry.

"That's how it is here," Helga wrote in her diary on October 2, 1943, "a poem for a piece of bread. One of the women in charge of the toilets writes poetry while sitting just outside the door. I asked her if she wouldn't like to write one for me. She did so, but the next day she demanded I pay her for it with a slice of bread."

Such dealings were not appropriate for the Home, and presumably Willy Groag knew nothing about them. Had he been aware of what was going on, he would have intervened. Willy Groag and Rosa Engländer ran a tight but friendly ship. One of Willy's easier tasks was making the evening rounds of the Home, casting a glance into each room to make sure no one was missing. There was trouble in store for anyone who was not there. Another escapee like Walter Deutsch would have been a catastrophe. To be sure, there was little danger of that in the Girls' Home, but there were plenty of prohibitions, restrictions, and regulations that had to be observed, and if they were not, the result could be severe punishment, either by the Ghetto Court or, worse, by the SS itself.

And so the children had to pay close attention to both daily orders and the General Order of the Jewish Self-Administration, including the rules for behavior on the street. They also had to be strictly reminded that:

- blackout regulations and times must be observed;
- open windows must be hooked and closed during strong winds;
- it is forbidden to walk on the ramparts or on the grass;
- any unauthorized departure from the ghetto will be regarded as an attempt to escape, in which case the police are empowered to make use of their weapons;
- children, whether in groups or marching in ranks, are to use the street pavement and not the sidewalk;
- it is forbidden to enter streets, squares, or parks that are barricaded, or to jaywalk; streets may be crossed only at corners or intersections;
- it is strictly forbidden to make loud noise;
- corridors, courtyards, and streets are to be kept absolutely tidy, and no paper or garbage is to be tossed aside or left lying around; likewise any spit-

ting on the street, in courtyards, or in corridors is strictly forbidden;

- everyone must be inside the Home at designated times and must observe nighttime quiet hours.

Friday, October 8, 1943

I would like to aim for greater self-control. I am going to fast all day tomorrow.

Sunday, October 10, 1943

I held out until a quarter to six. There was no unpleasant sensation in my stomach, no hunger, just a bad headache in the evening. Then I ate so much it made me sick. I wanted to freshen up, so I went for a bath in the Hohenelbe Barracks. Ela came along; we went together using one permission card. — Every young person in Theresienstadt had to write an essay. It was a competition.

Friday, October 15, 1943

Lea weighs 24 lbs 8 oz. Mimi is ill and is in the hospital at Hohenelbe Barracks. In the same room is a woman who tried to escape from Theresienstadt. She was caught and thrown into prison. While she was there she found several two-inch nails, smeared them with margarine, and swallowed a few. She was trying to commit suicide. They operated on her stomach. Papa says she's not in her right mind. He could tell from her eyes. How strange that I don't see it.

Then there's a woman who was put on a transport even though she was ill. She swallowed some kind of powder, but not enough to kill her. They pumped out her stomach. Outside the door is an O.D. man [abbreviation for *Ordnungsdienst* — police duty], and whenever one of the two women goes to the toilet, he accompanies them and waits till they come out in order to escort them back to their ward. They are prisoners from the Dresden Barracks prison and are in the hospital only for as long as they are ill.

Sunday, October 24, 1943

Yesterday some of the girls begged the counselors to ask us a series of questions. I answered eight out of ten, so eighty percent. Eva Stern and I have agreed to test each other once a month on our general knowledge.

Wednesday, October 27, 1943

Yesterday evening Rita criticized us in a roundabout way: "The person I have in mind is an intelligent girl who longs to learn things, who was once very spoiled, but has put that behind her, except that elements of her spoiled nature still appear from time to time. You can tell that she's an only child, because she is sometimes very moody." And then we had to guess who it was. It was me. — She told Fiška that she has a very poetic soul.

Fiška and I seem to spend more time thinking than any of the other girls in our room. I was steeped in thought well into the night. At about 11 o'clock I took out some paper and a pencil, and in the dark I wrote this sentence: Thinking and reflecting make you forget your poverty, and the world seems beautiful, mysterious, and unfathomable.

Thursday, October 28, 1943

Yesterday evening I spoke with Erica. We might be able to get along quite well. She gave me a little heart she had cut out. We have almost the same view of things. Erika doesn't have a close girlfriend, and neither do I. We both have Rita as a friend. My conscience has been troubling me of late, and I feel as if I'm doing everything wrong. But that's been the case only since I've begun to think a lot about everything. And I've been unsure of myself ever since.

But now Rita has explained to me that only stupid people are sure of themselves and their behavior. The smarter people are, the more they doubt. THINKING IS THE FINEST THING IN THE WORLD.

Professor Brumliková is a genius when it comes to lecturing. Although I was born after the First World War, I've found that her accounts bring this history to life for me. Today is the twenty-fifth anniversary of Czechoslovakia's independence from the Hapsburgs. And let's hope that there will soon be another "October 28th," be it in January or in May. And that it will come just as suddenly and unexpectedly as it did back then. When that day comes, we will all hug and rejoice. Benes and Masaryk will return, and Czechoslovakia will be a free country once again. Throughout the Czech lands, people will be singing "Where Is My Home?"

> Where is my home? Where is my home?
> Waters murmur across the meads
> Pinewoods rustle 'pon the cliff-rocks,
> Bloom of spring shines in the orchard,
> Paradise on Earth you see!
> And that is the beautiful land,
> The Czech land, my home!
> The Czech land, my home!

Yesterday evening I asked Papa whether he would be angry with me if I had myself baptized as an adult. I told him that I feel no real connection with the Jews, their history, and their sufferings. I don't feel I'm bound to them. Papa's answer was: "When you're an adult you can do whatever you want, and I won't forbid you to do anything, and certainly not try to change your mind." I'll never forget those words for as long as I live! I have a real Papa. If everyone had a father like him, the world would be a very different place.

Before I began to contemplate matters of this kind, I was restless and consumed with worry about Mama. But since I've begun to think so much, I've found an inner contentment. This peculiar feeling can't really be called tranquillity, since I'm forever coming up with something new to brood about — especially things that concern the world as a whole: people, races, and nations. In a word: everything.

And another thing — damn, I could fill a whole notebook today! At the moment I don't feel anything for our Home, just for Rita and Erika and for Fiška. But I'm so caught up in my own thoughts that I don't know what's happening around me.

Marta Fröhlich had been a resident of Room 28 since late September 1943. She had previously lived in Room 24, together with her sister Zdenka. The two sisters needed distance from each other, which was why the counselors decided to find another spot for Marta.

Marta and her four siblings — two sisters, Ruzenka and Zdenka, and two brothers, Jenda and Jarda — were no strangers to many of the children. In Prague the girls had lived in the orphanage on Hybernska and the boys in the orphanage on Belgicka. Hanka Wertheimer, who had lived nearby, often walked to school with Marta, whom many people called by her nickname, Frta, which was made up of the first two letters of her last name, Fröhlich, and the last two letters of her given name, Marta; it's the kind of abbreviation only Czechs are able to form and pronounce.

Only a few people really knew why the Fröhlich children were living in orphanages. In fact, Hanka didn't even know what an orphanage was. "But it was clear to me that the children who lived there were very poor."

Ela Stein had also known the Fröhlich children in Prague, if only in passing, but well enough to be taken aback when she noticed something odd while gazing out the windows of the Girls' Home in February 1943. "I saw five brothers and sisters being brought to Theresienstadt, accompanied by a couple of men in uniform. There was a barracks lockdown that day."

What could it mean? Ela wondered. Why of all people were the Fröhlich children being brought to the ghetto by special transport? Years later Frta related what had happened to her siblings the previous night.

It was early in 1943. The transports had been running in high gear for over a year. My brothers and sisters and I were living at the orphanage on Belgicka at the time. One evening, word suddenly came that the Fröhlich children were to report to the Gestapo the next morning. We didn't know why. The next morning we were all taken to Gestapo headquarters. Even Ruzenka, who was in the hospital on Lublanska with pneumonia, was fetched and brought to the Gestapo. Once we were there, we were locked in a cold, dark cellar. There was nothing to eat or drink. Only the several layers of clothing and the coats that we had put on just in case provided a little warmth. Late that afternoon we were taken to be interrogated. We didn't know what they wanted from us. They treated us like criminals. The first thing they did was to take my brother Jenda's lovely watch away. He had only recently been given this watch at his bar mitzvah in the synagogue on Maislova, where he had sung beautifully. He had received other gifts as well. Everything we had with us was confiscated: identification papers, rings, a little silver necklace, money. When my ring wouldn't come off, the SS man screamed at me and threatened to chop off my finger. The German was starting to come toward me when Jenda placed himself in front of me to protect me, and was given a hard kick by the SS man, while at the same time my little brother Jarda, only eleven at the time, threw himself at the SS man. Jenda had already tried to settle him down and told him to stay calm. But at that moment Jarda, who could get very angry and was a fighter by nature, could no longer control his temper and threw himself at the SS man and bit his hand, but the SS man just flung him to one side.

We were terrified of what would happen next. But the German didn't do anything to him and just said, "You're the only one I like. I'd like to have a courageous son like you." Meanwhile, I had been turning so hard at the ring on my finger that it finally came off. Then we had to sign something. The boys signed their names very quickly, but I took my time and scribbled mine. The Gestapo man grabbed me by the hair, banged my head against the wall, and shouted at me that my name wasn't Fröhlichová, but Fröhlich. My sister Zdenka signed correctly because Jenda told her to. Our youngest, Ruzenka, couldn't write yet. Besides, she had a fever of over 104 degrees. She lay on the stone floor, and the booted SS men kicked her. When we circled around to protect her, they kicked us. Then they put us all back in the cellar.

Marta Fröhlich had a special friend in Room 28: Eva Winkler. Marta liked this girl with her blue eyes and striking long dark eyelashes. Eva was a girl with a heart, considerate and loving — just like her father, Fritz Winkler, who took the Fröhlich children under his wing when he saw how vulnerable their situation in the ghetto was.

The first few days after their arrival in Theresienstadt, they had to spend their nights on a plank frame in an overcrowded barracks, in the farthest corner of a long hallway. Behind their sleeping quarters, separated only by a thin wall of boards, was a toilet bucket that could be reached only by stepping over the planks on which the children were supposed to sleep — and, of course, their sleep was constantly disrupted. They were liberated from "Hotel WC," as Marta calls their first quarters in Theresienstadt, a few days later by their uncle Franta, who was already living in the ghetto, only to wind up in an old barracks where the stench was not as intense, but where they suffered from the icy cold. What good was an old stove in a corner of the room, when there was neither wood nor coal to heat it — not even a match to light it?

It was Fritz Winkler who came to the aid of the Frölich children. He worked in a carpentry workshop, and now and then he was able to slip them some wood to heat the stove. And he soon became a fatherly friend — just what they so desperately needed. Their own father, who had arrived in the ghetto shortly after they did, was the same man in Theresienstadt as he had always been — angry and short-tempered. "We once brought him something to eat," Marta recalls. "And he went wild and almost hit us — because it was so little! The other men in the room came to our aid. They were furious at him, and almost clobbered him because he didn't appreciate what we had brought him."

Things were very different with Eva Winkler. She appreciated Marta's gifts. When Marta discovered her passion for collecting the slips of paper that Palmera razor blades came wrapped in, she asked her two brothers to "organize" as many as they could for her new friend, thus adding to Eva's already considerable collection. Eva treated this collection like a treasure trove. What a disaster it would be if even one of these prettily illustrated papers were to disappear! Eva would have been miserable, as is evident from a little song the girls made up and merrily sang sometimes: "Herr Winkler's daughter's sobs can be heard, / a tragedy has now occurred. / It's lost, it's lost — you ask what's lost? / The Palmeras have been lost. / Yes, yes, yes / it's as clear as day / Yes, yes, yes / it's true in its way."

One day Eva showed her new friend something quite different — the pictures she had painted with Friedl Dicker-Brandeis. "I'd love to learn to do that, too. It's lovely!" Marta said in astonishment. Shortly after that, Eva took her along for drawing lessons in Room 28.

For many children, art classes with Friedl Dicker-Brandeis were bright stars in the gloom of the ghetto. "During art class I was oblivious to everything else," Helga recalls. "There was only that big table with the painting supplies, even though the paper was nothing much, sometimes just waste paper or packing paper from some old packages. But at these moments I felt like a free human being."

The children painted and drew, did handicrafts, and made collages. Friedl supplied the paints, brushes, pencils, and paper, and often brought a few art books or objects that served as models — a vase, a Dutch wooden shoe, a teapot. One day, she would offer a theme — an animal in a landscape, or would simply say, "Storm, wind, evening — paint it!" Another day, she would sketch a fantasy story in a few sentences or would say nothing more than "Paint where you would like to be now. Paint what you wish for yourself. Paint whatever means a great deal to you." Or, "Look out the window and paint what you see."

There was usually a hush while the children worked. Friedl radiated a magical aura that inspired them. "You didn't have to draw well. That was not what really mattered," Helga says, describing her teaching method. "The crucial thing was that you developed your talents, that you learned to see. To recognize colors. To play with colors. To move your hand in time to music or a specific rhythm. For example, she would rap out a certain tempo on the table, and we were supposed to draw according to the rhythm. Her method of instruction gave us moments of lightheartedness. She had a capacity for awakening in us a positive attitude toward our condition, toward life in Theresienstadt. In her presence everything seemed to fall into place — more or less all on its own."

When she entered Room 28, Friedl did not always find calm, disciplined pupils who were eager to paint. Sometimes they were anything but. But in a flash, Friedl was able to engage the children in her subject. Most often it was rhythmic exercises that helped. "Besides making the painter's hand and whole person light and flexible, such exercises are an appropriate means by which to turn an unruly mob of individuals into a working group ready to devote itself cooperatively to a cause," she wrote in a report in mid-1943, on the first anniversary of the establishment of the Theresienstadt Children's Homes. "Moreover, they lift the child out of old habits of thinking and seeing [and] present the child with a task that can be fulfilled with delight and fantasy and yet with the greatest precision."[5]

Friedl loved children, and children loved her. This small, energetic woman with short, light brown hair, hazelnut brown eyes, and a gentle, bright voice was always cordial, always calm and patient with them. She did not reprimand the children, push them too hard, or coerce them in any way. Using fantasy and intuition, she set about her work in a playful spirit. She watched with interest her pupils' first, hesitant efforts at painting, cautiously asked questions, casually steered their attention. Above all, she encouraged the children to follow their own ideas and inspirations, and to give them graphic expression. One of her basic principles was: "Let the child be free to express himself."

Friedl Dicker-Brandeis was forty-four years old when she, her husband, Pavel Brandeis, and her friend Laura Šimko arrived in Theresienstadt on December 17, 1942, on transport "Ch" from Hradec Králové. In acknowledgment of her career as an artist, she was first assigned to the "Technical Department," a sort of engineering office whose official task was the production of whatever technical drawings the ghetto needed. But this SS-sanctioned activity produced creative work that documented the reality of life in the ghetto — studies, sketches, paintings, posters — hundreds of works in all. The department was headed by the painter Bedřich Fritta (aka Fritz Taussig). At his side were experienced colleagues: Otto Ungar, Leo Haas, Felix Bloch, Jo Spier, the young Peter Kien, and others.

The strict documentary realism characteristic of these artists was not really in Friedl's nature. Her understanding of art was nourished by other sources. Her interests moved her in a different direction, and soon, following her inner desires, she was to be found only among the children.

In her classes Friedl passed on her rich trove of experience in both artistic and human realms, rousing in the children latent energies that could function as a positive counterweight to their oppressive existence and that could restore their psychological balance. She awakened memories of what was good in the children's past and strengthened their hope for a better future. And she helped them recapture some of their self-confidence and build up their courage. In this way she lived up to her credo: "Wherever energy reflects upon itself and, without fear of appearing ridiculous, attempts to prevail on its own, a new source of creativity opens up — and that is the goal of our attempts to teach drawing."

Proof that she succeeded, if only for a few hours, is found in the more than three thousand drawings created by children under her leadership — each one a child's witness to life in the ghetto. They offer a message different from that of the drawings and paintings by Theresienstadt's adult artists, who were committed to documentary realism. This was the case not only because children painted and drew these pictures, but also because the work of these children reveals the influence of a particular school of art and of a very modern theory of artistic pedagogy. These children's drawings — some of which can be considered works of art — are the result of an ambitious professional method of instruction and the influence of an extraordinarily gifted teacher.

Born Friederike Dicker in Vienna on July 30, 1898, she began her education in art as a sixteen-year-old pupil of Franz Cizek at the Vienna School of Applied Arts. Cizek, whose drawing and painting classes were founded on the principle of the free devel-

Friedl Dicker-Brandeis (1898–1944)

opment of spontaneous artistic expression, helped give birth to what would ultimately become modern art therapy. Cizek and Johannes Itten, whose private art school Friedl attended a year later, gave her the crucial foundation for her own work. It was above all Itten's artistic instruction — which was based on chiaroscuro, color composition, and rhythmic drawing exercises, and on the principle of recognizing and appreciating individual expression — that provided the fundamental methodology for her work as an artist.

When Johannes Itten was invited by Walter Gropius to be part of the Bauhaus in 1919, Friedl followed her teacher to Weimar. The innovative concepts of this most influential art school of the twentieth century matched the ideas and expectations of the young art student eager to put theory into practice. "There is no essential difference between the artist and the craftsman. The artist is the exalted craftsman," Walter Gropius, the founder of the Bauhaus, proclaimed in a prospectus that called for an end to traditional idealized concepts of art and for the ennoblement of the work of the craftsman.

For the next four years Friedl studied all that the Bauhaus had to offer: textile design with Georg Muche, lithography with Lyonel Feininger, and theater design with Oskar Schlemmer and Lothar Schreyer. She learned bookbinding, graphic design, weaving, and embroidery. After Paul Klee arrived at the Bauhaus in 1921, she never missed one of his lectures — or any opportunity to watch over her revered master's shoulder as he worked. Along with Franz

313

Cizek and Johannes Itten, it was above all Paul Klee who became the inspiration for her remarkable pedagogical achievements, which ultimately reached their full maturity in her art classes in Theresienstadt.

"As the former director and founder of the Staatliches Bauhaus in Weimar, I followed the artistic work of Fräulein Dicker with great interest," wrote Walter Gropius in 1931 in a letter of recommendation for his former student. In that same year, in addition to her work in her design firm, Atelier Singer-Dicker, in Vienna, she also began her career as an art instructor for kindergartens. "During this period she always distinguished herself by her unusual and extraordinary artistic talent and thus attracted the attention of the entire faculty to her work. The variety of her talents and her great energy resulted in accomplishments and works that were among the very best of the institute."[6]

Indeed, numerous objects bear witness to her inexhaustible creative energies: posters, invitations, book designs, embroidered pieces, set and costume designs (for Berthold Viertel and Bertolt Brecht, among others), drawings, paintings, sculpture, furniture, interior designs, and photo collages. These works of art were created during her student days, in the Werkstätten Bildender Kunst (Workshop for Fine Arts) in Berlin, which she had opened together with fellow student and friend Franz Singer in 1923, and, from 1926 to 1931, in Vienna in the Atelier Singer-Dicker, whose renown soon spread well beyond that city.

Beginning in 1933, the changing times began to make themselves felt in Friedl's life. Sometime during the February 1934 uprising in Vienna, which resulted in several hundred casualties and imprisonments, Friedl was arrested for being a member of the banned Communist Party. Released from prison that same year, she fled to Prague, where she remained until 1938. These years were marked by two crucial turning points in her life. In the aftermath of her imprisonment and flight, and after having broken off a complicated longtime love affair with her professional partner, Franz Singer, Friedl underwent a period of introspection and inner withdrawal. Her new orientation found its artistic expression in a series of new paintings — portraits, landscapes, still lifes, cityscapes — that announced her emancipation from the influences of the Bauhaus and the development of her own unique style. On a personal level, it also led to a new partnership with Pavel

Brandeis, whom she married in 1936.

Following her inclination to work with children, Friedl set up a children's art studio in her apartment in Prague. It was attended mainly by children of German-speaking Prague families and by children of emigrants from Germany and Austria, among them Georg Eisler, son of the composer Hanns Eisler. One of Friedl's most talented students was Edith Kramer, who had moved to Prague from Vienna in order to stay close to her teacher and master. At the age of twenty she became Friedl's assistant. "I knew that I couldn't learn nearly as much from anyone else as from Friedl. She was an inspired and wonderful teacher," she would later say of her mentor.[7]

Friedl's circle grew smaller with each passing day. More and more friends were saying farewell. She herself could have emigrated; she had a certificate from Palestine in hand. But she didn't want to leave her husband and his family. "I cannot go," she said when saying goodbye to her friend Wally Fischer. "Theoretically I could leave for Palestine tomorrow. But I have a task to do here, Wally. I have to stay, no matter what happens."[8]

It is difficult to say today how she conceived this task. We know only one thing:

Friedl, who so desperately wanted a child, had a miscarriage during that time. This trauma might have led her to think that she was not meant to be a mother of a single child, but rather a teacher of art to many children.

"I believe," Edith Kramer would later say, "that it worked to the benefit of the children of Theresienstadt that she herself did not have a child. Otherwise she would have found a way to save herself. And the children of Theresienstadt would never have had those wonderful experiences with her."

In the summer of 1938, Friedl and Pavel moved to Hronov, a small town northeast of Prague, near the Polish border. They managed to lead a modest life there. And Friedl, though not used to life in a provincial town, enjoyed the picturesque surroundings, which became a source of new energy for her.

"This life has ransomed me from a thousand deaths by allowing me to paint with earnest diligence, and it is as if I have freed myself from some guilt whose cause I do not know," she wrote to a girlfriend shortly after arriving in Hronov.[9] Friedl threw herself into her painting with the utmost intensity. She painted to combat the suffering in this world and her own personal pain, creating her most beautiful, most personal works. "In those dark gloomy days," an acquaintance from the period reports, "she radiated energy, wisdom, and cordiality — emotions that seemed to come from another world and had almost been forgotten at the time. . . . And she was always drawing. Even while she was preparing supper she would sit at the window and draw, not wanting to waste a single minute."[10]

On December 9, 1940, Friedl wrote to her friend Hilde Kothny in Germany: "I have slipped through the net and am gratefully enjoying life. I only hope that if I have to pay for this, I will have stored up enough energy from it to do so."[11]

In December 1942 Friedl and Pavel received their transport orders. Composed and prepared for what was in store for her, she started on her way to Theresienstadt.

Helga's diary continues:

Wednesday, November 3, 1943
Ela cried. I could not at all believe that she's so fond of me and loyal to me and valued our friendship so much. I'm well aware that my friendship with Erika was a disappointment to her. But how should I have known that she and Flaška aren't

such close friends, that they only go to their rendezvous together because their boyfriends are pals and that's why they all go for their evening walk together? Flaška and Zajíček have exchanged friendship rings, and now Flaška also has friendship pendants with Hana Lissau and Eva Heller. Zajíček has left Flaška, just as Pavla once left Ela and I'm leaving Ela now. Flaška is all alone. Ela is all alone — her friends have betrayed her. Marianne doesn't have a friend, but she gets along well with Ela and Flaška. They're friendly with one another, but haven't offered each other real friendship. I told Ela just now that I'll always think of her as my best friend, even if she no longer wants it that way. I offered her my friendship again, to which she replied that she'd have to think it over seriously. I'm curious how it will turn out.

We lie packed together like sardines on our triple-decker bunks. Between the stench, the narrow confines, and the vermin, it's really terrible here. I've drawn a sketch of our bed, where two people lie on each level. We sleep in our beds, and live and eat in them like monkeys in a tree or chickens in a henhouse.

November 11, 1943, was a day of fear —

a cold, gray, rainy day. The evening before, an order had been given for everyone living in the ghetto to report the following day for a census to be taken two miles from Theresienstadt, in a low area just outside of Bohušovice that the Czechs called *kotlina,* the "hollow." The order had been preceded by the arrest of the deputy Jewish elder, Jakob Edelstein, and three of his colleagues from the Central Registry, the office assigned to keep a precise record of all arriving and departing transports and an accurate daily count of the population. The arrested men, who vanished into the camp prison in the cellar of the bank building, were accused of falsifying records and abetting the flight of at least fifty-five people.

In fact, it had become the practice among the Central Registry staff to occasionally enter the names of dead persons on transport lists in order to protect some people from being deported to the East. Sometimes births (beginning in 1943, abortions were obligatory)[12] were covered up by falsely entering the names of dead persons in the registry. And they attempted to hide the names of people who had fled the camp by listing them in the daily count as still present.

After several prisoners, including Walter

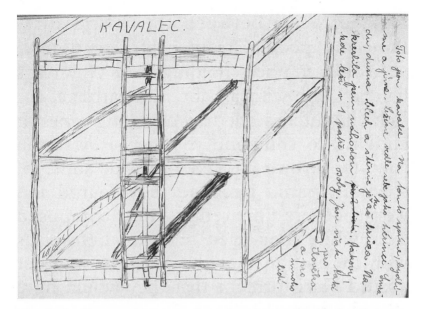

Beds in Room 28 — a drawing from Helga's diary

Deutsch, had escaped from Theresienstadt that October and were later arrested in Prague, the SS examined the records and, discovering all sorts of irregularities, sent some of those responsible to the camp prison. These events were known only to a small circle, and if the majority of the ghetto residents did learn of them, it was only by way of dubious *bonkes*. But there could be no mistake about the meaning of the orders issued for November 11, 1943.

Everyone had to get up at five o'clock in the morning and make themselves ready for the march. Soon afterward the ghetto's inhabitants were streaming from its buildings and barracks: between thirty and forty thousand people, from babies to ninety-year-olds, mothers holding their children's hands, some with a baby in a carriage, the sick on crutches, the frail clutching canes or clinging to someone younger. Row upon row, the crowd moved forward, some of them in panic because they feared the worst, others apparently more composed even while they tried to calm themselves with the notion that this was just another absurd Nazi torment that they would have to endure.

"I didn't sleep at all during the night of November 10th," Helga confided to her diary ten days later, after removing it from its hiding place. "First came the Home elder, then the doctor, then the nurse — and it was all about the census to be taken in the Bohušovice Hollow. We got up at five, had to put on the warmest clothes we had, and by half past seven we were required to be at the door and ready to march. We stood there for an hour, then we were sent back into the Home, only to be whistled for again ten minutes later and ordered to march back downstairs and line up out on the street. There were three hundred fifty children. Then we walked for forty-five minutes to the hollow. We had enough to eat with us, because that same morning we had been given our ration of three ounces of sugar, a pound of bread, half a tin of liverwurst, and two ounces of margarine. We stood in one spot from ten in the morning until five that evening."

"We were with the children," the counselor Eva Weiss recalls. "And we thought up games to play. Word games or the sort of guessing games you play with children when you don't have anything else, just to divert them and lessen their fear. But the whole time we were afraid they would shoot us. We didn't know if we would be coming back."

Today, the children who were under her care have no recollection of playing any games in the *kotlina*. Only a few of them managed to remember how they formed a little circle, facing outward, so that a friend could go to the toilet. Much stronger are memories of how cold it was, the pain in their frozen hands and feet, and how their legs hurt from standing for hours in one place. And they all share one memory burned forever in their minds — fear.

"I was terribly afraid," Flaška recalls. "I thought they were going to shoot us. The whole valley was surrounded by armed police and SS men, with airplanes circling overhead."

"I wanted to find my mother and grand-mother, but that wasn't possible. We weren't allowed to leave our group," Hanka says. And Handa remembers, "No one knew why we were there or what was going to happen next. And under those conditions you think of all sorts of possibilities. The worst part of that day for us was that we really didn't know if we would be returning home or what would happen next. We thought we would never return to the camp. It was a trauma for us all."

In the crowd were Alice Herz-Sommer and her little boy, Stephan, who sometimes played the sparrow in *Brundibár*. She sat on a blanket that she had brought and laid out on the damp, cold ground, with Stephan on one knee and another boy on the other. She told the two boys stories — how else was she to counter their anxiety, how else to make light of their questions of "why"? Why did they have to stand around here in the rain and cold? Why couldn't they go back to the ghetto? Alice told stories to fight against the increasing tension; she even managed to make the children laugh. And then suddenly came another booming command from the SS: "Line up in groups of one hundred!" In the distance Anton

Burger, the camp commandant, could be seen riding a black horse. A few gliders were drifting overhead, several SS men on bicycles were circling the large area filled with prisoners, Czech policemen held machine guns aimed at the crowd. Dogs were barking, whips cracked. Shots could be heard in the distance. What was happening to those left behind in the ghetto? It was late afternoon, and dusk was falling.

Suddenly the eerie rumor spread that it all might end in a mass execution by firing squad, or through some other kind of liquidation. Those who had lived in the ghetto since January 1942 recalled in horror the execution of the young men whom the SS made a point of hanging before the eyes of the members of the Council of Elders as punishment for their having tried to smuggle letters out of the camp.[13] The camp commandant wanted to set an example that would deter anyone else from disobeying camp rules. Was this so-called census in the Buhošovice Hollow merely a pretense for assembling everyone in order to murder them? An act of reprisal for some acts of disobedience? An act of revenge taken in the manner of the massacre at Lidice?

The Germans were capable of anything.

For those who were older, November 11 was a date that awakened the ghosts of the past. In Berlin on November 9, 1918, the Social Democrat Philipp Scheidemann had proclaimed Germany a republic. And November 11, 1918, marked the signing of the armistice agreement that later led to the Treaty of Versailles, which in the eyes of the Nazis had brought "disgrace and shame on Germany for all time." Ever since the early 1920s, these dates had been thorns in the side of all enemies of the Weimar Republic, especially Adolf Hitler and his Nazi Party, which was why they had repeatedly unleashed their hatred and thirst for power on their anniversaries. Their failed putsch in Munich occurred on November 9, 1923. And Kristallnacht — the pogroms unleashed against Jews throughout the German Reich, which by then included the Sudetenland — began on the night of November 9, 1938. The events of that night now lay five years in the past. But for those standing in the Buhošovice Hollow, those events were once again real and menacing.

"So I picked my boy up and held him tight, even though that was rather difficult," Alice Herz-Sommer continues in her report. "And now the moment was here. We are going to be shot. This is the end. Life is over.

Yes, and how does a person react in such a situation? One does not react at all. There is no way to react. Your own emotional life is no longer functional. It is more like a dark wall. Everything is black. The only thing I could feel was the warm body of my son. And I told myself, Well, he's here with me. Whatever happens to me happens to him. And that lies in God's hand."[14]

As the day drew to a close, people — especially the elderly — began falling to the ground in exhaustion, some of them fainting, others still quite conscious and yet incapable of staying on their feet. Many younger people were barely able to hold out, either, and — without arousing the notice of the police or SS men who were pacing along their ranks and bellowing numbers — they took turns slipping to the back of their groups of one hundred, where they could crouch down and relax their exhausted bodies for a few minutes. Several more hours passed. It was growing dark and still they were being held in check. When would this nightmare end?

Little Frta, Marta Fröhlich, was ill with bronchitis and in the infirmary in the Hohenelbe Barracks, so she did not have to appear for the census in the *kotlina*, as was the case with several hundred other patients.

Many of them, especially the old and frail, had been brought to the hospital early that morning. The hospital was overcrowded, and there was so little room that even those who were seriously ill not only had to share a cot with others, but many of them could not even stretch out and had to sit up. There they huddled, shoulder to shoulder, the entire day. Including Marta: "Sick as I was, I sat on my cot from morning to night. I couldn't even go to the toilet. They just kept counting us over and over — like cows. I heard airplanes and I heard shots, and I thought we would all be shot."

As the hours passed, her feverish thoughts were with her brothers and sisters in the *kotlina*. It seemed like an eternity. "What are the Germans up to? If only I could be with my brothers and sisters! If they shoot them, then I want to be shot, too."

"And then something happened that I will never forget," Alice Herz-Sommer recalls. "A loud cry, in Czech: '*Zpět do ghetta!* Back to the ghetto!' There's no describing the feeling. The ghetto had become paradise. The ghetto, that indescribable ghetto, that hell — in that moment it became paradise!"

Zdeněk Ohrenstein, the boy from Prague who had played the dog in *Brundibár* (and who later went by Ornest, the Czech version of his surname), described these events in an article for *Vedem:* "A great rush, as if a rope had slackened and everything gave way. People moved forward. No one knew who had given the order, but everyone started to walk. Like a slowly churning — and deadly — avalanche. Pushing and shoving. Loud cries. People ruthlessly trampling each other. Everyone just thinking of himself. Me, nobody else! My life is at stake. We rolled back to the barracks, which then stood in our way. This horde of people became one great mob. You couldn't breathe, and everything stood still. Each was carried along, scarcely aware even of himself. The strength and force of the individual no longer counted. There was only one awful force, the force of the mob, unstoppable and cruel. Yes, so it was — and yet we managed to get home. No one knows precisely how. Everyone fled, leaving everyone else behind. We escaped like flies from a spiderweb, our faces expressing only bafflement."

At nine o'clock the girls reached their Home. Flaška had fainted from exhaustion on the way back and had to be carried for a while. But that was harmless in comparison to those who were so old and weak that they did not survive this day of absurd census taking, or who later died from its rigors.

When the girls got back to "their" Room 28, Strejda (Handa's father) was already kneeling at the old stove. The fire was burning and spreading comforting warmth. Without a word, the girls took to their beds and fell asleep at once.

Helga's father kept a sober record of what happened: "Autumn parade. Census in the Buhošovice Hollow. Evidently a former drill-field. About thirty thousand Jews report for duty. Our building at nine o'clock in the morning. I've been on my feet for fourteen hours. I arrived home at a quarter to eight. Helga, who was standing at the other end of the field and held out bravely, arrived at her quarters at nine o'clock. We were let back into the ghetto at half past seven." His love of puns came through in his summary of the events of the day: "Open-air production on Buhošovice Field: *The Tallies of Hoffmann.*" Another musical allusion also made the rounds in whispers: Weber's *Freishit.*[15]

"The administration and the Council of Elders," stated Order of the Day #37 on November 13, "thank all those ghetto inmates, especially the staff of the barracks, the Ghetto Guard, the finance office, the doctors and nursing staff, the staff of Central Registry, and those working groups who assisted in both departure and return, for the discipline they displayed while the census was taken in the Buhošovice Hollow on November 11, 1943."

It was not until ten days later, on November 21, that Helga retrieved her diary from its hiding place and wrote, "I had to put you aside for a while, at the bottom of my suitcase, because I expected the Germans to do a search. I had to hide all my notebooks, hide you under dead things! Even now I cannot describe what had happened during this time."

"We're expecting some kind of inspection from the outside world," Helga wrote on November 29, 1943. "Everyone learned about it on the 27th. The entire ghetto is to be prettied up — the store windows, the barracks, and the children's homes. Shelves have to be hidden behind curtains. Nothing is to be left lying in the open. We're under quarantine. We're allowed outside, but no one is allowed to visit us. Encephalitis has broken out, thirty cases, four of them ours."

In Room 28 one bunk after the other stood empty, the sick bays were filled to their limit, and the Sokolovna was turned into a hospital for encephalitis cases. An inflammation of the brain, the disease is very infectious and results in both a high fever and narcolepsy, which is why it is also called sleeping sickness. There was hardly a girl who did not come down with it — Ela, Flaška, Handa, Helga, Frta, Marianne, Judith, Lenka, Hana, Hanka, Eva Winkler. One after the other they fell ill — as did the adults, and it was often worse for them than for the children. Tella suddenly could no longer move her fingers; it was as if she were paralyzed, and for a while she was absent from Room 28.

The disease caused great confusion and undermined the discipline that usually prevailed in the Girls' Home. Even prohibitions were ignored. Because of the contagious nature of the disease, no one was allowed in the Girls' Home except the residents, but this did not prevent a few boys from visiting their girlfriends.

"My boyfriend Polda put on girls' clothes and a fuzzy cap and managed to get all the way up to us on the third floor," Hanka recalls. Ela's and Flaška's boyfriends, Honza and Kurt, also wiggled their way through a hole in the garden fence right next to the compost heap. After a quick exchange of words, the two disappeared again the way they had come.

"Some of us did everything we could not

Marianne Deutsch (left) *and Hana Brady. Hana lived in another room in the Girls' Home. The two became friends when they were both confined to the same small sick-bay room. Hana had only her brother Jiři in the ghetto. "She was a very pretty blond girl. I liked her a lot and got along with her wonderfully," Marianne says. Marianne would have loved to live with Hana in that little room until the end of the war. She didn't want to return to Room 28.*

to be sent to the Sokolovna," Handa remembers. "When a doctor examined us we would sometimes fake reflexes. The knee reflex was no problem. But it was more difficult if he pricked us in the stomach. But we tried anyway and practiced producing the reflexes they wanted. I know I didn't want to miss a single performance of *Brundibár* for anything."

It was the same for the others. During this period they had a much better chance of being allowed to step in for one of the leads. Maria, who enjoyed playing the sparrow, much preferred, of course, taking over the role of Aninka, right beside her brother Piňt'a. She had proved herself in the part several times by now, and the girls in Room 28 were proud to have an Aninka in their ranks.

Everyone loved this pretty girl with the dark eyes and wonderful voice. Maria was three years younger than Rafael Schächter's first choice for the role, Greta Hofmeister from Room 25, whom, as Flaška puts it, "we younger girls regarded as something of a prima donna. She had a very beautiful, crystal-clear voice, like a bell. But our Maria was more childlike, more natural. For us, she was the real Aninka."

Stephan Sommer slipped into the role of the sparrow as often as he could. He was always close at hand, waiting for his chance. The little boy was the darling of the ensemble. "Everybody liked him, hugged and kissed him," Helga recalls. "He was so charming onstage, hopping about so marvelously, just like a sparrow."

By now the children knew every song by heart. It was no problem for Baštík to find stand-ins for any role. Some children were just lying in wait for the chance. Handa was given the role of the dog for one performance during this period, and Flaška even got to play Aninka. "One day both Aninkas, Greta Hofmeister and Maria Mühlstein, were sick," she vividly recalls. "And I asked Baštík, 'Please, can I can sing Aninka? I can do it, too.' And he let me. I sang it without a rehearsal — and didn't make many mistakes. Only when I was dancing with Piňt'a, he kept stepping on my toes. I did two performances on one day, afternoon and evening. And I was so happy that I could sing the role of Aninka!"

Each performance was a special event, a cultural and social high point in the daily monotony of camp life. The story and the music brought all the participants, both boys and girls, closer together. And there were such wonderful scenes! Whenever the little trumpeter played his solo, the children would waltz in time to it. "It always made us laugh," recalls Ela, who would never miss a show. "He was this little Danish boy — and he played so beautifully!"

The "Danish boy" was Paul Rabinowitsch,

Alice Herz-Sommer (born 1903) and her son, Stephan (1937–2001), who loved playing the sparrow in Brundibár. In 1949 Stephan adopted the name Raphael. "My boy was enchanted, bewitched by Brundibár," Alice recalls. "Whenever he returned from a performance he would sit on the top bunk with a ladle in his hand and conduct, and the other five children (there were six in our room) would sing along, and sometimes we adults sang along, too. The text is simply delightful."

born in Hamburg in 1930. He had emigrated to Denmark with his mother and stepfather, but had been deported to Theresienstadt in October 1943. Since then he had lived in Boys' Home L 414, where he was the only Dane among a majority of Czech and German boys. He owed his participation in *Brundibár* to a rare talent — he played the trumpet. And not badly, either. After all, he had already made his debut as a member of the Copenhagen Tivoli Guarde Band.

And now he was performing in a children's opera. He sat beside the pianist, the handsome Gideon Klein (or sometimes Baštík himself) and when it was time for his entrance, Paul stood up and played his trumpet with all his heart. "I vividly recall," he would report decades later, "playing that solo, that lovely *Valse lente cantabile,* and watching the children dance and laugh. It was fantastic."

Paul found other things fantastic as well — things that had greater meaning for him than they did for the other children, because he spoke not a word of Czech. "What was so wonderful for me," he recalls, "was that the plot was about milk and how the children were able to get milk, and that people stood there buying bonbons and cake and bread. That was incredible! They had cake and bread and milk and ice cream — vanilla, strawberry, and lemon ice cream. Croissants and buns and pretzels, and all the other things they sang about. And all we had, of course, was dry bread! We children hadn't had real milk to drink for years; no eggs, no cake, no bonbons, no ice cream. And suddenly there was someone selling every sort of ice cream imaginable, as if all these things actually existed. And the children acted as if these things were really there. That was fantastic. Reality was transformed, bewitched. And it was especially *Brundibár* that had that great creative power."

Sometimes when the new Home administrator Willy Groag made his evening rounds, someone would mention *Brundibár,* and he would treat the children to a special story — and Groag was a wonderful storyteller. He told the children how when he was a chemistry student in Prague between 1934 and 1936 he would pay his weekly visit — as a "boarder," as he liked to put it — to his uncle Heinz, Dr. Heinrich Fleischmann, a lawyer and bachelor who lived on Karlsplatz. "My uncle played the piano very well. He was an amateur of the highest level. And he played piano together with Hans Krása.

Willy Groag (1914–2001) and his wife, Miriam (1918–1946), whom he married in 1940. Their daughter Chava was born in the ghetto in 1944 and now lives in Israel.

Sometimes they would go to a coffeehouse together, the Deutsches Haus on Na Prikope, which was frequented by the good liberal left — many of them writers for the *Prager Tageblatt,* such as Rudolf Thomas, Ludwig Steiner, Max Brod, Egon Erwin Kisch, Anton Kuh, and Theodor Lessing."

It was from Groag that the girls learned many interesting details about the life of *Brundibár*'s composer, who was born on November 30, 1899, the son of a Prague attorney. They learned about his successful debut on May 4, 1921, when Alexander

Zemlinsky, the conductor of the New German Theater in Prague, performed his first work, *Orchestral Songs,* with texts taken from Christian Morgenstern's *Gallows Songs.* Groag told them about Krása's years in Paris, where he studied with Albert Roussell and where in 1923 he heard Roussell's Symphony for Small Orchestra and his String Quartet performed. And most certainly he also told them about Krása's greatest success, a musical rendition of Dostoyevsky's novella *Uncle's Dream,* which premiered under the title *Betrothal in a Dream* at the New German Theater in Prague in 1933 and for which Krása received that year's Czech National Prize.

"But you're barking up the wrong tree if you believe I would ever have thought that someday he would compose such a magical children's opera," Groag would conclude his special account of the life of Hans Krása. "You see, in those days, Krása seemed to me to be a rather odd bachelor, slightly introverted, at least in his dealings with me. But that may have been due to the difference in age. In any case, I was only twenty, and he was of my uncle's generation. But I remember him as a odd fellow, dressed in a rather old-fashioned frockcoat with tails that stuck out, but with an artist's lovely head of curly hair."

Hanukkah, the festival of lights and of hope, was drawing near. The children in the Homes set about preparing their gifts. This meant a great deal of craftwork and organizing. Helga had a Theresienstadt coat of arms made for her father, for which she paid five hundred fifty ghetto kronas, nineteen ounces of sugar, and two ounces of margarine — all of it saved up through an iron will. And although their friendship was falling apart, she wanted to give Ela a pendant. "It's all over with Ela. We've told each other that we aren't a good match. Nevertheless, I intend to treat Ela cordially, so she won't have a bad opinion of me. And I want her to have a memento from me, since I have one from her," she wrote in her diary.

Pendants and brooches were the two presents most girls could give each other. With a little skill, they could even make them themselves. As we learn from her notebook, Handa was planning the same sort of presents: she wanted to give Muška a brooch in the form of a dog. For Helga it was to be one with a horse's head, for Ela one with a cat's head, and a treble clef for Piňťa Mühlstein.

But during this time their thoughts were

also revolving around Hana Epstein — "Holubička." What had become of her? She had disappeared from their room a while ago. No one knew what had really happened to her. Some said she was in the Cavalier Barracks, among the mentally ill. But why? Something was not quite right with Holubička, they all knew that. She was slightly handicapped and a bed-wetter; she lisped and seemed naive. She usually had a smile on her face — even when the girls made fun of her, something she never seemed to really notice.

The girls missed Holubička, and Ela and Marta decided to try to find her. They set out for the Cavalier Barracks.

"As we were crossing the courtyard of the Cavalier Barracks, we suddenly heard someone shout, 'Elinka, Elinka,' " Ela recalls. "We looked around, and there among the other sad creatures, we saw an utterly gaunt, disheveled woman dressed only in her underpants. She stared at me distractedly and frantically waved her hands. I was close to panicking. Did this woman really know me?"

"Elinka, Elinka," she cried again as the girls walked on. Suddenly Ela recognized her voice — this woman was from her hometown of Lom. She had once been elegant and well-to-do, a hatmaker who had later lived on Na Prikope in Prague. Now she had ended up in the Theresienstadt madhouse. Just like Hana Epstein.

Ela and Marta finally found Holubička in a room locked to visitors. They could only peek at her through a large window. There she lay, side by side with other patients. She was in a straitjacket, staring into space, inert and apathetic. "She didn't recognize us. It was terrible. We felt so dreadfully sorry for her."

Transports! The news struck like a thunderbolt. "Transports! That terrible word brought Theresienstadt into a state of shock," Helga wrote in her diary on December 13. "Two transports of 2,500 people each will be leaving. The only people ineligible are those with infectious diseases. Four of us will be leaving: Irena Grünfeld and Eva Landa. Fiška and Milka are on the reserve list. But even though they're reserves and not on the first transport, they're sure to be leaving on the second. Papa and I are protected. The rumor making the rounds is that all Jews from the Protectorate are being sent to Birkenau."

Eva Landa was in sick bay when her mother came to tell her the terrifying news.

There was no escape. Eva had to pack her things and say goodbye to her roommates. And to Harry. Or was he going to be on this transport as well?

She kept a lookout at the window. Suddenly she saw her boyfriend on the street. She waved wildly and informed him by gestures that she had to leave on the transport. He pointed to himself. Eva understood at once: Harry would be among those on the transport, too. At least they would be together.

The Hanukkah celebration, which was now quickly moved up, left Eva in a kind of feverish trance. She watched as presents were taken from a small suitcase and distributed among the children — pendants, brooches, postcards, pictures, drawings, pencils, and, for each girl, a tiny booklet with pictures and a poem from their counselor Eva Weiss.

Saying goodbye was hard. "I still remember that big transport in December 1943," Hanka says, "and how so many of my friends had to leave, among them Eva Landa and Resi Schwarz. We kept saying, 'See you soon. See you again soon.' We always hoped and believed that the war would be over in a few days or a couple of weeks. We were firmly convinced that the

Germans would lose. And we told ourselves that it wasn't important who left or who remained — far more important was that we would all meet again after the war. And we agreed it would be on one particular day after the war in Prague, under the old astronomical clock on the Old City Ring."

Eva Landa packed her few belongings, placing a couple of drawings, poems, and her poetry album carefully between her clothes. She wanted to hold on to these things to remember her friends in Room 28, which had meant so much to her. She didn't cry. When they said their goodbyes, Handa told her, "After the war, be sure to call me in Olbramovice, okay? Our telephone number is simple, you know — just dial one."

"I wanted to be brave, had to be brave, and I did not want to betray our ideals," Eva wrote decades later. "I took with me my memories of our shared striving for justice, for a better life, for perfection."

And she wrote a goodbye message in Flaška's album: "Your path will lead you up the mountain and down the mountain, and sometimes through rocks, puddles, and snowdrifts. But whatever your path may be, walk bravely and hold your head up high, whistling a happy tune. Don't be glum, don't complain, hold out! Always remember your Eva Landová."

Milka said her farewell to Flaška in a letter:

Theresienstadt, December 14, 1943

My dear Flaštičko,

I have to say goodbye to you today. But we must be brave — there is no other choice. I hope we shall meet again somewhere. And that we shall once again be the good friends we were here. Flaška, you know how well we got along, but our time was short. I hope that even when I am far from you, we will remain the same good friends we were here.

I will think of you every day. And if it's possible, I'll write you right away.

And don't forget, Flaška: if I sign my letter "Milka" that means "things are bad for us." But if I sign it "Your Miluška," that means "we're doing all right." Flaška, if Freda goes out with another girl, write me about it. Flaška, I wish you much happiness in life, that you have a carefree life, and lots of little Buddhas. *[Buddha was the nickname of Flaška's boyfriend.]* Flaška, think of me and don't forget me. My head is so full of thoughts that I don't

know what I should write.
                                  So farewell, and remember
                                              Your Milka

Helga's diary continues:

Friday, December 17, 1943
  The first transport has left. Irena Grünfeld and Eva Landa were on it. Fiška was
taken off the list, and Milka is still here,
too. She was on the standby list to go but
has been left behind; she will be on the
second transport. Holubička's father has
learned that they are on the standby list,
too. Eva Weiss also. Fiška is writing
poems in bed next to Handa, who is sick.
They keep coming up with new topics.

Wednesday, December 22, 1943
  Eva Weiss is gone. Everyone in our
home who was on the transport is gone.
No one was released from the second
transport. Eva Weiss is traveling all alone,
without her mother, brother, or fiancé.
Helena wasn't able to get taken off the list
this time either. Her parents gave her an
injection that left Helena with a high fever
and diarrhea, just to keep her from being
included in the transport. But now Helena
is on her way to Birkenau with a high fever
and diarrhea — in a cattle car without a

toilet or even a bench to sit on.

Five thousand seven people left the ghetto on transports Dr and Ds. Among them were 115 children under the age of five and 500 children between the ages of six and fifteen. In Room 28, the bunks of Hana Epstein, Helena Mendl, Irena Grünfeld, Milka Poláček, and Eva Landa were now empty.

Only Eva Landa and the counselor Eva Weiss would survive Auschwitz-Birkenau.

ELA STEIN

Ela Stein was born in Lom, a small town in the Ore Mountains, on June 30, 1930, four years after her sister, Ilona. Her parents, Max and Markéta Stein, owned two shops on Školni Strasse, in the house where they also lived.

Max Stein was a man full of enterprise. On weekends he would often travel with his family to nearby Lány, the summer residence of President Tomáš G. Masaryk. They would sometimes cross paths with him there, and if the opportunity arose and Max Stein could exchange a few words with the president, he was overjoyed. "You simply can't imagine what Masaryk meant to the Czechs. And especially to us. Because he was a friend to the Jews." When Masaryk died on September

14, 1937, Czech Jews were among those who mourned the loss of a great statesman and symbol of hope. On the day he was buried, thousands of people, among them the Stein family, climbed the hill to Prague Castle. "We approached the Hradschin at a snail's pace, a long funeral procession ahead of us, a great many cars with flowers and wreaths. We stood in line outside the entrance to castle, where a black carpet had been rolled out on which was placed the catafalque with Masaryk's coffin. It took us four hours before we could pay our final respects."

The times grew more troubled. The Germans marched into Vienna, and cries for help from among the large circle of the Steins' friends and relatives became ever more frequent. Then came the first refugees from Austria. The border regions of Bohemia and Moravia, settled by a German majority, were still loyal to Czechoslovakia. But the invasion of ideology and anti-Semitic propaganda had long since begun. "I can remember my sister and me listening to Hitler's voice on the radio — the radio trembled! We couldn't listen to his screaming. And my father kept saying: 'Nothing's going to happen. Nothing can happen. It's not possible that they'll enter Czechoslovakia.' "

Then came a fateful day in the summer of 1938. Max Stein was having his hair cut as usual by a German barber, when a fierce argument about Hitler and the Germans broke out among the customers. The abyss that had opened between the two opposing parties grew deeper as they continued. On the one side were uncompromising Nazis who supported the Sudeten German Party (SdP) of Konrad Henlein, the strongest political movement after 1935, and on the other, Czech patriots like Max Stein, who finally became so excited that he shouted, "I'll give ten thousand krona to the man who'll kill Hitler." The next day he was at the top of the blacklist in Lom.

Shortly thereafter, the German army marched into the Sudetenland, and the National Socialist German Workers Party (NSDAP) and its ally, the SdP, seized power. Max Stein was one of their first victims; the Gestapo took him into custody from his home. A few days later, Markéta Stein was informed that her husband had died of a heart attack. When Ela and her sister, Ilona, returned from summer vacation, they no longer had a father.

The night of November 9 marked what has come to be known as Kristallnacht (Crystal Night, or Night of Broken Glass). That night and for several succeeding days, attacks on Jews and Jewish institutions reached levels never seen before — and not just in Germany, but also in the "Sudetengau," as the Nazis called the newly conquered peripheral Czech regions. Synagogues were desecrated, plundered, razed, and burned — in Liberec, Karlovy Vary, Mariánské Lázně, Chomutov, Znojmo, and Opava. A manhunt began. In Lom the hatred was directed especially at the Steins — one of four Jewish families in the town.

"It was a horrible night. A whole horde of maybe three hundred Nazis had assembled in town. Shouting and bellowing and beating drums, they began to march toward our house. I can still hear that *boom, boom, boom* even now. An old school friend of my father's came running to my mother, shouting that she had to close the shop at once. My mother could scarcely believe her ears. Then, all of a sudden, they were at our house, and began to break all the doors and windows. We ran up to the attic, where we hid." And so they waited until far into the night, huddled in one corner of the attic and clinging to one another in shock.

"My mother prayed while downstairs they smashed everything to smithereens — everything. The next morning the house was smeared with swastikas and graffiti that said things like JEWS GET OUT and SEND JEWS TO PALESTINE." In no time the Gestapo had confiscated the Steins' assets. The shop was handed over to a German commissioner. Markéta Stein was summoned by the Gestapo and interrogated for hours. Finally they threatened her, saying that if she did not leave town in the next twenty-four hours, "then we'll see you in Dachau."

On a late November afternoon, with a cold rain falling, Markéta fled with her children on a motorcycle with a sidecar. A relative drove, Ela and Ilona sat in the sidecar, and their mother sat behind the driver. Freezing and afraid, Ela began to cry. When they reached the border at Louny, they saw hundreds of people under SS guard. By this time it was known that their destination was Dachau. But no one knew what Dachau really meant.

While they were being checked at the border, Ela suddenly began to whine, "Mommy, I want to go home, I'm so awfully cold." "I don't know if the border guard understood me or not, but I can still remember what he said: 'Quick, drive on.' "

A few minutes before six o'clock, they crossed the border, just in time, because it would be closed at six sharp. That night they arrived at the home of relatives in Louny. Normally the confectionary factory belonging to her uncle Anton Krauss produced cookies and candy — one kind was even called Ilonetty, after her sister — but now production had been halted and the Krausses' home and factory had been turned into a refugee camp, which was already so full that there was no place for the Steins. They had to find a hotel room. The next day they took the bus to Prague, where Markéta's brother, Otto Altenstein, lived. Before the occupation he had been a state secretary in the Ministry for Social Welfare. His apartment in Prague-Holešovice was much too small to house them all, so the children were taken to Brno, where Markéta Stein's family lived.

Ela and Ilona were enrolled in the Czech School in Brno. After classes, they often went to visit their aunt, Kamila Korn, at Plotní 2, which served as a meeting place for Zionists who organized illegal refugee transports and gave agricultural instruction for Hachsharah. The youth counselors Fredy Hirsch and Franta Meier were part of this group; there was also a young fellow named Honza Gelbkopf, who a few years later would become Ela's first boyfriend.

March 1939 brought the occupation of what Hitler contemptuously referred to as the "Czech rump" (the remaining Czech territory, which had not been handed over to Germany under the Munich agreement), and the Germans seized power throughout the country. Markéta brought her two children to Prague.

They had plans to emigrate. Otto Altenstein already had an airplane ticket for New York, but he was turned back at the airport. "For us that was a signal that any plans to emigrate were doomed. We were already sitting on our packed luggage, and had to unpack it all over again."

It was the fall of 1941, and the first transports with Jews were leaving Prague. Ela and her family were living in two rooms of a five-room apartment at Šumovska 11 in Vinohrady. They got ready for their own impending transport. Feather comforters were sewn into sleeping bags. They bought backpacks, stockpiled bouillon cubes, oatmeal, bowls for eating, warm underwear. Then, in February 1942, they found their names listed for transport, with numbers 892 to 895 beside the names of Anna Altenstein, Dr. Otto Altenstein, Markéta Stein, and Ilona Stein. The last one, 896, was Ela Stein.

On February 14, 1942, they made their way through deep snow to the assembly point for Jews in Prague-Holešovice. Three days later they were led to the train station in a procession of about one thousand people. "My uncle Otto was ordered to lead the parade — Uncle Otto of all people! The Germans thought it was a good joke, because my uncle used a cane, the result of a childhood illness that left his legs too short. He could barely plod through the deep snow. I can still see myself in my heavy winter clothes walking beside him, and dragging a lot of luggage. First to the station in Prague-Holešovice, then once we arrived in Bohušovice, about a mile and a half to Theresienstadt."

EVA LANDA

Eva Landa. Her real name was Evelina, but everyone called her Eva. Eva Landa was born on December 25, 1930, into a peaceful and

auspicious world. Surrounded by her parents, Emil and Ilsa Landa, her older sister, Liesl, and her governess, Stási, she grew up in a large modern apartment in a stately building at U Smaltovny 18 in Letná, Prague. There was an elevator in the building, and a spiral staircase that led down to the courtyard, where street musicians played happy songs from time to time. Whenever Eva heard them, she would quickly wrap a few coins in a piece of paper and toss it down to the courtyard from the kitchen window, feeling confident that these strolling musicians were now playing their songs just for her.

Eva's childhood was one of affluence and security. Her father had founded the Landa Horsehair Fabrics Company. Her maternal grandparents, Nathan and Ernestine Klein, owned a wholesale pharmaceutical firm. Eva would later say, "Everything was just as it should be. My parents were hard workers. My life was well organized. I went with Stási to nearby Stromovka Park nearly every day. I spent most summer vacations on Mácha Lake in Tammühl. I have the loveliest memories of those days." At age six Eva was enrolled at the Czech Elementary School on U Studanky Street. She was a good student, especially because she was fond of her teacher, Josefine Littmann. And, like thousands of other

Czech children, she joined the Sokol Athletic Club.

It is difficult for her to pinpoint when the first major changes appeared on the horizon. The images of that period are a jumble, apart from one image that stands out clearly: "I was with my mother on the street, and airplanes with spotlights flew over Prague. And I suddenly felt sick — I think that was when I began to sense that something awful was going to happen."

But the strolling musicians who enjoyed playing in the courtyard of U Smaltovny 18 were still able to drive such gloomy thoughts away. "The Czech Guard stands at our borders. Don't think you can swallow us, Adolf," they sang at the top of their voices, setting these words to the melody of an old Czech folk song. This time Eva quickly wrapped a few more coins than usual in paper and tossed them down to the musicians in her courtyard.

Then came March 15, 1939, a Wednesday. Jutting out from the window of a building on U Smaltovny — neighbors called it Little Berlin because it was inhabited by Germans — was a large flag with a black swastika. It was snowing, and there was a cold wind. As usual, Eva went to school. "Everyone was upset, sad. Our teacher told us about what happened to Napoleon, about his ascent and deep fall, and about his horrible end. Although we were still very young, we immediately understood that she was speaking about Adolf Hitler."

From then on the Landa family was caught up in earnest discussions about whether they should emigrate. They had money and good business contacts in Zurich. They could have fled. "I can recall that I was very much against going to Switzerland, because I didn't want to go to a German school. But that of course was not the reason my parents stayed on. I think they simply found it very hard to leave their home, to give up everything and go off into the unknown. I understand now what a very difficult step that is."

Besides, the Landas were optimists, and they were Czech patriots. "We firmly believed that someone like Hitler could not stay in power for long. We believed the whole hullabaloo would soon be over." But then it really started. "We were forbidden to go to the movies, theater, concerts, even parks. Then we could board only the second car on the trolley, and even there we could sit down only if all the Aryans had first found a seat. Eventually we couldn't use the trolleys at all. We weren't allowed on the street after eight in the evening, weren't allowed to leave the town where we lived or to ride the train. All Jews were fired from the civil service, their entire fortunes confiscated. All Jewish doctors, lawyers, et cetera, had to close their offices. Jews were no longer allowed to have housemaids. Jews could not have anything to do with Aryans. Their bank accounts were blocked. We had to hand over all our valuables — jewelry, musical instruments, skis, radios. Even our pets. I had a little canary, Punta, that I had to give up. I can still remember the window on the street where I had to hand it over."

The transports began in October 1941 — first to Poland, to the ghetto in Lodz, then to Theresienstadt. When the two construction commandos left Prague for Theresienstadt in November and December, Eva's sister, Liesl, was among them. She volunteered to go because her husband, Franz Petschau, whom she had only recently married, was forced to join the transport. In the spring of 1942, Eva's grandparents Nathan and Ernestine Klein were on the transport list.

Then came the assassination of Heydrich in May 1942 and the Nazis' bloody reprisals, which filled the Czechs with fear and horror. On June 4, as part of their revenge for Heydrich's death, the Nazis ordered ten large transports in one fell swoop. The Landa family was on that list.

At six o'clock on the morning of June 28, 1942, they arrived with the prescribed hundred pounds of baggage at the Messepalais, the assembly point for Jews. On the morning of July 2, their journey continued in the direction of Theresienstadt.

It was a lovely summer day when they arrived. Many of the ghetto's inmates stood outside on the street, eyeing them with curiosity. Suddenly Eva recognized a former neighbor. "It was Herr Reiser. He was very thin and pale. He had a black ribbon on his sleeve, a symbol of mourning. My mother pointed to his sleeve, asking what it meant. He made a sign with his hand, and we understood right away: His little daughter Eva, age seven, had died of the measles. I had often played with Eva. The family had come from the Sudetenland and had been living with my grandparents. We had given the girl clothing, and supported the whole family. I was devastated — and afraid. I said to myself that day: I will do whatever I must to stay alive."

MARTA FRÖHLICH

Marta Fröhlich came from an impoverished family in the southern Bohemian town of Písek, where she was born on July 17, 1928. Her father, Leopold Fröhlich, was Jewish; her mother, Barbora Fröhlich, née Skřivanová,

was a Christian. Marta loved her mother. "She was very tidy and very hardworking, had a good heart, and was kind to everyone. She sewed us coats, shirts, and blouses, although she was no seamstress. But she knew how to help out with all kinds of work."

Barbora Fröhlich did not have much of a choice. Her husband was hardly a pillar of strength for the family. He was often ill, always hot-tempered, and had a tendency to tyrannize his family. This was also the reason why, with the help of better-situated relatives, the children were sent to Prague as soon as they reached school age — the boys to the orphanage on Belgicka and the girls to the one on Hybernska. Despite their poverty, they were to get a good education. Marta was enrolled in the Jewish grammar school on Masna Street.

Marta and her siblings soon felt at home in the Old City of Prague — until the day in March 1939 when the Germans marched into the city. "They sent us back to the orphanage from school. I can still see the huge crowds standing along the streets. Many people were crying. From that day on everything changed. Soon we weren't allowed to go to school anymore, Jewish institutions were closed one after the other, and we finally ended up in an overcrowded old people's home in Strašnice next to Hagibor, the Jewish athletic field." In one of the buildings in the complex, *Brundibár,* which had premiered in the dining room of the orphanage on Belgicka, started up again, and Marta and her sister Zdenka sang in the schoolchildren's choir. Shortly thereafter, when the inmates of the old people's home had been deported and the doors were locked, the remaining Jewish boys and girls were resettled in the Belgicka orphanage, and the five Fröhlich children were all under one roof again.

Then came the day in January when they

were taken away by the Gestapo. That same night, after having spent hours in a cold cellar, the Gestapo put them into a police van along with three other prisoners — a woman with two children. Guarded by six policemen, they arrived at Theresienstadt. It was February 1943.

EVA WINKLER

Eva Winkler was born in Brno on October 12, 1930, the daughter of Fritz and Edith Winkler, née Rosenblatt. She spent her childhood in Miroslav, a little village in southern Moravia,

where her parents owned a sawmill.

When Hitler's troops marched into the Sudetenland in October 1938, the family left everything behind and fled by night to Brno, where Eva's grandparents Adolf and Wilma Rosenblatt lived. They also owned a sawmill with extensive grounds and quarters for workers. The family took refuge in one of these buildings, and Eva soon got over the shock of their sudden flight. Eva liked her new surroundings. She admired her grandmother, "a generous and elegant lady. Actually, it was very fancy there, quite special, and it made a huge impression on me."

Life seemed to return to its normal course, and while she attended school or played with her cousin Bed'a, her father spent his time in a little workshop making stack upon stack of crates for the many people who hoped to emigrate or flee the country. The demand for them kept growing.

The Winklers were also thinking of leaving. They were weighing the idea of Montevideo, and also of putting Eva on a children's transport to England. But these plans came to naught, in large part because their sawmill in Miroslav had been Aryanized and all their assets confiscated.

In March 1939, when the Germans occupied Brno and the rest of the Czech lands, everything was as it had been in Miroslav. Eva's grandparents' sawmill and assets were seized. Close neighbors turned out to be vicious Nazis, and even the supervisor in their building suddenly showed up in a brown shirt. "We were afraid of these people."

Eva and her family moved a total of four times, until finally they were living in one room of a small apartment, which they had to share with other families. It was there that she often got together with a friend she had made in Brno — Flaška. There was still some space for children to play in Flaška's apartment at Adler Gasse 13, and they made use of it as often as possible.

Then the transports began. The eleven thousand Jews of Brno were summoned in alphabetical order. Flaška was on one of the very first lists. By April 1942, it was the letter *W*'s turn, and the Winkler family began the journey early on a cool Sunday morning.

"Why a Sunday? Why so early in the morning?" Eva asks, when describing that day years later. "Because most people were still asleep at that hour. Because there was no one on the street, no one to see us moving through the streets loaded with our backpacks, on the long walk to the Brno school that served as the assembly point. Only the SS guards watched us closely, some of them young fellows who mocked and laughed at us. And my father said to them, and I can still hear him even today, 'Just wait. One day those grins will be wiped right off your faces.' "

CHAPTER SIX:
APPEARANCE AND REALITY

December 21, 1943, was the day on which Hanukkah actually fell, but no one was in the mood to celebrate. And yet who would want the flame of hope to go out? After all, Hanukkah is the festival of hope. It commemorates the uprising in 165 B.C.E. in the Land of Israel of the Maccabees against the occupying Syrian Greeks, and the rededication of the Temple in Jerusalem (*Hanukkah* is Hebrew for "dedication") following its desecration by the occupiers. Just enough purified oil was left to light the menorah, the Temple's candelabra, for one day. But a miracle occurred: The menorah burned for eight days, during which time new oil could be produced, and the flame was kept alive.

As 1943 drew to a close, the question of whether there could still be miracles was often asked in Theresienstadt. Most everyone believed that there could be. What would be the point of maintaining the opposite? But there were also some pessimists among the girls. The following verse can be found in Handa's notebook:

Pessimists live by one rule —
The optimist's mood must be spoiled.
But the optimists smile and wonder
   instead:
Might it be true? Might it yet happen?
The scowling pessimists reverse the case
And laugh in every optimistic face.

Otto Pollak was an optimist; there was no doubt about it. Before an assembly gathered to celebrate Hanukkah at the Home for Invalids he read from a collection of poems titled *Songs of the Ghetto* by Maurice Rosenfeld. Helga, he reports in his own calendar diary, "listened wide-eyed."

"I am really proud of Papa," Helga wrote that same evening. "I just heard him read poems aloud for the first time — and so beautifully! It was at the Hanukkah celebration at the Home for Invalids, which lasted until nine o'clock. I couldn't stay past eight-thirty. Papa read three very beautiful Jewish poems with such liveliness — Papa is a treasure. Not because I received gifts from him — a little notebook with a picture of a menorah on the front and a velvet cover for

The Sokolovna, which before the war had been the clubhouse of the Sokol (Czech for "falcon") Athletic Club

my diary — but because Papa has reminded me that it is Hanukkah, even here in Theresienstadt."

Three days later Helga was lying in sick bay with encephalitis; the old year passed into the new without any fanfare. On January 5, Helga, along with Hana Lissau and Ruth Gutmann, was transferred to the Sokolovna, the former clubhouse of the Sokol Athletic Club. It was a very busy place.

Wednesday, January 5, 1944
Today is my first day in the Sokolovna. I

have encephalitis, or sleeping sickness, a kind of brain flu. I've been sick for ten days now and spent the whole time in sick bay. There are so many cases that one of the rooms in the Home had to be cleared to accommodate them. It was really awful there. The door wouldn't close, the windows were broken, the blinds ripped, the stove wouldn't heat, and there was a thick layer of dust everywhere. No one looked after us because it wasn't a real sick bay. It was just so that we could be isolated from the healthy children. I am so happy to be here now.

Thursday, January 6, 1944

The Sokolovna is a beautiful, modern building full of laboratories. The former gym is now the sick bay for all encephalitis cases. There are four rows of beds, with twenty patients in each row. Each row has its own doctor. One doctor and one nurse are on duty at night. There are five or six nurses during the day. When Pfeiffer, the head doctor, makes his rounds, he's joined by four other doctors and all the nurses.

They wake us at six o'clock and take temperatures. At nine the doctor in charge makes his rounds, and at eleven the head doctor makes his. This afternoon Prof. Sittig, a nerve specialist, came to examine the new patients. We new arrivals are lying just outside the ward in a separate room with only nine beds.

We are all in love with Dr. Herling, the physician assigned to us, but it's hopeless because he's already married. He's so handsome and dashing. He has a very special smile, probably because he knows we all have a crush on him.

During visiting hours today we were allowed out on the balcony and I spoke to Papa from the second floor.

The next day Helga passed a little note to her father — let down from the terrace at the end of long thread. No visitors were allowed inside the Sokolovna, so there was always a crowd outside the building during visiting hours. Naturally, there was a loud muddle of voices, and it would have been impossible for Helga to shout everything she wanted to say to her father.

January 6, 1944

Dear Papa,

We're finally here. It's nice here and the main thing is: it's CLEAN here. The girls who were already in the Sokolovna were

The note that Helga let down to her father on a thread from the terrace of the Sokolovna

so happy to see us — it's a miracle that they didn't hug us to death. We had to bathe and wash our hair. There was a concert in the evening. Someone played the violin and someone else an accordion. They played Dvořák's *Humoresque, Poem* by Fibich, a medley of songs from the operetta *Gypsy Princess,* plus some

Czech folk songs. They ended the concert with Gounod's *Ave Maria.*

Nine o'clock is lights-out. My blanket is so heavy that I thought I'd end up flat as a pancake by morning.

I'm lying next to Ruth Gutmann. She's a great girl from our room. I had already laid beside her in 17a *[the sick bay at the Girls' Home].* We've become fond of each other since that time. Please, write me, I'm a little afraid here. I'm reading a book in German now: *The Jewish Millionaires.*

When I look out the window I can see the Sudeten Barracks and a barbed wire fence. It looks as if I'm right at the border. Everything is covered with snow, and I can see forests and mountains in the distance. There's a guardhouse and a policeman stationed at the fence.

When Hana Lissau was discharged on January 10, Helga moved to the vacant bed beside Eva Heller. Eva also came from Vienna and, like Helga, had been taken in 1938 to Czechoslovakia, where she lived with her aunt in Brno until her deportation. Her parents had fled to Palestine and, like Zajíček's parents, they had hoped to have their daughter follow later. But it hadn't worked out, and Eva remained with her aunt, who treated her like her own daughter.

A deep friendship developed between Helga and Eva Heller. The two of them founded a "commune," shared their food and anything they got, and occasionally buried themselves in the books that were passed around the Sokolovna: *Quo Vadis, The Microbe Hunters,* and *Pierrot,* Francis Kozik's biography of the French mime Caspar Debureau. Sometimes they did handicrafts with the help of a girl in a nearby bed, making little dolls out of rags, wire, and yarn. Helga gave her first creation to her father. "In case you don't recognize it, he's supposed to be a sailor, and that's an accordion he's holding." For her cousin Lea she put together a snowman, and for Trude a girl in winter clothing, in a dark blue dress with a muff, a cap, and a scarf.

And so the days passed with naps, chatting, reading, handicrafts, and visits by the doctors. The fears and anxieties that sometimes faded away during the day hit doubly hard at night: "Every day the actress tells me what I did in my sleep; that she tucked me in like a little child and that I scream a lot. Today I was lying with my head on Eva's stomach, and she woke up because she couldn't breathe. What's the political news? Write and tell me. I would so love to see

Mama even for just a little while."

Illness still held Helga in its clutches. "I have a real encephalitis head. I forget everything. I go to the bathroom and suddenly realize I don't know why I went there. It is so bad that when I write to you and put my pencil aside for a second, I fall asleep at once. I hope that I can come home in a week or two. I couldn't write to Mařenka yesterday because my eyes hurt too much."

January was drawing to a close, and there was still a blanket of snow when Helga was finally released. "Left Marta at three-thirty to see Mimi," Otto Pollak noted. "A marvelous surprise when I got to House L 410 — Helga came shooting out the door. She's been released from the Sokolovna. She wanted to surprise me by playing her little trick. When I visited her yesterday she said the doctors were figuring it would be two weeks yet before the infection was gone. With a cry of *Tati!* she hugged me and smothered me with kisses."

February 20, 1944, was, as Otto Pollak recorded enthusiastically in his diary, "the most beautiful winter day of the year. No fog, no clouds, an azure sky, cold, but with a wonderfully bright winter sun, and with freshly fallen snow thawing on Monte Terezino."[1] News from the front indicated that the Germans were suffering huge losses on a daily basis. At the start of the month, according to the *bonkes* making the rounds of the ghetto, fifty-four hundred airplanes were involved in a maneuver in North Africa, and the roar could be heard all across the south of France. "They were American and English planes," Helga confided to her diary in code, reversing all the letters of the sentence.

In the meantime, a new girl, Miriam Rosenzweig, had moved into Room 28. She shared a bunk with Hanka Wertheimer. The two had become acquainted in the Dresden Barracks, where Hanka's grandmother and Miriam's mother shared a room. Hanka liked this blond girl who was, like herself, a member of the Zionist organization Tekhelet-Lavan. Their pleasure in spending time together quickly grew into a friendship that was deepened at the meetings of Hanka's little Zionist group, Dror, which Miriam also joined.

Miriam had long been familiar with Room 28. She had regularly attended Friedl Dicker-Brandeis's painting classes there. And she also loved to join in the girls' other activities, because there was usually something interesting going on in Room 28. The latest rage was scouting.

By this time a group of girls had joined with the boys in Room 9 to form a scouting troop. Inspired by *The Boys from Beavers' River,* a book by Jaroslav Foglar, they called themselves the Beavers. The Beavers were divided into teams: the Wolves, the Sharpshooters, the Foxes, and the Lions, each with its own flag and battle cry. "With lion-like strength we pounce like the king of beasts. Forward, young Lions, forward, ahoy, ahoy!" was the cry of the Lions, the group that Helga had halfheartedly joined. "At first I didn't want to join the scouts," she noted, "because I know how it always turns out when our girls do anything together with these guys. Many of them don't take the whole thing seriously — they just want to be around the boys. But then I reconsidered and joined the group, because I do love nature."

When Helga heard that a couple of the girls intended to organize parties with the boys, though, she regretted her decision. "Yuck! Dancing, body against body. The smell of sweat and makeup. I'm against it. This isn't allowed according to scouting rules."

Judith Schwarzbart was in total agreement with her. Weren't there enough scouting activities — like not speaking for a day, or not eating all day, or not laughing, even when others did everything they could to make you laugh? What was all this to-do about boys? Some girls were now also suggesting ideas for future parties: a sketch, a game, something amusing. Had their comrades gone completely crazy?

Others saw the funny side of the matter. Handa and Fiška used this opportunity to write what they called an "ironic song." It can be found in Handa's notebook:

One day Gelbec [Honza Gelbkopf] came to us and said: "I'm supposed to tell you that our scout troop will be meeting this afternoon." He was hardly out the door when everyone began shouting, "Hurrah! There'll be lots of boys there!" Lenka: "Which blouse should I wear? This one's all wrinkled, and my best skirt has a big spot on it." "So what?" one of the girls said. "Why are you always going on about your blouse!" "Lenka, calm down. It's not important." Lenka: "But I've got to look good because my boyfriend will see me there." Another girl: "You're so silly. Gelbec isn't even your boyfriend anymore. So don't try that on us, and stop worrying about your outfit all the time."

The next day the stillness of Home 9 was broken by a deep sigh. "Who would like to exchange 2 ounces of margarine for Ela? She jabbers so much I don't even like her anymore." And one of the boys says, "You don't think I'm crazy, do you? I can eat margarine. But what can I do with Ela?"

Suddenly Chamičurgl's bald head comes into view. And he raises one finger and says menacingly, "Gelbec, I'm warning you. You stick with Ela, or I'll make mincemeat of you."

Although Judith and Helga both loved to laugh and were amused by such foolishness, they could not make heads or tails of the excitement this partnership with the boys in Home 9 was occasioning among their roommates. "For all I care this scouting thing can fall apart. It's really just silly stuff with boys, and it has no deeper meaning at all," Helga told her diary. "Ma'agal full speed ahead would be better." Or education. "I've been unfaithful to you, haven't I?" reads her entry for February 24. "But I really haven't had any time to write. I have so much to learn if I want to stay in group A. I was second in geography with a grade of 95, and in history I had a 100, and Hana Lissau and I are the best in the class. We have a new teacher in Czech, a regular Xanthippe. She taught the eighth grade. Things are getting lost here. Tella is carrying out a search to find out why."

Something quite shocking was happening in Room 28. Bread, margarine, sugar, and even buns and dumplings kept disappearing somewhere along the way from the children's kitchen to the Home. "I'll never forget that moment," little Frta, Marta Fröhlich, recalls. "I was a suspect! And then two more buns disappeared, and two girls would have to go without lunch. They searched everywhere and took my bunk apart, but didn't find anything. Then the counselors came up with a plan. Before our meal all the girls had to go down to the courtyard, and a counselor hid behind the curtain of our closet. The counselor who accompanied the girls getting the food placed the bucket in view of the hidden counselor. We were called in for our meal. And two buns were missing again. 'That just isn't possible!' I can still hear it today. And suddenly a girl pointed at me and said, 'She's blushing. It's probably her.' I started to cry. It was horrible. It wasn't me, and it was such an awful feeling. It weighed on me for a long, long time, even after the war. The counselors insisted that the thief confess and admit what she had done. But no one stepped forward. Since two portions for our noon meal were missing again, there was an inspection. They searched everywhere now, in our blankets, which we always kept rolled up, and what do you know — two buns appeared! They were not in my things, but no one apologized to me. They probably thought it didn't matter if you make life difficult for such a stupid girl."

The story about the pilfering cut Marta to the quick. Had it not been for Eva Eckstein, their new counselor, she would have had a hard time getting over it. But Eva kindly took her under her wing. She sensed that Marta was not held in high regard by Tella, and she didn't want to make her life any more difficult than it already was. She herself had reservations about Tella. "I always had the feeling that whatever I did wasn't enough. She also pointed out to me that Eva Weiss did everything better than I did."

Eva Eckstein was nineteen and more emotionally connected to the girls than Tella. She treated her wards with great kind-

Eva Eckstein was born in Louny on November 7, 1924. She arrived in Theresienstadt in February 1942 and began working on the cleaning crew. Then, during the hard winter of 1942–43, she was assigned to a commando in the forests of Křivoklát. After Eichmann's visit to Theresienstadt in April 1943, tents were set up in Market Square as a place to assemble crates for the army, and Eva was assigned to this "essential war production." In the wake of the transports of December 1943 and with the help of her friend Kamilla Rosenbaum, she was transferred to work in Youth Welfare.

ness, especially Marta, whom she often took along when she visited her mother and two sisters. Marta had finally found someone who offered her trust and maternal affection, and who helped restore her self-confidence. Eva did her best to make life easier for the children. "The time I spent in Room 28," she would say half a century later, "was the best part of my stay in Theresienstadt."

By March the blue skies of February had long since yielded to Theresienstadt's typical gray weather and low-hanging clouds. Showers alternated with snow flurries, and no change seemed to be in sight. But life went steadily on. "It seems almost incredible to me," Helga wrote on March 18, 1944, "that in only one month and twenty-eight days I will be fourteen. I was talking with Papa yesterday and I asked him what he would have given me on my birthday in peacetime. He said that if he had the money, he would give me a globe, a microscope, and lots of books. It made me so happy that he had guessed what I wanted."

On April 3 she wrote: "The finest time in Theresienstadt is when I can debate with Papa. I learn so much. Yesterday Papa read me a few paragraphs from Schopenhauer;

he's in favor of everyone keeping a diary. It makes me so happy that I can write to a good friend who will never desert me if I don't want it. At first almost all the girls kept a diary. Now it's only two or three."

By mid-April, Helga found that she had lost her appetite and her stomach was aching — symptoms of jaundice. She was put back into sick bay. Her spirits plummeted. "Any idiot can see that this weather just won't end," she said during a visit to her father, who recorded her words in his own diary. "The sun is moving away from the earth."

Life in the ghetto seemed to be improving. "Assembly this evening at eight o'clock about the new mail regulations. Permission to write every six weeks. All packages allowed except for tea, coffee, tobacco, cigarettes, and money, which are forbidden. In the future packages will be passed on in the presence of the receiver," Otto Pollak noted on February 6. And one month later: "Cancellation of the rule that we must greet anyone in uniform."

March 6 to March 12 was spring-cleaning week. "Our Invalids' Home won a prize," Otto wrote. "My share was two pounds of bread, half a tin of liverwurst, three ounces of margarine, and three ounces of sugar."

At six o'clock on the evening of March 11 he visited the coffeehouse: "Orchestra concert, sixteen musicians, with Professor Carlo S. Taube. They played selections from Mozart's *Magic Flute,* Fantasia from Schubert's sketchbook, Kreisler's Praeludium and Allegro, a solo by Fröhlich, Dvořák's Fourth, two Slavic dances."

Change was in the air in Theresienstadt: "There is to be a new central medical library with a large reading room," Dr. Munk, the head of the health department, wrote on March 13, 1944, in a letter he sent to Jakob Edelstein on the assumption that Edelstein was in good health in Auschwitz-Birkenau. "The building that adjoins the Infants' Home is being added onto it; on the block set aside for small children a toddlers' nursery is being built in the movie hall, and the wooden barracks have become the living quarters for working women. The park on Market Square is making great progress, and within a few weeks there will be a fountain in the middle of a large flower bed. According to the plans, a music pavilion to be located opposite the coffeehouse seems to be very promising."[2]

The coffeehouse was one of the first additions meant to turn Theresienstadt into the Potemkin village that the Nazis were about

Entrance tickets to the coffeehouse

to build. Opened in December 1942, it marked the beginning of musical activities that were officially permitted and encouraged by the SS. At first it was Carlo S. Taube and the Ledeč Orchestra who usually played there along with the Weiss Jazz Quintet, which was directed by Fritz Weiss and featured musicians Pavel Libensky, Wolfi Lederer, Coco Schumann, and Franta Goldschmidt. As time went on, and as more musical instruments arrived in the ghetto and concerts were now performed on the explicit orders of the SS, additional ensembles were formed. In the winter of 1942–43, Karel Fröhlich, Heini Taussig, Romouald Süssmann, and Freddy Mark formed a string quartet, which initially performed with the world-famous Viennese cellist Luzian Horwitz.

Once the second floor of the coffeehouse was opened for concerts, a group calling itself the Ghetto Swingers had great success with their first revue, titled "Children Not Admitted." This orchestra, whose membership constantly grew and changed, played in the style of an American swing band — even though jazz was forbidden within the Third Reich — and was instantly the most popular ensemble in Theresienstadt.

Upon closer inspection, the coffeehouse did not offer what its name promised; it was anything but a warm, pleasant spot to enjoy swing music and a selection of delicious cakes and good coffee. First, you had to have an entrance pass, which you might be issued once or at most twice a year, and which designated the date and duration of your visit. "Authorization for a visit to the coffeehouse from noon to 2:00 P.M., ground floor," it might read. You could spend a maximum of two hours there over a cup of ersatz coffee. "But," as Thomas Mandl, who at age sixteen was a talented enough violinist to be a member of the coffeehouse orchestra, said, "the good thing was that this cup of ersatz coffee was sweetened with a teaspoon of real sugar. And as a musician in the coffeehouse I was permitted one cup of coffee per shift. Usually I saved up my coffee rations from three shifts and then on my fourth shift had them give me a cup with four teaspoons of sugar. And that, of course, was an incredible way to fight off hunger."

Visitors, however, had to make do with just one cup of ersatz coffee and one teaspoon of sugar — definitely not enough to combat the agony of hunger. At best they managed to forget it for a while, thanks to lovely music by Lehár, Waldteufel, Béla Kéler, Johann Strauss, or, when Busoni's brilliant pupil Carlo S. Taube was directing, challenging arrangements by Ravel and Saint-Saëns.

The coffeehouse was reserved for adults and was essentially off-limits to the girls of Room 28. But the music often found its way up to them, for it came from Q 418 on "Neue Gasse," as it was now called, a building that stood kitty-corner to the Girls' Home. From their windows the girls could watch people coming and going, although they could not observe what was happening inside.

But other unusual changes in the ghetto were not hidden from view. "The barricades are being taken down on Arische Strasse, the barbed wire fence is being removed from the main square," Otto Pollak noted on April 1. And two days later: "Daylight saving time begins tomorrow. Evening curfew has been extended until nine o'clock."

Sometime during the night of April 11, one of the writers for *Vedem* sneaked into the "brain of the Theresienstadt rumor mill." Using the pseudonym Syndikus, he reported his discoveries as follows: "The first thing I learned was that our Father [Karl Rahm] intends to issue an order, the gist of which is that all work squads will be forced to send their youngest personnel to do so-called maintenance work. To assure the rapid reconstruction of our town, it was our Father's wish that specialists of all kinds should participate to the fullest extent. For this purpose Father Bedřich had the gymnasium, which had been turned into a hospital, cleared to have it converted into a synagogue, theater, and future cinema. According to the latest news, which I obtained just a few hours before writing this, an open-air café is to be established on the roof of the gymnasium. He had the barbed wire fence on the square removed and the square transformed into a park, where he had a music pavilion erected to give the inhabitants of Terezín an opportunity for entertainment and refreshment during their lunch hour and in the evening after work."[3]

Sure enough, between noon and one o'clock on April 13, a bright and sunny day, the town orchestra began to play for the first time under the alternating direction of Carlo S. Taube, Peter Deutsch, and Karel Ančerl. It was scheduled to play on Market Square daily, if the weather was good, between eight and nine in the evening, an innovation that gave Syndikus cause for further speculation: "It is said that a restaurant is also going to be built beside the garden on the town square. The bill of fare has not yet been decided. Our town council has also ordered a fleet of hackney cabs for our international spa. The working people of Theresienstadt will also be provided for. There is to be a trolley line laid to make it easier for them to get to and from work."

Theresienstadt was well on its way to being turned into a sham show-piece, very much in the style of the village of facades that Prince Grigory Aleksandrovich Potemkin had quickly assembled to deceive Catherine the Great on her 1787 trip to inspect the south of Russia and observe the prosperity of the Crimea. Great swindles need just a little paint and a few false labels. The banal premise of this Nazi propaganda campaign in Theresienstadt — it's not the contents but the packaging that count — had as its sole purpose deceiving the world as to the true goals of the Nazi regime.

And so as of April 15, the daily decrees

were now published, nicely illustrated, as *Communications from the Jewish Self-Administration.* The camp high command was renamed the SS Service Office, and the commandant became the head of the SS Service Office. The Jewish elder was transformed into the mayor, and the ghetto court was now the community court. The guards posted outside the barracks were no longer ghetto guards but community guards. And there were no longer any deportation trains leaving Theresienstadt, but workers' deployment transports. After all, Theresienstadt was not a concentration camp or a transit camp or a ghetto, but a Jewish settlement area — the "town that the Führer gave the Jews."

There was even a contest — "Who Can Come Up with the Best Name?" — that was announced in the *Communications from the Jewish Self-Administration* for April 23. "The following streets and squares are to be renamed: Rampart III, the lane around the former sheep barn behind Haupt Strasse 2, the lane behind the building at Wall Strasse 8 . . . There are eight prizes in all: first prize, two tins of sardines in oil and a loaf of bread."

The opening of the community center at the Sokolovna, on 3 West Gasse, was celebrated on April 30, 1944, in the presence of the Council of Elders, the heads of all camp departments, and work brigades appointed by the town's administration. As the chronicler of the town's musical events, Viktor Ullmann, wrote, "To the delight of music lovers there was an ensemble composed of Messrs. Taussig, Kling, Süssmann, Mark, and Paul Kohn, joined by Karel Ančerl for the performance of a Brahms sextet, which deserves special praise for its precision, clarity, beauty of tone, and unity of style."[4]

"Beautification" was the new slogan that turned all of Theresienstadt upside down and marked the implementation of a critical new phase that began with the introduction of camp commandant Karl Rahm, who arrived on February 8, 1944, as the replacement for Anton Burger. Born in Austria and trained as an auto mechanic, Rahm had been a member of the Nazi Party since 1934, had worked closely with Eichmann in the Central Office for Jewish Emigration in Vienna and Prague, and was very well prepared for his assignment, which Adolf Eichmann summed up succinctly at his trial in Israel as one of turning the ghetto of Theresienstadt into "a billboard for the outside world. He [Himmler] evidently

Watched over by their guards, the prisoners prepare for the visit of the Red Cross Delegation. Drawing by Alfred Kantor

wanted to have some evidence on hand, so that when special delegations from abroad addressed him on the issue of the murder of Jews and so forth, he could say, 'That's not true; go have a look at Theresienstadt.' "[5]

While the ghetto was undergoing these strange changes, the prisoners in it were increasingly gripped by mistrust, fear, and sadness. Where had their friends gone? Where were they now? How were they doing — Pavla, Zdenka, Olile, Poppinka, Holubička, Milka, Helena, Irena, Eva Weiss, and Eva Landa? Those were the questions the girls in Room 28 kept asking over and over. No postcards had arrived, no signs of life that might have eased their fears. "Eva, why did you leave?" Lenka Lindt wrote on a slip of paper on March 26, 1944. She missed her friend Eva Landa very much.

Eva, Eva, why did you leave?
Why have you left an open wound behind?
Why did you leave
For a land so far away?

Lenka, are you angry with me?
What could I have done?
I had to go away
I could not defeat the Germans.

I'm not angry with you, Eva. I do under-
   stand.
I know that if you could
You would fulfill my wishes.

You know, don't you, Evička
That all will be well after the war
And we will never leave one another.
After the war we shall meet again
And renew our friendship.

Eva Landa had been deported to Ausch-witz along with her mother, father, and friend Harry Kraus on December 15, 1943. "The 'trip' was horrible," she would report decades later.

We rode in a cattle car for about three days. In each sealed car were fifty people and their baggage. There was one small barred window. We couldn't lie down; there wasn't enough room. Some people died on the way. At one point I began to wail terribly. It was a genuine case of hysterics. They asked me what was the matter. And I said that we'd been traveling for so long and so far and that we would never come back. I had a premonition.

On the third day we arrived in Auschwitz. Suddenly the door opened, and we saw a wide area garishly lit with spotlights and surrounded by barbed wire. There were strange creatures running up and down along the platform. They were wearing pajamas and little caps on their shaved heads; they shouted something and took our baggage away. They looked as though they were crazy. Then we were divided up: men on one side, women and children on the other. We were led to a building called the "sauna." That was a new word for me back then and I didn't understand what it meant. There they took all our remaining things away, our clothes and shoes. Then we had to stand under a shower that ran cold and then very hot, for about fifteen minutes. SS men walked back and forth the whole time — even though we were all completely naked! When it was over we were given old tattered clothes and wooden slippers. Only the soles were wooden, the rest was just old rags. Each of us got two slippers that didn't even match. Then we had to line up for "tattooing." We were ordered to hold out our left arm to be tattooed. My number was 71266, my mother's was 71267.

That was how we spent the first night. The next morning we were led to the camp. There we met people from the transport that had left Theresienstadt in September. They told us how lucky we were that everyone had been taken to the sauna, that no selection had been made, and that no one had been sent directly to the gas chamber. We — the entire December transport — were assigned to the so-called Family Camp B II b, where men, women, and children could remain together, although in separate barracks. In the opinion of the experienced prisoners, we were lucky in that as well, since in all the other camps, except the one for Gypsies, the separation of the men from the women, of the elderly and children from those capable of work, took place immediately on the ramp.

The Family Camp at Auschwitz-Birkenau had been set up by the prisoners of the September transport. As a few historians have noted (something that Eva Landa could not have known at the time), Himmler's goal here was the same as with his model ghetto of Theresienstadt. It was intended as a tool of cunning Nazi propaganda in case it should become necessary to deceive foreign visitors about what was really going on in Auschwitz. That was why families in Camp B II b remained together. And that was why Fredy Hirsch was allowed by the SS to organize the children's block.

The September transport had been stamped with the secret directive "SB six months," which meant "*Sonderbehandlung* [special treatment] after six months of quarantine." SB was the Nazi euphemism for "death by gas."

"It was December 1943 and my life in

Auschwitz-Birkenau began," Eva Landa continues.

December twenty-fifth was my thirteenth birthday. I was sick and terribly unhappy because I had been separated from my friends in Theresienstadt. I remembered my days in the ghetto as a happy time in my life. I couldn't shake the feeling that we would never go home again.

It turned very cold, and we were poorly dressed. We were hungry. In the morning we were given a dark green liquid that was called "coffee," in the evening turnip soup and a piece of bad bread. The provisions we had brought with us were left on the train. We had to stand for hours of roll call. They would count us over and over again. It was torture.

The quarantine period passed, and we had to start working. My father had to pave a road, and my mother wove cloth for the German military industry. I was taken to the children's block run by Fredy Hirsch, where a life similar to the one we had in Theresienstadt was organized for us. We played sports, theater, and wrote poems. And we sang: "Alouette," "The Ode to Joy," Handel's "Hallelujah Chorus," and many more. I remember that one day we were singing a song in Latin and an SS man asked Fredy Hirsch what it was we were singing. And he replied, "God, give us bread and peace." To which the SS man said, "You've already got it." And Fredy replied, "That's why they're singing about it."

The food in our block was better than in the others. Fredy Hirsch had seen to it that we got the same so-called children's soup that they had in the Gypsy camp. It was the same as the adult soup but with barley groats added, plus white bread. We thanked him with a little poem before meals: "In our *taba'at* group [Hebrew for 'ring'] we all are very hungry. / There's nothing to laugh about, because we have to wash our dishes, otherwise Fredy will shout at us. / And now we can sit down and — eat!"

A vague hope sprang up — maybe we would somehow succeed in leaving Auschwitz alive, although we knew what was going on around us. We even wrote skits about it. I remember there was a twelve-year-old named Štepan, a cousin of Handa Pollak's. We had been in the same class in Prague. He was small and very talented. He and his friends in the Auschwitz-Birkenau children's block enacted this scene for us: After the war Štepan is walking along in Prague, and someone asks him what time it is. He looks at his arm and answers with the number tattooed there. And the passersby say, "This fellow is crazy!" and grab him and take him to the madhouse. And he replies, "I knew I'd end up in Heydebreck." Heydebreck — that was a special term for us children. We didn't know any town by that name. We thought it was a Nazi invention. For us going to Heydebreck meant being sent to the gas chambers.[6]

March 6, 1944, was my boyfriend Harry's thirteenth birthday. I made a little heart out of the clay of Auschwitz for him and inscribed it: "To Harry on his birthday from Eva, March 6, 1944." The next day — it was T. G. Masaryk's birthday — there was a lockdown, and no one was allowed to leave our block. Those from the September transport had to move to a neighboring camp. Someone called over the fence, *"Fredy je otráveny,"* which in Czech means both to be in a bad mood and to be poisoned. I can still recall my father trying to comfort me with the first version. But we soon learned the terrible truth.

Fredy Hirsch had taken his life. When he saw that resistance was pointless, he swallowed poison. The next day, March 8, 1944, the entire September transport, except for those with infectious illnesses, were gassed, including four girls from our room — Pavla Seiner, Olilie Löwy, Zdenka Löwy, and Ruth Popper. My father died on April 13. Only our December transport was still left in the Family Camp. People talked quite openly about how we were to be gassed six months after our arrival.

Eva Weiss, the girls' counselor, had also arrived in Auschwitz-Birkenau with Transport Dr on December 15. Her orders had come as a shock to her — she was the only one in her family to be transported. And so she had to set out by herself, "on the most mysterious of all journeys," as she says when she begins to describe her experiences. "It was a trauma." To this day Eva has tears in her eyes when she remembers the day she had to say goodbye.

A great deal has been said and written about that trip in cattle cars, and it's all true. It was horrible. Locked up for three days without food, without water, barely enough air to breathe. I'll never forget the moment of our arrival, it was deepest winter, the ground covered with snow. It was like a sudden storm sweeping over all our senses: blinding spotlights aimed directly at our eyes, which had grown used to darkness after three days in the cattle cars; shouts and — this was the worst part — the barking of savage, fierce dogs. We could barely see and couldn't understand what was happening. All I wanted was — water! Despite all the threats I clung to my little backpack, which contained my most cherished things — above all my photo album. In the forced march to one of the buildings I managed to scoop up a little snow and put it in my mouth — what a wonderful relief that was.

They crammed us into an empty block, where a few girls were sitting behind a table. They were wearing striped uniforms, and their heads were shaved. We didn't know where we were. Then some of the girls — they spoke mainly Polish and Slovak — came over to us and demanded our valuables. They said that we wouldn't be needing them anymore.

It was like a dream, and I gave them my watch. I don't know when or how, but my precious backpack vanished at some point. The girls at the table registered us one after the other and tattooed a number on our arms. Mine was 73673. I told myself that this number wasn't the worst possible number.

Then we were led to the so-called sauna; we had to undress and leave our clothes behind. We were searched in every possible spot for any valuables, and then we had to stand under the shower, which poured out ice-cold water. Since I didn't have my mother with me and was feeling feverish, I joined up with my friend Eva Schlachet, whose mother was with her. I was sick, and they were both very kind to me. Time passed, and I can see myself in a blue coat and with shoes that felt very strange, walking along a path between barbed wire fences. Because I had a fever, I have only a vague recollection of it all. Then I ended up on a bunk beside Zuzanna Ržičková — who is now a famous musician in Prague. She and her mother looked after me. I must have contracted dysentery from that snow I ate. I fainted at the first roll call.

We were housed in separate blocks — men, women, and children. Our camp was called B II b in Birkenau. I don't remember much, except that I felt terribly abandoned without my mother. Slowly I recovered and began to take part in the "activities."

A few days later Fredy Hirsch came and took me with him to Block 31 — the so-called children's block. I was greeted very warmly. I knew most of the counselors from Theresienstadt, and many of the children as well, some of whom were from Room 28. I remember being so happy to see Poppinka [Ruth Popper] and Pavla Seiner and Olilie again. They had been in the camp since September, and some, like Eva Landa, had arrived on my transport. I remember Eva very well, because she was an anchor in my group, very pretty and full of energy. I know there were other girls as well, but I don't recall their names.

I was a substitute mother to many of the orphans, a substitute mother under extreme conditions. It was my job to play with them and give them lessons — without books or any other materials. The important thing was to make them forget where they were and what was happening around them. We played word games, sang, danced, even memorized parts for plays and skits, which the children then put on. One of these was *Snow White and the Seven Dwarfs* and another was *Robinson Crusoe.* There were lots of optimistic songs, always with a happy end. Sometimes the SS men would come by and watch us; some of them, or so it seemed to me, turned sentimental. Maybe they were thinking of their own children.

All the older children, and, I think, many of the younger ones, understood only too well what was happening around us. There was no way not to see the chimneys with flames shooting out at the top. The smoke permeated the air. "No one leaves here except up through the chimney" — how often we heard that statement!

The neighboring camps were used as transit camps. We could see across the fence. One day we discovered a friend from the Zionist movement. It was Dov Revesz, a Hungarian. He was too exhausted to call back to us. The next day the camp was empty.

We heard Russian prisoners nearby for a few days, singing their beautiful, melancholy songs. At times we even chimed in. Sometimes we sang Czech and Hebrew songs. But soon the Russian soldiers were no longer there.

We celebrated Jewish holidays and even solemnly observed the Sabbath. When someone had a birthday, we threw a little party. We didn't have much to eat, but we saved up something from our tiny rations — a little slice of our bread, which seemed as though it had been made from sawdust, a bit of margarine, and, when we had it, a smidgen of turnip marmalade. Those were the ingredients for our "birthday cake." I recall that I once decorated a couple of them to look like dominos.

Directly across from our block was the hospital where Dr. Mengele conducted his experiments with twins. And there were twins among us as well whom he was interested in. When Mengele showed up, the cry passed from barracks to barracks like a jungle telegram, "Twins to thirty-two," and then all the twins had to report to him. I remember the Salus twins from Brno, who both had one blue eye and one brown eye. That shout of "Twins to thirty-two!" was almost something of a joke. We had no idea about his awful experiments. And I suppose we simply didn't want to believe the rumors about them.

In February there were rumors that the entire September transport would be sent to a labor camp — to "Heydebreck," as the SS put it. The rumor came from the Auschwitz underground movement, whose members were mainly Communists. Although it all looked quite hopeless, Fredy Hirsch and some of his counselors — I remember one of them, Hugo Lengsfeld — discussed plans for an uprising. I seem to recall that someone had smuggled a hand grenade and some matches into the camp. We were told what to do if worse came to worst.

Early in March, the SS gave each of us a postcard. We were told that we could write to our relatives on the outside. We were allowed only thirty words, and we had to date them about one or two weeks ahead. I think the date was March 26. Of course we all tried to guess what this was about. It was quite unusual. We tried to use the thirty words to say where we were and what was happening to us. We had to write our messages in code and hope that they would be understood. For example, we used the name of someone who was dead and wrote that we had met him. Or we wrote that we had met *Mavet* — which is Hebrew for "death." All the cards arrived. But by the time they did, most of the people who had written them were already dead.

March 7, 1944, will always remain in my memory. The day began with a lockdown, a sure sign that something was about to happen. All the people from the September transport, and also some children of my group, had to move to the neighboring camp. There was a lot of shouting. I can still recall that I was in Fredy's room, but I no longer recall what we spoke about. I didn't know that all of them were to be gassed. He knew; that's for certain. But he didn't say a word.

Our rebellion never took place. And Fredy, our leader and inspiration, took poison, fell into a coma, and was carried out. The camp was very quiet afterward — as though after a defeat.

The news that spread through the camp the next day was horrifying: the entire September transport had gone to the gas chambers. They died with many of them singing the Czech national anthem or "Hatikvah" or the "Internationale." We knew the same fate awaited us at the end of June, six months after our arrival.

We had lost a good many counselors, but we kept up our work, mourning for all those we missed. Fredy Hirsch's position was taken over by Seppl Lichtenstein, who was also connected with the underground. We had to get used to the idea that we didn't have long to live. We made jokes about it, and even laughed — because that was the only way we could bear it.

We went on singing and playing just as before. We had a little space outside where we could do sports, jump around, and dance. Off to one side we could see the chimneys, the embers of their flames against the sky, and sometimes terrible screams would reach us — at one point children were simply tossed into the fire. On the other side we could see barbed wire and the railroad tracks beyond, where trains arrived day and night. By then it was primarily Jews from Hungary. Most of them went directly into the gas chambers.

Fredy Hirsch. There is no way today to find out for certain whether Fredy Hirsch committed suicide or if, in order to prevent an uprising, camp doctors intentionally gave him an overdose of the sedatives that he had asked for. There are several contradictory versions. One thing, however, is certain: Fredy Hirsch faced a hopeless situation. He was aware that no uprising could save the lives of the children under his care.

■ ■ ■ ■

It was around noon on May 11, 1944, when news of more transports to the East exploded like a bomb in Theresienstadt. On the streets, in the barracks and Homes, the dreaded word haunted every conversation: "transport." It was said to be for seventy-five hundred people. Who would be included this time? And the guessing began all over again as to who would receive that ominous slip of paper. Some said it would be mainly old people and TB patients, while others said that it would affect men of working age.

Only a few could lull themselves into a sense of relative security: the so-called *Mischlinge* (children of mixed marriages), those who had been awarded important medals during the war, their families, and those who had been designated as "prominent."[7] Rumor had it that the municipal orchestra, the community guards, and the fire department were also protected — they were still needed. But all the others?

The transport orders had already been prepared. "At 7 A.M. on May 13th," Otto Pollak wrote, "Joška arrives with the bad news that Hermann, Trude, and Lea are on the transport. Helga arrives with Lea at the office unannounced. At the sight of that beaming, smiling childish face and at the thought of such an innocent creature departing for who knows what, I start to cry. I go out on the veranda. Helga, with tears rolling down her cheeks, follows and says in real pain: 'I feel as if my little sister will be leaving.' "

Seventy-five hundred people got ready for transport. In Room 28 it was Erika Stránská, Alice Sittig, Ruth Schächter (Zajíček), Miriam Rosenzweig, and Hanka Wertheimer who packed their suitcases and bags. "My mother told me that we had to leave. She was very sick at the time," Hanka recalls. "She had always hoped that Jakob Edelstein, the chief Jewish elder, would help keep her off the transports. She knew him personally, from Brno, through her membership in the Zionist organization Blue-White. But he had long since left the ghetto. On May 15 we all boarded Transport Dz — my mother, my grandmother, my great-aunt, and me. My friend Miriam from Room 28 was on it, too."

The many goodbyes began. "You know, after the war: Olbramovice 1," Handa said while she hugged her friend. And Hanka replied as she had so many times: "After the war I'll wait for you under the Old Bell Tower on the Old City Ring." Nothing could shake her faith: the war would soon be over, they would all see each other again in Prague, and one day they would emigrate to Eretz Yisrael. Others were less confident. It was hardest to say goodbye to Zajíček, who was being deported along with her brother Alexander.

Tears. Hugs. Words of comfort — imparting brave or forlorn serenity in the face of an inescapable fate. And some final gift for a comrade — a slice of bread, a piece of gingerbread from a recent package, a warm sweater. Those "departing" needed to know that they were all still bound together.

It was almost impossible to sleep. Everyone was depressed, even Marianne Deutsch, although she had an unusual reason. She felt almost a little envious that she "wasn't allowed to go," that she could not get away from Theresienstadt, which she detested, from the involuntary community of Room 28, where she did not feel at all at home. Wherever they were going, it couldn't be worse than here, she thought. "I was naïve, a child," she would say later. "I didn't know what those transports to the East really meant."

Handa, by contrast, was filled with deep

forebodings, as a poem in her notebook
reveals:

I walk down the stairs
Alone, lost in my thoughts
Outside peace and quiet reign
The quiet of the night
That I so love

The moon rises
Shining through the fog
Stands there, alone
Like an eye that's weeping

The cross on the church
Shimmers silver
Here and there a ray of light
Pierces a window

I keep on walking
Down the stairs
The moon emerges from the fog
Adorned with a wreath of tears
Every puddle sparkles like a star
I keep on walking
Lost in my thoughts

I watch as the wind
Brushes through the trees
As the town sleeps

As everything sleeps
I keep on walking
Lost in my thoughts.

The light behind the windows
Has gone out
My eye is lost in the fog
Of the beauty that surrounds me
My thoughts
Twist and turn inside my head
And my head burns
Like white-hot iron

> Handa Pollak, from her notebook,
> *Všechno,* 1944

The suitcases and the backpacks were packed. On May 14, Otto Pollak noted: "Said our early morning goodbyes to Hermann, See Strasse 16, and to Trude and Lea. They are all calm and resigned. At ten o'clock last night Hermann and I agreed upon a code for our letters."

"We watched people moving down the street, dragging their bags and suitcases, their transport numbers hung around their necks, and we were terribly afraid," Judith Schwarzbart recalls. "No one knew where they were going. No one knew what the Germans had in mind. No one knew if we would ever see one another again. And the people passing below us there, they were afraid, too."

Among them were Mimi Sander and her mother, Frau Porges. "Unforgettable sight," Otto Pollak wrote in his diary that same day. "Hugo in the little wagon. Mother Porges bracing herself at the rear. Mimi, composed and holding her head up high, linking arms with her stooping mother. Gustav is pulling the wagon. Hugo's steering shaft breaks. Let's hope it's not a bad omen."

Miriam and Hanka also made their way to the Hamburg Barracks. Everything was in an uproar. In one part of the building people were assembling to be transported out; in another part were new arrivals from other transports. Suddenly amid the throng Hanka spotted Eva Ginz, a friend and former classmate from the Jewish School in Prague and the sister of Petr Ginz. "I can still see her there before me," Hanka recalls. "I'm standing under the porch and we wave to each other from a distance. I'm leaving Theresienstadt and Eva is just arriving." It was a reunion and a goodbye all in one. Neither knew what lay before her.

May 15. "Hermann, Trude, and Lea left in a cattle car at two o'clock." The total number was twenty-five hundred people; this was the first group. The lists for the second were already prepared. Another mass of people moved toward the assembly point in the Hamburg Barracks, where both L 2 and the train tracks ran along the rear facade. Countless trains, loaded with thousands of human beings, had been rolling in the direction of Auschwitz. These transport hubs for transports were referred to as "sluices."

In reality, the entire ghetto had become a sluice. "An endless stream of hundreds of thousands of lives poured in," Jindřich Flusser has written, "slowing down for a moment as the water level rose, seemingly calm, until it reached the brink of the sluice. This space had the capacity for up to 35,000 naked human lives. They were herded here from Prague and Vitkovice, from Hamburg and Vienna. The water level kept rising — until the sluice was emptied. Men and women and children were washed by the thousands, even tens of thousands, out of this dusty basin and borne eastward on a river of death."[8]

Flaška, Helga, and many of the other girls had volunteered to lend a hand. Wearing white headscarves and red armbands, they sneaked into the Hamburg Barracks to do the one thing within their power: to give comfort to their families and friends.

The transport list for the third group was posted. Judith's brother Gideon was on the list. "It all went very quickly. Suddenly he was assigned to his group. We didn't even see each other. We couldn't say goodbye to him."

At the last moment, camp commandant Karl Rahm unexpectedly intervened in the transport procedures and crossed out the names of a few young people on the list. Why? The answer was soon apparent: They were needed as walk-ons for the great hoax. But by now the elderly and the frail had no chance.

"Poor things," fourteen-year-old Šáry Weinstein wrote in her diary. "They will die soon enough in any case, and they could do that here just as well. This is supposed to be a model ghetto after all, so why do they send people away, especially old people? Maybe because it wouldn't seem so nice if others saw them begging for a bowl of disgusting soup? The town is overcrowded, and that doesn't leave a good impression either."[9]

"In this one week, 7,500 Jews have left the ghetto and are being taken somewhere into an unknown future, but we don't know where that is," Gonda Redlich jotted in his diary. "They're leaving in order to make more room. And now a 'commission' will be visiting the city and will render its verdict: Everything is fine. The town is so lovely, with a whole lot of children's homes, coffeehouses, wonderful halls and green gardens; the Jews live in spacious rooms."[10]

Transport Dz (May 15), Transport Ea (May 16), and Transport Eb (May 18) bore their cargo of 7,503 people toward the East. The town's population sank to about 28,000 — less than half of what it had been at its highest point in September 1942. There was a little more air in the ghetto, but no one was breathing a sigh of relief. "After the commotion of the last few days, calmness has returned," Otto Pollak noted on May 19, "a mournful calmness and loneliness."

The paralyzing calm that reigned in Theresienstadt after the May transports gave way to a phase of hectic activity. Anyone who could change to a better bunk or better quarters did so. Some of the prominent people were assigned to a room of their own, so they could live together with their families. Improvements were made in the living arrangements of the Danes, and a couple of rooms — all on the ground floor of buildings visible from Haupt Strasse — were nicely furnished, with pictures on the walls, flowerpots on the windowsills, and pretty curtains at the windows.

But in the larger rooms of the barracks, in the attics and rear courtyards, and on the third floor of the Girls' Home, in Room 28, everything remained just as it was.

The sole objects of the beautification campaign were public buildings and those quarters that were sure to strike the eye of the upcoming visitors — a delegation from the International Red Cross, which everyone had been talking about for months[11] — or that could be strategically called to their attention. Along with the quarters of a few prominent people and the Danes, these buildings included the Bank of the Jewish Self-Administration, the town hall, the post office, the children's nursery, the coffeehouse, and the Sokolovna. And of course the "mayor's office" in the Magdeburg Barracks — the headquarters of the Jewish Self-Administration and the Council of Elders.

As part of this short-lived deceptive maneuver, these buildings were scrubbed until they shone, as were a few streets, courtyards, and pathways. "Everyone was assigned to the cleanup," recalls the pianist Alice Herz-Sommer, who herself was ordered to join a street-cleaning brigade. "We mopped the streets, we cleaned the coffeehouse, and there was one shop that had to be cleaned

The Bank of the Jewish Self-Administration was founded on orders from the SS and opened on May 12, 1943. It was the crowning achievement of the hoax and played the key role in the entire fraud. Even bank notes were printed — ghetto kronas.

as well, and its displays tidied up. The bank and the hospitals, too. It all had to be clean as a whistle. Picture this little town with its usual population of five thousand — it was full of people wherever you went; it was black with people! It was such a little place that you could hardly move. There was no possible way to clean it up properly."

Theresienstadt, "the face of an involuntary community," as H. G. Adler has called it,[12] was a perfect deception, built on smoke and mirrors. Else Krása wrote a poem about it with a telling title: "As If." She dedicated the poem to Leo Strauss, son of the "operetta king" Oscar Strauss and one of the chief writers for the Theresienstadt cabaret:

> I know a little town
> A town that has some spiff
> I'll not betray its name
> So let's call it "As If."

Leo Strauss set this little verse to brilliant music. In Theresienstadt these words came to form a kind of running joke, but also a philosophy of life and survival, and a motto. And so when Helga's fourteenth birthday came around on May 28, 1944, it was celebrated in accordance with this motto — much to the surprise of the birthday girl, who only a few weeks earlier had said to her father, "If there are transports and my friends have to leave, my birthday will be a very sad one, because we have lived like sisters in our Home."

Now it was all turning out very differently. Helga was invited to a "festive seven-course banquet in the Grand-Hôtel Hecht, Bahnhof Strasse 31." One course after another was served in the "as if" mode: "Bean soup with noodles, spring vegetables, snow-peas and carrots with roasted potatoes on onions, sardine snacks on toast, open-face sandwiches with sausage and bacon, pineapple pudding, mocha à la ghetto with pastries, ending with a selection of desserts." Only a wisp of these delicacies actually appeared on the table, but where quality and quantity were not what they should have been, imagination came to the rescue — daily life in the camp offered lots of opportunities for that.[13]

"The child wasn't expecting such a lovely party," Otto Pollak wrote that same evening in his diary. "At five o'clock we distributed presents. The festive dinner, then, was at half past five. All those courses made us forget our Theresienstadt misery. During the meal Hecht [house eldest in the Home for Invalids L 231] gave a stirring speech."

Helga returned to Room 28 laden with gifts. By Theresienstadt standards, what she held in her hands was a small fortune. We know this from Otto Pollak's list of her presents: "From Maria, a blouse, a winter and a

Alles Liebe und Schöne
zu Deinem 14. Geburtstag.
Dein Onkel
Fritz.

Theresienstadt, 28.V.44.

Birthday card for Helga's fourteenth birthday

summer dress, and a cake; from Hecht, a necklace and three chocolate bonbons, Odol mouthwash and Nivea cream; from Schmitz, two large notebooks and a wooden box; from Hugo, a travel manicure set; from Leuchter, the engineer, a bouquet of lilacs with two tulips; from Papa, a belt, a handbook, a bar of Palmolive soap, a chrome and nickel bracelet with a watch, and a Pelikan fountain pen with a fourteen-carat-gold nib."

Unfortunately, we have no direct account from Helga about how she felt that evening. In 1956, during the Suez Crisis, when Helga was moving from Addis Ababa to London, fire broke out in the ship's cargo

Menu for Helga's fourteenth birthday: "A banquet served in the spirit of 'As If!' "

room, and the container carrying several of her most precious possessions, including the third volume of her diary and her poetry album, was destroyed.

It seems quite likely that once the birthday celebration had passed, Helga quickly reawakened to the reality of Theresienstadt, just as she did after a concert given on April 5, 1944, as can be seen in this last entry in the second volume of her diary:

Wednesday, April 5, 1944
Today I attended a Beethoven concert. They played a violin sonata. Taussig played the violin and Professor Kaff was

426

at the piano.[14] Then came a piano sonata that Kaff played by heart. He lived the music. He played with his eyes closed. For me it was like a fairy tale, with fairies dancing and singing on a meadow at the edge of the woods. There were small animals, too. Then came a loud rumble, and someone said that a dragon was coming down the road in search of prey from the Kingdom of the Forest. They ran off in all directions, looking for a place to hide. The fairies fled into their subterranean kingdom, the animals dashed into their subterranean homes and up into the trees, etc. And now the dragon arrived in the meadow. And what does he see, right under his nose? A little fawn who couldn't get away in time because it had slipped and fallen and wasn't able to get up again. The dragon grabs the fawn and takes his prey back to his castle.

The forest dwellers return to the meadow and sing and dance. But then the fawn's mother appears, weeping. She tells them that she couldn't come sooner to join the others because she was not feeling well, and had sent her fawn on ahead with the idea that she would follow as soon as she was feeling better. Now that she is here — she cannot find her child. They all join in the search, but don't find the fawn, and they realize that the dragon has it.

So they decide to break into the castle very early the next morning while the dragon is still asleep and to slay him, thereby freeing the fawn and liberating their land from this evil creature. They all return to their homes and settle in for the night. Now only the owl hoots and the moths flap the air with their wings and fly, fly — black velvet with red stripes, gorgeous and glorious.

Dawn breaks, and the sun rises. Sunbeams shine through the branches onto the meadow, and a pleasant, gentle breeze rustles through the leaves. Everyone slowly wakes up. The small animals stumble to the well for a drink, and then the large animals go and slurp up the remaining water. Once they have all had their fill, they set out to free the fawn.

There are between ten and twenty small animals — rabbits, hamsters, and others of that sort — accompanied by the larger ones. Eagles and falcons fly above them. They belt out their song of war. They arrive at the castle and enter the courtyard. In single file the animals, both large and small, climb the stairs cautiously and quietly, looking for the dragon's room.

There they hide behind curtains and furniture. An eagle, who has been appointed by the fairies, gives the sign. All the animals come out of their hiding places and run to the bed where the dragon lies sleeping. They pounce on him — all the foxes, the eagles, the falcons, the weasels, and many more. The dragon wakes up, but he is dead on the spot. They free the fawn and return home singing a happy song.

In the nearby village the bells ring the noon hour, which can be heard on the meadow and in the forest. All the animals are in their homes or basking in the sun. The war has been won. You can see the sunlight falling through the branches, just as it did that morning, and a gentle wind is blowing from the south. The doe is lying peacefully beside her fawn. She licks it, and showers it with maternal love. And the fawn tells his mother all about what happened with the dragon, until it falls asleep.

And now the fawn is sleeping. Its mother gently licks its face. All is peaceful. The music comes to an end. The people leave their seats.

I don't want to leave. Why am I in Theresienstadt? Here? Everything was so beautiful — and now this dark, gray Theresienstadt. I would like to slip inside the piano, where there is music. And here on the outside is the prison.

The main square in the center of Theresienstadt shimmered in lush green, interspersed with flower beds and snapdragons that Judith's father, Julius Schwarzbart, had planted on orders from the SS. The newly sanded paths were lined with freshly painted benches. The bright yellow of the music pavilion stood out against other facades now repainted in soft pastels.

"The park area in Market Square, previously surrounded by barbed wire, is gradually being made available to Jews," Otto Pollak noted on June 1. "The residents are sitting down gingerly on the new wooden benches set on concrete supports — about seventy-three of them in all, which will provide a spot for a siesta for three hundred sixty people."

Every day around noon, and again toward evening, the town orchestra gathered in front of the pavilion for a "promenade concert," under the direction of either Carlo S. Taube or Peter Deutsch, the former conductor of the Copenhagen Radio Orchestra. The girls watched in amazement from their window. What did this strange hubbub mean? All the activity around the main square? Even signposts had been put up: TO THE BANK, TO THE POST OFFICE, TO THE COFFEEHOUSE, TO THE BATHS. Near the construction office was an old school, which until now had been used as a hospital; the hospital was cleared out, the rooms were given a fresh coat of paint, and school benches were installed. The next morning there was a sign in gold letters above the main entrance: SCHOOL FOR BOYS AND GIRLS. "It looked very nice, like a real school, except there were no students or teachers," Helga Weiss noted. "But that little problem was resolved with a piece of paper posted on the school door, which read simply VACATION.[15]

The "shops" were given new signs and their display windows were decorated; the goods on display were expanded and extolled on advertising boards. No one in the ghetto was taken in by this sham. Everyone knew what was going on with these "retail stores," as they called the shops. A witticism began with the question: "Where do you find the finest luxury shops in the world?" The answer: "In Theresienstadt. Because if you're lucky, you can buy a shirt there with your own monogram already on it."

The items for sale were nothing more than

leftovers from what the SS had confiscated and plundered from the prisoners on their arrival. It was much the same with the goods offered in the grocery store, about which people also poked fun. "Try to buy sugar, and there won't be any sugar; try to buy flour, and there won't be any flour. Try to buy a map of Germany, and there won't be any Germany."

Helga had a new line of her own to add to this joke: "Try to buy ketchup and there won't be any ketchup." One day she had seen a bottle of ketchup on the shelf and could hardly wait for her turn to buy something. "But when I got there, there was nothing left in the shop but paprika and mustard. I gave the mustard to my father. I kept the paprika for myself and sprinkled it on my bread. I remember that I was very unhappy about it."

And now, as if to mock the inmates, there were shiny, deceptive new signs on shops all around the main square: PERFUMERY, DRUGSTORE, GROCERY, SHOES, CLOTHING, LADIES' UNDERWEAR. And the display windows suddenly contained a startling array of goods: fresh meats, sausages, fruit, and vegetables.

"It's absurd, but it looks as if Theresienstadt has been transformed into a spa,"

Helga Weiss wrote in her diary. "I don't know why, but it reminds me of the fairy tale *Table, Set Yourself.* That's what it seems like. The orders go out each evening, and the next morning everyone looks around in amazement and asks where this or that has come from all of a sudden."[16]

"We had to vacate in the middle of the night," recalls Eva Herrmann, who lived in Home L 414, where a spruced-up ground floor housed the post office. "We didn't know why. They put us somewhere else, and we were told that everything was being renovated. And when we came back a few days later, there was nothing but bright new furniture — tables, benches, shelves. The bunks were made of new wood, and we had white sheets and blankets — it all looked very pretty. And the hallways were all freshly painted and decorated as well. Suddenly there were whole rows of cabinets, each a different color, each hung with a curtain featuring a different animal emblem — just like in kindergarten, so that you know which chest belongs to which child. And behind the door was shelving for our food, and suddenly there was lots of food — more bread than usual, chocolate, and a jar of Ovaltine! We didn't even know what that was."[17]

There was even an art exhibition on the

second floor of the Magdeburg Barracks. The paintings all had Theresienstadt motifs. "My favorites were those done by Spier, *A Telegraph Worker, View of Litoměřice,*" Otto Pollak wrote on June 9. "And by Karas, Haas, *The Old Commandant's Office.* Helga's *Girls' Home.*"

At half past eight on the evening of June 13, Otto Pollak found himself for the first time on the roof of the Kavalier Barracks, which had been renamed Eger Platz. "It's a splendid evening. I can see the sluice mill, the highway, mountains all around. A village to the right of Litoměřice, near the top of the mountain. A glider is circling in the air. Birds are flying to their nests. A view of freedom! I am filled with a longing to embrace nature."

During this same period, Helga felt drawn again and again to visit one of the ramparts with her new friend Ruth Gutmann, whose father was employed in a workshop there. At the edge of the ghetto they found a path that previously had been barricaded, "but somehow we were suddenly allowed on it. All by ourselves we walked out onto a meadow where flowers were blooming. I still dream of that place."

Summer weather, cheerful music, and curiosity about all these changes lured many people out of their quarters. On June 11, Otto Pollak went to see the new children's pavilion, "with a nursery for the smallest ones, designed by the architect Kaufmann. An excellent piece of work in its structure, utility, and proportions. All made of glass and wood. The square transoms have splendid sketches of animals done by Spier, the Dutch artist. A brand-new merry-go-round for the playground, swings, and monkey bars."

The girls took in the changes in the ghetto with amazement. What could it all mean? Was the war almost over? No one had an explanation. "Maybe they're worried about the commission?" Helga Weiss guessed. "Maybe we don't know just how favorable the situation really is."

Meanwhile, the SS set about deciding which of the many cultural events in Theresienstadt might be offered to the commission from the International Red Cross. The choice wasn't easy, since, as Thomas Mandl put it, "offerings that were few and far between in civilian life were available in incredible abundance: lectures, from the most arcane subjects to popular themes; recitations of the Greek classics in the original; theater, opera, operetta, chamber and solo music; and cabaret acts of every conceivable kind."[18]

The SS had no problem scheduling excellent presentations for the day the foreigners would pay their visit, and they did not have to worry about a lack of posters around town to highlight the flourishing cultural life. One poster announced an extraordinary soiree for June 22, 1944: an evening of lieder sung by Karel Berman, with Rafael Schächter at the piano. The program offered songs by Hugo Wolf, Beethoven's "To a Distant Beloved," Pavel Haas's *Four Songs on Chinese Poetry,* and Dvořák's *Gypsy Melodies.*

But what would the visitors see and hear on June 23? A cabaret revue with the stars of the Theresienstadt Cabaret: Karel Švenk, Leo Strauss, Kurt Gerron, Josef Lustig, and the duo of Hans Hofer and Anny Frey? A play by Molière (*George Dandin*), Gogol (*Marriage*), Chekhov (*The Proposal*), Karel Čapek (*The Fateful Game of Love*), or Molnár (*The Play at the Castle*)? An opera — *Carmen, Tosca, The Magic Flute, The Marriage of Figaro, The Bartered Bride*? An operetta — *Ghetto Girl, Die Fledermaus*? Or a piano concert with a virtuoso such as Juliette Arányi, Alice Herz-Sommer, Edith Steiner-Kraus, Renée Gärtner-Geiringer,

Gideon Klein, or Bernard Kaff? A string quartet with Egon Ledeč, Fredy Mark, Karel Fröhlich, and Romouald Süssmann or Paul Kling? Karel Ančerl's string orchestra? Or a choral work, with Karl Fischer directing Mendelssohn's *Elijah,* Haydn's *Creation,* or Rafael Schächter's choir and its radiant performance of Verdi's *Requiem?*

Even with all these options, the opera *Brundibár* was on the short list. As Rudolf Freudenfeld recalls in his memoir, it would first be presented to the camp's high command:

We had to transfer the opera from our little hall in the barracks to the large hall in Sokolovna. At that point the building lay outside the ghetto barricades. The hall had a full working stage, an orchestra pit, changing rooms — everything that we needed.

The day of our performance approached. The auditorium itself was completely empty this time around, and the choir and orchestra were ready. Then the whole SS gang entered at the balcony level. They remained standing, did not remove their caps, and the camp commandant gave his usual order: Get cracking!

After a few scenes I turned around. They were all sitting now, not a man budged, and the caps had been set aside. When the opera was over, they made no move to leave. Even these unfeeling cynics had been touched for a moment by this sweet music. Maybe these criminals even had children at home — who knows?

The order came that same evening: *Brundibár* had to be performed. But, the troupe was told, the stage was too dark, not cheerful enough for the children. By morning an entire city would have to be visible behind the wooden fence. All the necessary materials — canvas and paints and so forth — were to be distributed at once.

We worked all night. Zelenka supervised a crew of assistants, and by morning the backdrop was finished and in place. A whole section of a town, including a school — the future!

The high command also ordered that the visitors were to see the finale.[19]

By early June 1944, Hanka Wertheimer, her mother, and her friend Miriam Rosenzweig had been in Auschwitz for three weeks. After traveling for three days, they had arrived in the middle of the night.

Suddenly we heard shouts — there was so much shouting there! Everybody out! Everybody out! Leave your baggage! We'll send it after you. Quick, quick, quick! We saw barbed wire, and there were big, bright spotlights shining on it — it's a scene I will never forget. The SS men kept shouting: Out! Fast, faster! Move, move! Because there were no steps, you had to jump down from the cattle car — even my old grandmother. And the voices kept shouting: Leave your baggage behind in the car! It was horrible. It was a shock. It all happened so quickly. The spotlights, the dogs, and the SS men with their clubs. And such fear! This was a scene that, I believe, even the best movie director could never capture. Then we were in the camp. My mother said at the time, "This can't be intended for us. We're sure to be taken elsewhere, to a labor camp."

The next morning I met up with my girlfriends who were already there. Those who had arrived on the December '43 transport, as Eva Landa and Resi Schwarz had, knew about the September transport and that about a month before we arrived they had all been sent to the gas chamber, and Fredy Hirsch along with them. I remember what terrible news it was to hear that he was dead. They didn't know if they should tell us or not. But I found out. I saw the tall chimney. I don't know just how far away it was, but I can still see that tall chimney, and the fire at the top. Not just smoke — fire, flames. I see it before me now. And my friends were sure that they'd be there soon themselves. And that it would be our turn, too, in six months.

I never, ever mentioned it to my mother. I knew that she knew, and I'm certain that she knew that I knew. But talking about it was taboo. My mother's brother and his whole family had been on the September transport. We never spoke about it. Maybe because we couldn't have done anything about it. What good would it have done to speak about something so terrible? It was like a well-kept secret. You feel better just not saying a word. When I think back to it now — I believe that I wasn't even afraid. I couldn't imagine that something like that could happen to us. We always said that the war would soon be over.

Six months were a long time for me. And besides, we were brought up to believe that good wins out in the end. "The truth will prevail," that was the motto of the Czech president Masaryk, whom we revered. And it was our motto as well.

Those six weeks in Auschwitz-Birkenau — I cannot forget them! It ran so counter to every humane instinct, that only a bizarre individual could even think up such things.

My mother was very sad that I wasn't getting any schooling. Sometimes we lay together on her bunk, and she would use her finger to trace a map of Europe on the underside of the bunk above us: Berlin — Hamburg — Paris — London — Madrid. We used little knots in the wood as orientation points. And I learned, without pencil or paper, and saw the map of Europe in front of me.

Twice a day was roll call, for hours on end. They counted and counted, counted, counted. I still don't know: Were they constantly miscounting or was there some method to it? Once there was a special roll call. That was in the women's camp. I don't know if it was meant as a punishment, but at any rate, we were naked and had to kneel for a long time with our hands in the air.

I also remember how during roll call one day they called out the name of Jakob Edelstein's son, Arye — he was our age. It was June 20th, at ten in the morning. Later we heard that they had killed him. He and his mother and grandmother were shot in front of Jakob Edelstein's eyes.

It was late in the morning on Friday, June 23, 1944, a pleasant summer day, when the delegation pulled up in front of the Theresienstadt commandant's door. "We were looking out the window the whole time," Handa recalls. "Then we saw them walking down Haupt Strasse, together with the Germans and the Jewish elders. They were talking. They never tried to approach anyone else or venture in a different direction. It was clear that we could not expect anything from them."

They were Dr. Maurice Rossel, the delegate from the International Committee of the Red Cross (ICRC); Frants Hvass, director general of the Danish Foreign Ministry; and Eigil Juel Henningsen, head of the Danish Ministry of Health. Viewed from the top floor of the Girls' Home, they were just the outlines of three figures, barely distinguish-

The music pavilion, with the Girls' Home in the background

able from the Germans around them: SS *Sturmbannführer* Rolf Günther, Adolf Eichmann's deputy in Section IV B 4 in the Reich Security Main Office; his brother, SS *Sturmbannführer* Hans Günther, head of the Central Office for Resolving the Jewish Question in Bohemia and Moravia; Hans Günther's deputy, SS *Obersturmführer* Gerhard Günnel; Eichmann's adjutant, *Hauptsturmführer* Ernst Möhs; Dr. Erwin Weinmann, security police chief for the Reich Protectorate; Dr. Eberhard von Thadden, section head in the Reich Foreign Ministry; and F. von Heydekampf, the representative of the German Red Cross.

The girls could identify only two of these men with certainty: Karl Rahm, the camp commandant (he was the only one in uniform), and the gentleman in the dark pinstripe suit and top hat. That was Dr. Paul Eppstein, the Jewish elder — their "mayor."

The entire entourage came from the direction of the Magdeburg Barracks, from "the Jewish Mayor's Office," as Dr. Rossel wrote in his minutes, "where the Jewish elder H. [*sic*] Eppstein briefly described for us the organization of the ghetto and suggested we begin our tour at once. His concluding words were 'You will be visiting a normal provincial town.' "[20]

And so they did. To the eyes of twenty-five-year-old Rossel, the ICRC's chief representative, "it looked like a town for privileged Jews."[21] Later he would say: "At the time I was, I must say, naïve, very naïve, just a simple fellow from a village who had studied in Geneva, who knew nothing except what he had learned firsthand along the way."

Things had in fact been spruced up nicely: the sparkling little main square with its pavilion, where they all stopped for a few moments to cast a glance at the pretty facades, at the shops, the church, the town hall with its Bank of the Jewish Self-Administration, and the coffeehouse. Seated around tables were people specially selected for this show — men, women, and children who, if you didn't look too closely, did not manifest the ravages of ghetto life.

"My parents received tickets for the coffeehouse that day, and I was with them," Vera Nath recalls. Vera's mother was a beautiful woman and Vera a very pretty girl. Her father was the manager of the *Kleiderkammer* ("clothing warehouse"), the department that was in charge of the clothing that came principally from the baggage of the deportees.[22] It was no problem for him to come up with appropriate outfits for the day.

"The elegantly dressed women all had silk stockings, hats, scarves, and stylish handbags," Rossel noted. "The people we met on the street were all well dressed."

These same people, according to Rossel's report, also appeared to be properly nourished. And how did he determine that? "It is sufficient for this purpose," he wrote, "to examine the photographic evidence, especially of the children's groups. . . . The people who live in the large barracks prefer to eat in the communal canteens. These canteens are pleasant and quite spacious. The people who eat here are served

One of the photographs that Maurice Rossel attached to his report. Decades later Paul Rabinowitsch (1930–2009), who played the trumpet in Brundibár, *recognized himself in it; he is the third boy from the left. June 23, 1943, was the one day that he and the Danish children were allowed to eat their fill. Rabinowitsch, who later called himself Paul Aron Sandfort, incorporated his experiences into his novel,* Ben: The Alien Bird.

promptly by a young girl in an apron and a starched bonnet just as in any restaurant."

A dining room had been created expressly for this occasion, in a wooden barracks adjacent to the Magdeburg Barracks. Thirteen-year-old Paul Rabinowitsch, one of 466 Jewish prisoners from Denmark, whom the delegation wanted to have a special look at, ate in the dining room on June 23, 1944. He remembered the day clearly:

> For me the main thing was that we Danish children were selected to eat as much as we liked that day. We were taken to a special restaurant that had just been built, with new wooden tables and chairs, and that was used only this one time. We were told we were to eat there, and we were served pea soup and potatoes with gravy. We could eat as much as we could manage. I went back for thirds, and ate my fill.

"My sister worked outside the ghetto at the Kursawe villa," Vera Nath recalls.[23] "She was looking after a group of young Dutch children who had arrived on a transport from Westerbork. These children had been coached on what they were to say if the camp commandant offered them some chocolate or a tin of sardines: 'Thank you, Uncle Rahm, but not chocolate again.' Or, 'Thank you, but not sardines again.'"

The ruse with the sardines worked perfectly. The SS high command was, of course, well prepared for Rossel's special interest in the delivery of international mail, which was known to function very poorly. Now the International Red Cross delegate was able to see with his own eyes and hear with his own ears that despite any shortcomings in the postal system, the many packages from Portugal — paid for by funds from the World Jewish Congress and sent through the United Relief set up by the International Red Cross — had reached their destination. "We were present in the large post office as the packages were being distributed. We saw many parcels containing sardines that had been sent from Portugal," he wrote in his report.

The delegation moved on from the post office to the Young People's Home in the building's second story, which had recently been turned into a model home with new, top-quality wooden furniture. Eva Herrmann recalls:

Then six or seven men entered, including some SS men in uniform, but most in civilian clothes. They were touring the whole building — the post office was downstairs. They now entered our room. We had been warned beforehand not to say a word. We just stood there and thought to ourselves: Are they just plain stupid, or don't they see that all this is new? The wood was shiny and still had the scent of new furniture; that's how fresh it was. There were eight of us girls, fewer than before the May transports. And we had a kind of commune, by which I mean we always shared our food equally among ourselves. And they could tell that from our bread. Each person got a piece of bread every third day, and the normal practice was to ration it out and store the remainder. But we did it differently. Instead of dividing up all our bread into individual portions at the outset, we distributed only as much as each was to receive for that day. As a result, entire loaves of bread were still on our shelf. And one of the visitors noticed this and asked, "Why do all the others only have a quarter of a loaf, and these girls whole loaves?" Then a girl from Ostrava who spoke German (most of the girls didn't understand what she was saying, since we were almost all Czechs) spontaneously remarked, "That's because we're a commune. We're Communists, you see." I can still see how our visitors cringed at that, although they stood there very stiff and erect. And I thought to myself, Oh my, now she's said something she shouldn't have.

The men left very quickly and right away someone came bounding up the stairs and said, "Well, that was some disaster! Something will happen now. Don't you realize what you said?" We were all flabbergasted. We didn't really know what that was — Communism.

But thank God — nothing came of it.[24]

On the contrary, Rossel was quite impressed, especially by the Children's Homes: "They are furnished quite nicely and reasonably, with very decorative murals that are also of remarkable educational value." And perhaps it was in fact the comment made by the brave girl from Ostrava — presumably the only person among all the prisoners to speak a single word to the delegation — that prompted him to conclude his report with this bold assertion: "This Jewish town is truly astounding. In view of the fact that these people come from many different places, speak different languages, arrive from different stations in life and with different degrees of wealth, it was necessary to establish a unity, a spirit of community, among these Jews. That was very difficult. The Theresienstadt ghetto is a

Communist society, led by a 'Stalinist' of great merit: EPPSTEIN."

What else could one expect of a Maurice Rossel? Of a young man who took his job so literally that, unless it was demanded of him, he never looked to his right or his left and certainly never peeked behind the scenery? "During this visit I was supposed to view what they showed me," he declared in a conversation with Claude Lanzmann. And that is exactly what he did. No more and no less. And to make sure that Rossel would also be able to tell the world about the astonishing cultural life in Theresienstadt, he was driven through town alongside the "mayor" in a limousine chauffeured by Hans Wostrell from Linz, a brutal SS officer who, in order to look more like Paul Eppstein's driver, dressed in civilian clothes.

As the bells in the church steeple began to toll at the stroke of five o'clock, the town orchestra, under the direction of Carlo S. Taube, began to play a medley of cheerful tunes. One of them was a song, so Otto Pollak tells us, from the operetta *The Czar's Diamond* by Granichstaedten: "For you, my dear, I've made myself beautiful." But who among the visitors could have or would have wanted to take that obvious musical hint?

■ ■ ■ ■

Everything was in place at the Sokolovna when the visitors finally arrived. Upstairs there was a rehearsal for Verdi's *Requiem.* In the main auditorium the children were performing *Brundibár,* from which, according to the plan, the visitors were to see the finale. "We stood on the stage and they told us that when given our cue we should start with the finale," Eva Herrmann, who was in the chorus of schoolchildren, recalls. "We waited a long time, and then someone came running in and said, 'Now.' And we started. And then someone else came running in and said, 'No, not yet.' And so it went, back and forth. We knew, of course, that we were putting on a comedy act for somebody. But of course, since this was a commission of the International Red Cross, we also thought and hoped that this would help us in some way. They might say, 'These children sing so beautifully we just have to help them.' We always hoped. Or at least most of us hoped — that maybe something would come of it after all."

"I was given the first signal as the car turned the corner," Rudolf Freudenfeld noted in his report. "The second signal meant that they were coming up the stairs, and at the third signal I dropped my raised hand and gave the downbeat. The music that greeted the visitors was: 'We have defeated Brundibár because we weren't afraid. We didn't let ourselves be defeated.' The children had been told that at one specific point they were to hold up high whatever they had in their hand — books, schoolbags, notebooks. But, like children everywhere, most of them had forgotten their prop. And so they simply raised their balled fists. As I was told later, the visitors liked it."

"We would like to say," Rossel added at the end of his report, "that we were greatly astonished to find the ghetto to be a town that lives an almost normal life; we had expected worse. We told the officers of the SS who escorted us that the difficulty we had encountered in obtaining permission to visit Theresienstadt was the most surprising thing of all."

"There was that whole farce with the Red Cross," Judith Schwarzbart comments, decades later, when recalling that remarkable day, "and my father was ordered to beautify the park, to set out flowers. Once the Red Cross hubbub was over, I was astonished to see that nothing whatsoever came of it. Why didn't these men see anything? Why didn't they look behind the facade? If they had just taken a peek, they would have seen all the old half-starved people who weren't allowed out on the street. If they had just opened a door to one of the barracks, they would have seen what was going on there. But they didn't do any of it. They walked down the street, through the lovely park. The coffeehouse had been made to look nice and pretty, with a few tables set outside, where young attractive women in elegant clothes were ordered to sit and drink a cup of coffee; and in the park was a pavilion, where they played music, and the Red Cross people never went over to have a peek at what was behind this farce. And that astounded me. It shocked me. Yes, it robbed me of a bit of my faith."

One week after his visit to the ghetto, Rossel sent his companion, Dr. Eberhard von Thadden, legation councilor in the Reich Foreign Ministry, copies of two photographs taken during the Theresienstadt visit, accompanied by these words: "We would like to take this opportunity to express to you, in the name of the International Committee of the Red Cross, our sincere gratitude for organizing our visit to Theresienstadt. Thanks to your efforts our visit was facilitated in all respects. We shall always have fine memories of our trip to Prague, and we are happy to assure you yet again that our report of our visit to Theresienstadt will come as a relief to a great many people, inasmuch as we found conditions there satisfactory."

The real satisfaction, however, was felt by those who had initiated and directed this successful production, primarily because of this key assertion in Rossel's report, which could now be disseminated around the world. At a time when thirty-two thousand people had already died in Theresienstadt and approximately sixty-eight thousand people had been transported to the East, Maurice Rossel wrote: "The camp at Theresienstadt is a 'final destination camp,' and normally no one who has come to this ghetto is sent on to somewhere else."

A visit to a "Jewish labor camp," which had already been authorized by Himmler, had now become superfluous. The inspectors had no further questions, so no other Potemkin villages needed to be put on display. The family camp at Auschwitz-Birkenau could be eliminated.

On July 2, 1944, all the women that Mengele had selected as being capable of work were sent on foot to the women's camp, which was not too far from the family camp. Eva Landa recalls:

For several days we could still look through the barbed wire and see the people who were left behind in the family camp. Then it became very quiet and empty there. There was heavy smoke coming from the crematoria chimneys. New selections were being made on a constant basis. The weak and sickly and those who had succeeded in bringing their children to the women's camp had to go back to the family camp. Then came the last selection in Auschwitz that I was part of. One row ahead of me were Helena Mendl and her mother, who told the SS man that Helena was not completely healthy, that she had had meningitis as a child. And I think Holubička's mother said something similar. They hoped that this would keep their daughters from being assigned heavy work. They were separated out and had to stand off by themselves. And then there was also our block elder, Marika, a beautiful young woman. She had a three-year-old child. And the SS man told her, "Leave the child here. Do you know where they will take you if you stay with her?" And Marika said, "Yes, and I'm staying with my child." So they stood off from us at a little distance, in an extra group — Helena, Holubička, and Marika with her little daughter. It was the last time I saw them.

My mother and I were almost the last to be chosen for work and put on a new transport. We were on the train again, though we didn't know where we were headed. But we did know that we were leaving Auschwitz, leaving the horror of the gas chambers. We knew what those words meant. And we thought that it was a good thing to get away from Auschwitz — far away — because it was very easy to perish there, and very hard to escape death.

We rode on the train for a long time. Then we had to change to a small train with open cars. We all had to stand; there wasn't enough room to sit. The region we were riding through was very beautiful — forest all around us. It was summer, the sun was shining — and we were far away from Auschwitz-Birkenau.

"After this final selection in early July 1944, nothing happened for ten days," Eva

Weiss recalls.

Life in Block 31 went on. Then there was another lockdown — disruption and goodbyes. I saw many of the children for the last time. I remember how terribly sorry I felt for Zajíček. It was impossible for her to make it through the selection — she was so small. She had always clung to me. She was such a poor, lovable thing, such a forlorn child. She radiated warmth. There was a special aura about her, as if she were trying to say, Come, help me! She knew what awaited her. All the children knew. We knew that we would never see each other again.

Our group was taken to the Auschwitz women's camp. We huddled very close together. The chimney was still a real possibility for us. We thought it was some evil joke by Mengele to let us think that we would escape the gas. We spent several days under dreadful conditions in the women's camp before we were led to the "sauna" again. We thought — this is it. But instead of gas, water came out of the showerheads. What an immense relief! Then they threw a pile of dirty clothes and shoes at us, and we had to quickly grab something that looked more or less like it might fit, with them bellowing at us the whole time. After we were dressed we looked around — and broke into loud, uncontrollable laughter. We simply couldn't believe that we had escaped the worst. We still had our hair, which was a major exception in the camp. There we stood, howling with laughter and waiting for what would happen next.

On July 2, 1944, they gave us different clothes, a kind of khaki uniform, and we were put on cattle cars. We couldn't believe our good luck. We were all young women. We were in a hopeful mood, and through the chinks in the car we could make out a green landscape. We appeared to be getting closer to Germany and we thought nothing from here on could be as bad as the time we had spent in the shadow of the chimneys. After a day traveling on the train, guarded the whole time by female SS personnel, a few of the cars were uncoupled. Then the train moved on.

In early July 1944, Hanka Wertheimer and her mother survived a selection. It was their last one before they would leave Auschwitz, and before the family camp at Auschwitz-

Birkenau B II b was eliminated during the night of July 10, 1944. Hanka remembers:

We had to walk past the SS men and give our age and profession. Eva Landa and another girl from our home, Gerty Kersten, were in front of me. I can still hear an SS man saying as he pointed at Eva and Gerty: "Look at those pretty Jewesses." They were sent to the right. I was directly behind them and I said, "Agriculture, sixteen years old." I was lying because my mother had told me to. She had also managed — I don't know how — to get hold of a dab of lipstick and had rubbed it on my cheeks so that I'd look healthier, because I was very pale. Like Eva and Gerty I was sent to the right. As were my friends Miriam Rosenzweig and her sister Vera. We didn't yet know what it meant to stand on the left or the right. Next to the SS men were two *kapos* — Jews who had to help see that the orders of the SS were carried out. One of them was a Dr. Wehle, a lawyer my mother knew. When he noticed her and saw that although she gave her age as forty — in reality she was forty-three — she was sent to the left, he gave her concealed signals to slip into the line on the right, which she immediately did. I didn't notice any of this because I was already past the SS men and was standing with my back to them. That's how it came about that my mother stayed with me and we finally made it out of Auschwitz together.

After this selection we arrived in the women's camp. It was on the other side of the railroad tracks. We met a lot of women from Poland who you could tell had been there for a long time. . . . But we were soon loaded onto freight cars and sent elsewhere.

Theresienstadt, August 19, 1944: "A cultural documentary is being filmed this afternoon," Otto Pollak noted in his diary, "in a hollow on the road to Litoměřice — an open-air cabaret that accommodates an audience of about 2,000. About sixty swimmers of both sexes are to be filmed at the SS swimming pool outside the ghetto. Dita Sachs from the Nurses' Home, slender, about five foot nine, blond, blue-eyed, was excluded, along with two other blond girls. I've also heard they've excluded a Danish actor, a blond giant of a man. Gerron, who enjoys making inappropriate jokes about Jews, is directing."

"Crazy things have been happening during the last few days — they're making a film!" Eva Herrmann noted with astonishment in her diary the next day.[25] "The town orchestra, the children's pavilion, our performances, and life on the streets and even outside of Theresienstadt. Five girls from each room are to report for the filming. I managed to be one of them, and so we were able to get out of the ghetto, to Travice, where a stage was set up."

The scenery was in place, the dress rehearsal had worked perfectly, a director was found, a script authorized, and a film crew hired. The filming could begin. It was an enterprise that had long been planned by the top echelon of the SS in Prague. *Theresienstadt: A Documentary of a Jewish Settlement* was a piece of Nazi propaganda that has since come to be known as *The Führer Gives the Jews a Town*.

Kurt Gerron — an actor, cabaret performer, and former star of Germany's preeminent film studio UFA — was both the producer and the director. His 1928 recording of "Mack the Knife" from *The Three-penny Opera* had made him a sensation, and when he appeared as the vaudeville director Kiepert in *The Blue Angel* alongside Marlene Dietrich, his international career was launched — and then derailed by Hitler. In January 1944 he was deported from the Westerbork Camp in the Netherlands and sent to Theresienstadt, where he soon established a cabaret called the Carousel. One of Gerron's leading lyricists, Martin Greiffenhagen, was assigned to be his scriptwriter for the film, and from Prague came the team from *Aktualita,* the weekly Czech newsreel. The main actors and walk-ons were already on location — the inmates of the Theresienstadt ghetto.

"In those days I was working in the fields," Vera Nath recalls. "And we saw people going for a swim in the Eger. It looked like a summer camp, like a shore resort."

"My sister Zdenka and I and some other girls," Marta Fröhlich recalls, "were brought to a swimming area along the banks of the Eger. We had to put on bathing suits, then sing a song, jump gleefully into the water, and then keep on ducking underwater and pretending that we were so very happy. There were swings that we had to swing on. Then they gave us some bread spread with margarine — not to eat, but to hold so that they could film us. And my brothers had to climb up on a horse-drawn wagon. And the wagon was full of fruits and vegetables — apples, pears, potatoes, carrots. But during the entire ride they weren't allowed to bite into a single apple."

"I remember one thing," Handa Pollak says. "The bigger girls from our Home were working in the vegetable gardens. Of course, eating any of the vegetables was strictly forbidden. While they were making the film the girls were painted brown so they would look tanned and healthy. Every girl got a basket of vegetables to dangle from her arm, and then they had to walk along the road toward the camera in a group, singing. At one particular point they had to pick up an apple or some other fruit and bite into it, then turn a corner, where the basket and even the fruit they had bitten into were immediately taken away. I still recall them telling us about it. It made them laugh so hard, and we laughed along with them. We just made fun of the whole charade."

"When someone gave a whistle, we had to march off with rakes in our hands and walk past the church," Helga Pollak recalls. "And there on the steps stood Kurt Gerron. Then there was another whistle, and we had to take a few steps back, stand stock-still, and then came the command again: Keep marching and be cheerful."

"We were afraid of Kurt Gerron," Ela Stein comments in describing the general atmosphere. "The Germans were constantly circling around him. We didn't know whether he was in cahoots with them or not. There was a lot of tension in the air. The Czech film people weren't even allowed to speak with us."

The team filmed every inch of the Potemkin village: the Bank of the Jewish Self-Administration; the post office, where the walk-ons had to stand in line waiting for packages to be distributed; a meeting of the Council of Elders, which was moved from the gloomy Magdeburg Barracks to an elegantly furnished room in the Sokolovna; firemen extinguishing a fake fire; doctors performing surgery. And, of course, the central library, managed by Professor Utitz, had been "spruced up beyond recognition," displaying the splendid spines of the *Encyclopaedia Judaica* and the *Jewish Lexicon*.[26]

On the Sokolovna terrace, where Helga had lowered her notes down to her father while she was ill with encephalitis, the camera captured people dancing past, dressed in their finest evening clothes; people sitting convivially next to each other under parasols, sipping from champagne glasses with straws. In the garden, prominent people were strolling and engaging in lively conversations; frolicking children played in the children's playground; and laborers in the workshops — carpenters, cobblers, launderers, tailors — went merrily about their work. On the outskirts of the ghetto a cabaret program was performed before an audience of about two thousand.[27]

"In a village near Travice, where they had set up a stage, I watched them film a scene that didn't come out right," Eva Herrmann recalls, "and saw Rahm, the camp commandant — I think it was Rahm — slap Zelenka, the architect and famed set designer from the Prague National Theater. And that started me thinking: Oh my, something's not right here. The whole thing is really just one huge sham. They also had young people get up on the stage, and then they pointed to this one or that one. Suddenly it became clear to me that they were looking for particular types, Jewish types, and SS *Scharführer* Haindl pointed at me — I had black curly hair. And at that moment I knew I didn't want to have any part in this hoax, made myself scarce, and mingled in with the crowd."[28]

Despite both a heat wave — the temperature soared to 104 degrees Fahrenheit on August 21 — and a plague of bedbugs, the filming proceeded according to plan. As in the previous year, many of the living quarters, including the Girls' Home, had to be freed from bedbugs and lice. "Helga is sleeping in Frau Mandl's room at the Home for Invalids, above Frau Heilbrun's bed," Otto Pollak noted on August 24. "At nine in the evening Helga takes a cold bath in the bathtub. Altenstein looks for bedbugs with a cigarette lighter. I watch his silhouette from the courtyard. Helga has slept well during the first night here with us. Her sleep wasn't disrupted by bedbugs. She has words of praise for our washing facility, which reminds her of peacetime."

On August 28, Otto Pollak likewise had to flee the bedbugs. The night before, he had turned on the light every half hour so that he and Schmitz, from the adjoining bed, could hunt down and kill hundreds of bedbugs. Now he was sleeping in the open air for the first time. "A dark blue sky sown with stars, cool air. After weeks of not being able to sleep, I slept like the Lord God himself, until five-thirty. I served Helga her breakfast — coffee and bread with margarine — in bed. She was absolutely delighted and said that this was the first time she'd ever been served breakfast in bed in Theresienstadt."

Meanwhile, the shooting went on. They filmed the town orchestra playing in Market

Square; a soccer game before about four hundred spectators in the courtyard of the Dresden Barracks at three o'clock on the afternoon of August 31; the first act of *The Tales of Hoffmann* in the auditorium of the Sokolovna; and the premiere of Pavel Haas's *Study for String Orchestra,* played by the symphony orchestra under the direction of Karel Ančerl. And against the backdrop of a town created by František Zelenka, they filmed the children's opera *Brundibár.*

"I recall those days only vaguely," Flaška says. "We were very agitated. It was hard work to put it on for the Germans, even though we knew the opera very well. But there was Kurt Gerron, who was very energetic, and there were all the camera people, and sitting up in the balcony was the SS. I remember the SS sitting up there, watching us. It was different from usual — a tense atmosphere."

"We weren't used to the large stage of the Sokolovna," Handa explains. "There was a lot more room than in the Magdeburg Barracks. I didn't feel at all comfortable on this stage. It was all too new, too big. From time to time we had to move to the music and arrive at a particular spot on the stage. And I was afraid sometimes that I wouldn't end up where I was supposed to end up, and would be standing in the wrong spot."

And yet the children performed their opera with growing enthusiasm. As always, many of their fans were in the audience. They all wanted to see *Brundibár* and were eager to see how it was going to turn out this time, under spotlights and cameras. In spite of everything, it was an extraordinary event, both for those in the cast and for the audience. Let the Germans do what they wanted with their hoax and their film, let them present the world with their fairy-tale lie about Theresienstadt as a cultural paradise and model ghetto — they could not lay a finger on *Brundibár.*

Up in the balcony, on the side reserved for the Germans, unexpected guests were seated: the wives and children of the SS men.

Now they could show them. The children could show them what people degraded as subhumans and often cursed as "Jewish swine" were capable of. *We,* their message seemed to be, *we poor, starving, caged children can put on a show like this. With music that pleases even you, and your children!*

"The music is simply enchanting," Thomas Mandl, the young violinist for the coffeehouse orchestra, wrote, describing his

FREIZEITGESTALTUNG

Flach Anna

Kenn.Nr. _____ Adr L 410

Betr.:Filmaufnahme

Wir bitten Sie, sich zu der Brundibar

am _____ um 12 30 Uhr

in   20.8.44

stattfindenden Filmaufnahme(Probe)
Westgasse 3
pünktlich einzufinden

Diese Aufforderung dient als Ur-
laub beleg für die oben angegebene
Zeit und ist der Arbeitsstätte
vorher zur Kenntnisnahme und Ab-
stempelung vorzulegen.

Da die Aufnahme-(Probe-)zeit als
Arbeitszeit gewertet wird,ist
dieser Beleg nach Beendigung der
Aufnahme(Probe) dem Beauftragten
der Freizeitgestaltung abzuliefern.

                    Freizeitgestaltung

2545-X-44/k

This notice required Flaška to participate in the production of Brundibár, *which the director Kurt Gerron was filming for the Nazi propaganda documentary.*

470

impressions after a few performances. "The music is of such high quality, so wonderfully varied and demanding and thrilling and evocative, that anyone with a spark of musicality is carried away from start to finish. There are so many subtle and clever melodic devices and the instrumentation is so intelligent and at the same time so deftly written that these children could really sing their roles. They certainly weren't professionals. They were just 'ordinary' children. But with that ordinary set in quotes."

On August 20, the children put on their beloved opera for one of the last of a total of fifty-five performances. And little Paul made his trumpet ring for all it was worth. "When the SS was present, I always had this shadowy feeling at the back of my head. I knew I could not play wrong, and you can hear every wrong note very clearly on a trumpet. Rahm would notice, I thought to myself, and be mad at me, and put me on a transport. And in those moments it was as if I were playing for my life."

MIRIAM ROSENZWEIG

Miriam Rosenzweig was born in Košice, a town in eastern Slovakia, near the Hungarian border, on November 7, 1929. When she was six, her family's serious financial problems

drove them to move to Ostrava in the hope of
making a fresh start. But the Nazis soon put
an abrupt end to their efforts. On October 18,
1939, Miriam's father and 901 other Jews
from Ostrava were forced to board a transport
for, as it was called in the official jargon,
"voluntary resettlement to a reeducation
camp." It was the first transport to leave the
German Reich and its annexed territories. Its
destination was the little Polish town of Nisko
on the San River, in the district of Lublin. Miriam never saw her father again. Three years

later, in early October 1942, Miriam, her mother, and her sister arrived in Theresienstadt. "I was ill all that winter. I had dysentery and an ear infection. There were no medicines. The doctor could only puncture my eardrum every day to drain the pus. It got worse and worse, and I had a high fever."

Finally, vital medicines found their way into the ghetto, and Miriam recovered. It was spring, however, before she could join her mother in the attic of the Magdeburg Barracks, where she lived until the end of 1943, when she moved into Room 28.

CHAPTER SEVEN:
GHETTO TEARS

The evening of September 2, 1944, did not bode well. Around eleven o'clock that night, a severe thunderstorm broke out above Theresienstadt, drenching the town in heavy rains. The bad weather caused a power outage and left the ghetto in terrifying darkness, relieved only by repeated flashes of lightning. "After that, swarms of starving bedbugs flooded the entire camp," Otto Pollak wrote.

By this time people were caught up in a mixture of euphoria and fear. The tension that had prevailed during the visit of the International Red Cross delegation and the unrelenting frenzy surrounding the propaganda film still seemed to hang in the air and charge it with explosive force. Artistic pursuits also took on a feverish, almost superhuman intensity.

In the Sokolovna auditorium, in the town hall, in the Magdeburg Barracks and the

This poem, "The Vintage Wine of 1944," written by
an unnamed fellow prisoner of Theresienstadt, was
saved by Otto Pollak.

old movie hall, in the gymnasium of L 417,
in the coffeehouse, and in many attics —
there were performances everywhere, some
of them of the highest artistic quality. Edith
Steiner-Kraus provided the accompaniment
on a spinet for a performance of *Carmen*

directed by Franz Eugen Klein; Karl Fischer conducted Mendelssohn's oratorio *Elijah*. In the attic of the Magdeburg Barracks, Norbert Frýd presented a dramatic version of the biblical story of Esther with music by Karel Reiner, and Hanus Jochowitz directed Mozart's *Bastien and Bastienne* on a different stage. There were evening song recitals with Karel Berman and Rafael Schächter, chamber music concerts, and solo concerts by several piano virtuosi — Bernhard Kaff, Gideon Klein, Edith Steiner-Kraus, Renée Gärtner-Geiringer, and Juliette Arányi.

The Vintage Wine of 1944

When there will come the time you seek a
  name
For a drop of vintage wine,
A name to capture what's within, not
  watered down, but dry
(I mean someday, at home — in Palestine)
Then call it: "Ghetto Tears 1944."

Like "Henkel Dry" or "Tears of Magdalene,"
This brand will gain renown
Nor let its drinkers down
There is no water in these tears,

Just purest wine,

The name itself is guarantee.
"Vintage 1944."

And you must search the years long past
And far ahead your eyes must cast
To find that kind of tears
So dry, and none with peers,
As "Vintage 1944."
                    Theresienstadt, October 1, 1944

One of the final opera premieres, *La Serva Padrona,* an opera buffa by Giovanni Batista Pergolesi, was performed in the Sokolovna auditorium. The conductor was Karel Berman, Rafael Schächter played the piano accompaniment, and, as Viktor Ullmann noted, "it was a pleasure to hear Hans Krása at the harpsichord."[1] Karel Švenk played the role of the servant Vespone, and Marion Podolier and Bedřich Borges gave brilliant performances as well. "It was the last premiere I was able to mount in cooperation with František Zelenka," Karel Berman wrote in his memoirs. "Our ensemble was dissolved after three performances."

As on several previous occasions, Alice Herz-Sommer gave a solo concert of Chopin's études in the town hall. "To play all twenty-four études in one evening is to take both a physical and an artistic risk,"

Viktor Ullmann wrote. "These are, after all, 'études,' exercises for the development of Romantic piano technique. Alice Herz-Sommer is a justly admired pianist, short perhaps in stature but great in artistry, and her rendition of certain études was phenomenal, but the program as a whole is to be rejected."[2]

What Ullmann did not know and would never be able to learn was that this concert left a strong impression on many of those who heard it and would later survive the war. "We were gently lifted out of our narrow, starving Terezin and taken to another time and world," Zdenka Fantlová said of this concert in her autobiography. "Sitting on a wooden bench I listened as if in a trance. Forever unforgettable!"[3]

Alice's playing remained unforgettable for Flaška as well. Indeed, for her it became a crucial inspiration. "The Chopin études by Alice Herz-Sommer left such a deep impression on me that I decided that very evening to become a pianist. And I did."

Meanwhile, in the cellar of L 411, rehearsals had begun for the chamber opera *The Emperor of Atlantis, or the Refusal to Die*, which Victor Ullmann had composed the previous year, basing it on a libretto by the young painter and poet Peter Kien. This allegorical ballad/opera about life and death and a tyrant named Overall reflects the inner spiritual revolt of its creators and of those who participated in the production.

Shortly before the dress rehearsal in late summer 1944, the project was canceled. Paul Kling, the violin prodigy from Opava, who had just turned fifteen and was already part of the string quintet, had only vague memories of the moment. "No one knows just why the cancellation came about, whether the camp administration decided the premise was too risky, or the camp commandant himself prohibited it, or the Council of Elders ordered the production terminated — no one today can say. Someone at the time knew of course. But these people are no longer alive. I am almost the only one who survived, and I of course know the least, since I was the youngest."[4]

And so no one heard Death's aria from *The Emperor of Atlantis:* "I am the gardener Death, I sow sleep in furrows plowed with pain. I am Death, the gardener Death, and pull up wilting weeds of weary creatures."

Only Verdi's *Requiem* was heard one last time, sung by Rafael Schächter's legendary choir — *"Requiem aeternam, dona eis, Domine. Libera me."*

The earth is red with blood
The year advances wearily
It is war
My God, it is war

The battlefields
Overflow with blood
The earth is so tired
The moment of hopelessness
Stands on the horizon

Even the sun
Shines through the blood
And says:

Brothers, stop
Murdering one another!
Have you not had enough of war
Do you not know
That you are human beings?
There is no point
In finding human beings
If the world no longer exists

The moon moves calmly across the sky
And it too gazes in sadness down at the
    earth
And says: God, do you not see
How the world suffers
Everything is bathed in blood!

It is impossible to recover from this
When the heart of humankind
Is bullet-riddled.
> Handa Pollak, from her notebook,
> *Všechno,* 1944

It was a period that alternated between hope and despair. When word spread through the ghetto that the Allied armies had successfully landed in Normandy on June 6, 1944, hope was on the rise. The end of the war no longer seemed far off. The overwhelming force of Allied troops was bearing down on the German Reich from all directions. In the West, the final phase of the liberation of France from four years of German occupation had begun. The Red Army was approaching from the East. In January it had reached the eastern border of Poland, and had been advancing in a steady series of offensives ever since. By the middle of August, the border of East Prussia had been reached, and the Red Army was headed in the direction of Warsaw and to the great bend in the Vistula. "Telegram from Stalin," reads Otto Pollak's diary. " 'Send ten million mattresses. Our soldiers are right at the border.' "

But whenever hope budded spontaneously, it was always overshadowed by other ominous events and news. As before, the general mood was dominated by worries that were grimly confirmed when, on July 17, three boys fled from the ghetto, including, as Otto Pollak reports, "young Sklarek from Berlin. Presumably in reprisal, five renowned artists were arrested along with their families for defaming the ghetto and are confined in the Little Fortress."

The Theresienstadt painters' affair left the ghetto in great agitation and even greater fear.[5] Everyone knew these painters, especially Bedřich Fritta (Fritz Taussig), Otto Ungar, Felix Bloch, and Leo Haas, whose works are among the most valuable extant documents from the period of the Theresienstadt ghetto. Many people also knew Bedřich Fritta's three-year-old son, "droll, chubby-cheeked Tommy," whom Otto Pollak had often enjoyed entertaining. The child likewise vanished on July 17, leaving behind only gloomy forebodings.

And yet — the pendulum continued to swing to the side of hope. Everything was in flux; there was no doubt that the Allied armies were advancing. The residents of Theresienstadt could see that with their own eyes. "The first swarm of silver birds, flying in the bright sunlight across the southwest," Otto Pollak wrote on July 21, 1944, "were

482

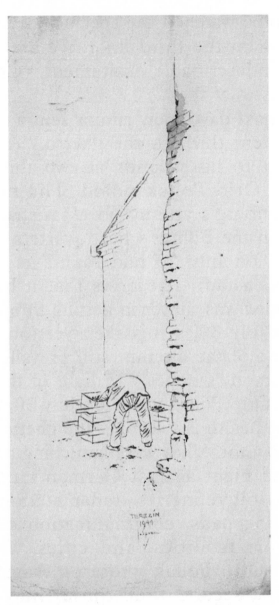

Man at the Well, *pencil drawing by
Jo Spier*

observed between eleven in the morning
and one in the afternoon. The children in

the Home watched the spectacle from their window on the third floor. We are caught up in indescribable excitement. (Children blew kisses at them.)"

The next day a new rumor sent a wave of excitement through the ghetto. "AH succumbed to his wounds at two this afternoon," Otto Pollak noted. The news of Stauffenberg's attempted assassination of Hitler in the Führer's headquarters in East Prussia on July 20 had found its way to Theresienstadt. The news that it had not succeeded was slower in getting through. As late as July 30, a mistaken version of the outcome of the attempt still prevailed, lifting everyone's hopes. "In light of the good news," Otto Pollak wrote on July 30, "a tide of good health is sweeping the ghetto."

By now the Allies were launching air raids day and night against German munitions depots, oil refineries, radar stations, V-1 launching pads, communication centers, transport facilities, and cities. "Twelve noon," Otto Pollak wrote on August 24. "For the second time those shiny silver birds . . . in the east, moving southwestward."

The effect of such events was enormous. And now that the air-raid alarm was sounded once or twice a day, there were happy faces and optimistic conversations everywhere. Was it not obvious that the Germans would soon be defeated and would finally lay down their arms?

> People are blind and helpless
> And the good ones lie buried in the earth
> When will peace finally
> Fill the hearts of men?
>
> Open your eyes, you blind people
> Look upon it and do something
> To make the awful booming cloud of war
> Be swept away.
>
> And one day, perhaps
> All nations will shake hands
> They will triumph over evil
> And be friends again.
>
> And they will defend the truth
> And call out in their happiness:
> "Evil is banned;
> We no longer need to fight."
>> Handa Pollak, from her notebook,
>> *Všechno,* 1944

For prisoners wavering between hope and fear, the New Year's message of the Jewish elder Paul Eppstein, issued on September

16, 1944, in the name of the Theresienstadt Council of Elders, must have seemed like an ominous tipping of the scales. Eppstein wished them all the best for the year 5705 of the Jewish calendar, and thanked them for the work achieved in the year just past and for their discipline in carrying out their duties. Then, as reported the next day in the *Communications of the Jewish Self-Administration,* he added: "In a time of great decisions that are changing the course of world history, when it has been our fate to live as if on an island, our own resiliency is crucial for us in shaping our lives and in recognizing our historic task of meeting our responsibilities for our community."[6]

"These times do not allow me to speak openly." These words as well, according to an eyewitness account, were included in an address in which the chief elder fervently appealed to the ghetto residents for their trust. "I would nevertheless like to employ a comparison that may help you understand our current situation." And he likened Theresienstadt to a ship nearing its harbor. "The harbor is, however, encircled with mines, and only the captain knows the course, which, though not direct, is the only one that will bring us safely into port."[7]

On Saturday, September 23, more swarms

of silver birds passed over Theresienstadt. "Gazing at those airplanes coming from who knows how far away, Helga has been caught up in strong longings for her mother, which she told me about this evening, trying to hold back her tears," Otto Pollak wrote, and then continued, "There is a rumor that during the Jewish holy days, 5,000 Jewish men between the ages of eighteen and fifty will be sent on two transports to D. How can the ghetto manage if nearly all the men capable of work have to leave? What lies behind such a measure?"

The next day, the SS issued a written decree — in the *Communications of the Jewish Self-Administration* — that every resident of the ghetto needed to know:

With a view to total employment of all forces, it has been decided . . . that opportunities for work needed to meet current demands in Theresienstadt will be expanded. Men capable of work will therefore be employed in priority tasks outside Theresienstadt, much as the "outside work brigades for constructing barracks" were employed. To this end, on Tuesday, September 26, and Wednesday, September 27, following instructions of the appropriate office, 2,500 men between ages sixteen and fifty-five will be processed each day and sent from the settlement to other districts of the Reich. . . . All such men must therefore immediately prepare for transport and assume they will be summoned.[8]

The transport lists were now announced and the orders issued. Riesa, near Dresden, was the place of employment, at least according to the rumor that the SS had made a point of circulating. No one trusted such information anymore. People were aware of just one thing: A catastrophe had overtaken them.

"The ghetto is caught up in great unrest, since in a few days so many men will be leaving their wives behind, fathers their children, sons their mothers," Otto Pollak wrote on September 24. And a day later: "Helga is helping her chemistry professor, Miloš Salus, pack his things, since he has to leave on the transport, as does a teacher who, she says, always wears an ironic smile and whom she describes as an 'elegantarium.' Felix is saying his goodbyes, since he will be confined to holding barracks tomorrow. He is calm and composed."[9]

In all the uproar, only a few people noticed that sometime between three and four o'clock on the afternoon of September 27, Paul Eppstein vanished into a closed truck. He was taken to the Little Fortress and murdered that same day. No one in the ghetto learned of this, not even his wife, Hedwig, who came to the SS headquarters every day with a pot of food for him. "Gentlemen," Heinrich Jöckel, the feared commander of the Little Fortress, who spared no effort to torture and murder his victims in the cruelest ways possible, said to his accomplices, "I expect you to maintain the strictest silence about this matter; it is an issue of far-reaching significance."[10]

One day later, at noon on September 28, 1944, Transport Ek was the first to leave, with 2,499 men on it. Engineer Otto Zucker, the designated "leader of the labor camp," was on this transport, along with other members of the so-called staff of Theresienstadt. Almost without exception, those who left were men in their prime, among them the singer Karel Berman, the young violinists Paul Kling and Thomas Mandl, Rudolf Freudenfeld, who had directed *Brundibár,* and Karel Pollak, Handa's father, whom the girls called Strejda. Their last moments together are burned forever into Handa's memory:

"The day before my father had to board the transport was Yom Kippur. We sat on the ramparts above the Cavalier Barracks — Tella, my father, and I. We talked about our life after the war. And we promised one another that when we were all reunited we would always observe Yom Kippur as a day of fasting. But my father never returned."

At eight o'clock that evening, Otto Pollak went to the sluice. Alongside the tracks, "four arc lamps on the side of the building illuminate the street bright as day. A locomotive with the second train of cars is pulling in. The first cars are large cattle cars refitted with big windows."

"And then came the moment when five thousand men between twenty and fifty-five, in the best years of their adult lives, were sent away all at once," Alice Herz-Sommer recalls. "Among them were my husband and the husband of my best friend, Edith Steiner-Kraus. That goodbye — it was a terrible shock for my son! I had to give my husband my word of honor that I would not volunteer for a transport. The transport pulled out, and then, only two days later, another transport was ordered and we were told: 'Wives can now follow their husbands.' "

The SS circulated a flyer stating that only a limited number of family members would be allowed to join this labor transport that was so important for the war effort. So it was a labor camp after all? "Many of the women volunteered," says Alice, "but my friend Edith and I did not."

Five hundred women fell into the SS's trap. They voluntarily joined two subsequent transports, El and Em, that left Theresienstadt on September 29 and October 1. Rahm and Haindl amused themselves — and not for the first time — by striking and cursing the prisoners in order to move them onto the cars more quickly.

Eichmann's adjutant Ernst Möhs was already handing out typewritten lists of names with special instructions to the newly appointed chief elder, Dr. Benjamin Murmelstein. One of them stated that high-ranking officials in the ghetto administration, officials in the Jewish organizations, former officers in all armies, important inventors, and prominent individuals would also be transported.

Summonses were issued day and night without a pause for one whole month — almost nineteen thousand orders for transport. Hardly anyone was able to sleep now. The residents of the ghetto were petrified.

"They just wept, wept, wept. No one said a word. So many people were gone," Marta Fröhlich says. "My older brother, Jenda, our protector, was gone. I almost left with him. Our counselor Eva Eckstein left voluntarily to be with her sister and her fiancé."

"Most of my friends, boys and girls, went away," Ela Stein says. "Honza Gelbkopf was gone, and nearly all the boys from Home 9. My uncle Otto left with the last transport on October 28. There was no time to say goodbye. There was no pause. Everything happened so quickly."

"One transport after the other left," Flaška recalls. "One girlfriend after the other left. Our counselors. My brother Michael left on September 28 and my sister Lizzi on October 19. I accompanied them as far as the sluice, which was forbidden and very dangerous. Sometimes people who weren't on the list were shoved onto a car at the last moment and the doors were closed behind them."

"You cannot imagine the kinds of things that happened there at the sluice," says Eva Herrmann, who wore a red armband as a transport aide. "And it was organized so that everyone had to line up by number — everyone had a number. Then they walked toward the cars and the numbers were called out, from one to one thousand, to one thousand five hundred, to two thousand. . . . You had the feeling that as long as they were in the barracks they were still in Theresienstadt. But when they went out that gate — there stood the SS, who took charge with their shouting and stomping, with boots and clubs and everything else! If one of the older people didn't move fast enough or there was someone with children — the scenes we were forced to watch were lessons in horror. People didn't really know what was happening to them. They only knew that they were leaving, but didn't know where they were headed."[11]

Thursday, October 12, 1944 (Otto Pollak's diary)

Sunny day. At eleven in the morning I manage with some difficulty to make my way to the Hamburg sluice. Last goodbyes with Marta and Fritz. Marta deeply touched. Weeping, she expresses her fear that we'll not see each other again. Helga and I remain behind alone.

Sunday, October 15, 1944

The Hechts, Hugo, Grünbaum, Kopper, and Helga's best friend Hanna Lissau are summoned. At three-thirty in the afternoon a difficult goodbye with the Hechts. With them I lose my last friends. From the steps I call out to them not to lose heart. Helga is on night duty and visits the Hechts at the sluice. I look out on the street early in the morning. The boarding of the cars is in high gear.

Monday, October 16, 1944

Around five in the morning Helga quietly enters the room. I turn on a light. My child, breaking into tears, reports that the train rolled out at five o'clock. The pain in Helga's soul is very great. She stopped at Genie Barracks and watched the train pull out, until the last car was lost from sight. She saw Hugo being boarded on a litter and noticed how all the baggage of the blind was left behind.

Tuesday, October 17, 1944

Hugo's will, made as he said goodbye on Sunday: My heirs are my brother's three children. Amid his tears he told me this while gazing out the window. Another transport leaves tomorrow. Helga remarks about these summonses: "A single piece of paper decides a person's fate."

"I received my orders to be transported in October," Eva Winkler recalls. "Just me. Not my mother, not my father. My father did everything he could to get me removed from the list. He went to the Council of Elders and told them either the whole family goes or I have to stay here. It was my good luck that my father was needed. I was already in the Hamburg Barracks. I can still see the lines of people with transport numbers on the tags around their necks, and I can hear them being called out, one, two, three . . . and then watching as people climb into the cattle cars. Then, at the last moment, my father arrived and pulled me off the transport."

"It was one of the last transports in late October. And needless to say, as a fourteen-year-old girl, I was put on it alone," says Vera Nath. "I wasn't doing any important work. My sister was working at the Kursawe villa, my mother in the mica works,[12] my father in the *Kleiderkammer.* Their work was very important. I received my summons for a transport leaving on Sunday, October 22, 1944. When they put me on the list my father went to Murmelstein and begged him to take me off the transport. And Murmelstein said, 'You can go as well. You and your wife and your daughter.' And he put us all on the transport list.

"We were in the sluice for two days, and our things were already loaded and our numbers had been called. As my father passed by Rahm, Rahm said, 'Nath, what are you up to?' My father said that I was on the transport and he couldn't let me go alone. And Rahm said, 'I need you. Stay here with your family.' And so we stayed."

"My father didn't even try to get us off the transport," recalls Judith Schwarzbart, who also received her orders to be transported in late October. "My mother didn't want him to. She hoped to see my brother Gideon again, who had left in May. And shortly before we left, my father called me to him — he probably guessed that he wouldn't be coming back — and he said just these words to me: 'Stay just as you are.' And then we all boarded the transport."

Of the girls in Room 28, the following boarded the October 1944 transports: Jiřinka Steiner and the counselor Eva Eckstein on October 1; Ruth Meisl on October 4; Ruth Gutmann on October 6; Eva Heller on October 12; Eva Fischl, Hana Lissau, and Maria Mühlstein on October 16; Emma Taub on October 19; Marta Kende, Helga Pollak, Handa Pollak, Eva Stern, and Marianne's friend Hana Brady on October 23; Lenka Lindt and Judith Schwarzbart on October 28.

Room 28, all the Girls' Homes, the Boys'

Transport summons dated October 22, 1944, from the papers of Otto Pollak

Homes, the Children's Homes, the barracks, and all living quarters — they were all being emptied out, day after day. Left behind in the ghetto were the Danes, a few Dutch, women and girls who labored in the mica works, and those who, like Ela's mother, worked in the fields under the Czech supervisor Karel Kursawe. Experts who were important to the SS and highly decorated or wounded veterans from the First World War, such as Leo Flach and Otto Pollak, also remained.

The dedications and good wishes in Flaš-ka's poetry album were left behind as well:

Just as this big mushroom protects the little mushroom, that's how our Home protects us. But after a while we will have to protect others. And so prepare yourself, for you will have to pay back the loan someday. Never reflect for long if you can do a good deed, and never lose hope. Without hope you cannot exist. And keep remembering those you were fond of. And never forget those who are like me.

Your Fiška
Terezin, October 5, 1944

Think back now and then to our Home in Theresienstadt and don't be annoyed if I annoyed you sometimes.

Ruthka (Plzeň Bezovka 9)
Ruth Gutmann
October 5, 1944

Always remember our Room 28, think of what we learned there, what we strove for, and organize your life according to the rules that we learned there.

Tella
October 5, 1944

Dear Flaška,

Never forget what we have experienced together. The way we sang and dreamed, and the concerts with Baštík. Never forget what was beautiful about our Home. Good luck, and don't upset your mother.

Kisses from your
Maria Mühlstein

P.S.: Don't be annoyed that I've written such nonsense. You wanted me to write something.

October 13, 1944

I am sorry, but I have to write similar thoughts for you as I wrote for the other girls. But you need to know that Theresienstadt was also a good school for us, despite all the bad things. You came here as a little child, without character, but under the influence of our Home you have acquired character. And I believe you have the will to be a good person.

Hana Lissau
October 14, 1944

There is no end. A new era always follows. Each person has his goal, and whoever wants to achieve that goal has a great many difficulties and a long struggle ahead. A person has to struggle in the face

Fiška's entry in Flaška's poetry album

of adversity. People who have no will
never achieve their goals. But if you keep
up the struggle and never stop, even if you
are defeated, you come closer to your
goal. This struggle is the struggle of the

Milá Flaško!

Doufám, že se shledáme v nějakém takovém
kraji, kde je vše svěží, vzdušný a ne tísnivý
jako vězení. Kde budeme moci volně dýchat.
a při tom vyplníme své ideje. To již budeme
starší rozumnější. A když se pole bude tmí-
vat a nebe bude temné, hvězdy budou vychá-
zet a jezero neb moře se bude třpytit tu se-
sedneme si v břehu a budeme přemýšlet o
našich radostech i starostech, které jsme mě-
ly v Terezíně před několika lety

Helga

Terezín 22. X. 1944

Helga's entry in Flaška's poetry album

501

will. Even an individual who is physically quite weak can have a strong will.

Eli Mühlstein
October 15, 1944

Human beings are in this world to do good. Anyone who does not abide by that has no right to be a human being. If you want to fulfill your mission on this earth, act accordingly and live by the principles that Tella has taught us. Whenever you're in doubt, think back to what she would have done. I believe that she is the most flawless person I know.

In memory of my sweetheart,
Lenka Lindt
October 15, 1944

Always remember, dear Flaška, that there were times here in Theresienstadt when we lived lazily through each day and never gave up hope that peace will come.

Handa Pollak

Dear Flaška!

I hope that we will see each other again out in beautiful nature, where everything is fresh and fragrant, where we can breathe free and realize our ideas and not live as we did here in this prison cell. And when we are older and a little wiser, there will perhaps come an evening when the stars shine in a dark sky, lending the sea its silvery luster, and we shall sit beside the shore and think of our friends and the cares that we once had so many years before in Theresienstadt.

Helga
October 22, 1944

"After the transports left that autumn, we came back to our room one evening and didn't know what to do. Almost all the girls, all the counselors were gone. It was eerie in the ghetto," Ela Stein recalls. "A lot of the windows stood wide open, and many of the rooms were completely empty."

"The last days in Room 28 were very depressing. All our friends were gone. The Home stood almost empty, the whole ghetto felt deserted," Marianne Deutsch recalls. "Nothing functioned anymore. And then Willy Groag came and told us that whoever had parents or someone else in the family should move in with them."

"All the bunks were empty," says Flaška. "And at the end there were only four of us in the room. So we took down our flag and cut it into quarters, and each of us took one. And we promised each other that after the war, when we all met up again, we would sew it back together as a symbol of our friendship."

Ela, her mother, and her sister moved into a building that housed many of the people who worked in agriculture. They were given a small room with enough mattresses to go around, and they could arrange things relatively comfortably. The 18,402 prisoners who had gone with the transports had to leave many possessions behind. There were now only about 11,000 people living in Theresienstadt.

It took a while for the ghetto, which had come to a standstill, to be reorganized and begin functioning again. Only a few hundred men capable of work had remained in the camp, among them Willy Groag and the fathers of Marianne Deutsch, Vera Nath, and Eva Winkler. Women took over the jobs of the deported men, and children did the work of adults. Flaška, who moved in with her parents in the Magdeburg Barracks, worked in the fields at one point, then in the mica factory, and for a while as an errand girl for the administration. Marianne and Marta, like most of the children, were assigned agricultural jobs, but they did all sorts of other work whenever the need arose.

Chapter Eight:
Liberation

November 8, 1944 (from Otto Pollak's diary)

On awakening, the first snow. Meet with Marianne Deutsch, Helga's friend from Room 28. She tells how she got out of being transported. How her father intervened so that M. gave P. the order to switch papers. In fifteen minutes she was off the list.

November 19, 1944

Four weeks ago today Helga entered the sluice. Quarter after nine, last goodbye from my child.

November 20, 1944

Forty-nine Dutch arrive, nothing but rags and neglect. Most don't know their own names or where they have come from.

November 22, 1944

Spent a bad night, constantly thinking of

my child. Does she have all her things? Is she perhaps freezing? This morning at six, as a kind of symbol, a young black and white kitten came running into the room; wouldn't leave my side.

In mid-November 1944, the commandant ordered that urns with ashes of those who had died be disposed of. The task was assigned to a group of about twenty children, among them Ela Stein and thirteen-year-old Horst Cohn from Berlin. As one of the boys who had hauled the wagon for corpses and bread through Theresienstadt, he was immune to death.

"Death didn't frighten us," he recalls, "and certainly the ashes of the dead didn't. We knew that there was a crematorium where the dead were incinerated, and that the ashes had been kept. We knew that each corpse was burned individually. It was pushed in at one end by a Jewish prisoner; the temperature was close to forty-five hundred degrees. Everything burned, even the bones. And at the other end stood another prisoner with an iron pole, who swept out the ashes, put them in a cardboard box, and closed it up. Next to him was someone who filled out the label: name, place of birth, date of birth, date of death."[1]

And now these children were to see those boxes, the urns of the dead of Theresienstadt, with their own eyes and feel them with their own hands — thirty thousand boxes, stacked on shelves that reached from floor to ceiling, all in strict alphabetical order.

"The moment I entered the columbarium," Horst says, "my eyes were drawn almost magnetically to the letter *H* — my grandparents were named Heller. And I walked over and in the very same moment I spotted two boxes side by side, at eye level. One read 'Gustav Heller,' the other 'Ettel Heller' — my grandpa and my grandma!"

Upon his arrival in Theresienstadt in May 1943, Horst had found his grandparents in the last stages of starvation. They had begged him for something to eat, and he had been unable to help them. A few days later they both died, on the same day, in separate hospital rooms. Their grandson had felt both shock and relief. "Because they were released now from the agony of starvation," he says. "It is one of the worst torments a human being can know." He continues:

I grabbed both boxes, took Grandpa and Grandma under my arms, and kept

By the end of the war some thirty thousand Jewish prisoners had been incinerated in the crematory that stood in the Jewish cemetery. Their ashes were kept in cardboard urns.

them there while I loaded other boxes on the wagon outside. No one said a word. None of the other children had bothered with the names.

Then the wagon started to move and I helped pull, but always with both boxes firmly under my arms. Then we came to the Eger, where we were ordered to open the boxes and empty the ashes into the river. We formed a chain and passed the urns from hand to hand. But I was standing down at the river and emptied the ashes of my grandpa and grandma into the river with my own hands. I'm glad I did. I buried them with my own hands. And I watched as the ashes from all those boxes spread out into the river, watched the river carry them away. And the Eger flows into the Elbe, and the Elbe flows into the North Sea, and the North Sea merges with all the oceans of the world. And I know that Grandpa and Grandma circle the world forever and ever. They are there. They will always be there for me. In my mind, the spot where I emptied their ashes into the river is my grandparents' cemetery.

During the late autumn of 1944 — it was already very cold — the Germans ordered some of their young prisoners to carry out another special job. Ela Stein was among them. "We were supposed to help them hunt. They gave us two sticks and chased us out into the cold water, where the animals were swimming — I think they were pheasants — and we had to drive them off. And when they flew away, the Germans shot them. It was Rahm and Haindl and a couple other SS men. I think they had visitors from Prague. We had to do this for a long time. There we stood in the ice-cold water. Some girls were very ill afterward."

Ela was lucky, because her mother, Markéta, did all she could to keep her healthy. Markéta was a thoroughly practical woman and was assigned to all kinds of work. Now and then she managed to "organize" food of one sort or another — cautiously and at great risk. Sometimes she made pickles for the SS, sometimes she plucked geese for them. And when the sheep from Lidice — they had been brought to Theresienstadt after the massacre in May 1942 — were slaughtered in the winter of 1944, she helped butcher the meat and was able to smuggle a piece of it into her room. She preserved most of it in fat. " 'We'll keep that for the day our family and friends return. They'll need it,' my mother always said. And we began to save all sorts of things for that moment."

In the winter of 1944, Eva Landa and her mother arrived in Gutau, which was then a Polish village. Auschwitz and the concentration camps at Stutthof and Dörbeck, on the Vislinskij Zaliv River near Gdansk, were behind them. Their numbers had been reduced, and the work they were forced to do — digging tank trenches ten feet wide and twelve feet deep — was much too hard. For Eva, the worst part of the war years began now, in Gutau. She remembers:

The first freeze came early that year, and it began to snow. We had no warm clothes, sometimes not even shoes. Wooden sheds were built, but we had to sleep on straw strewn over the bare ground. There was a stove in the middle of the shed, but we had nothing to heat it with. It was terribly cold. There was a brook not far from the sheds, where we could wash until it froze over. We were given no food until our work was finished — turnip soup and a piece of bread. Many of us came down with typhoid, diphtheria, and other diseases. We were plagued with lice, but had neither the strength nor the means to do anything about it. There was no light, and it got dark early.

On November 22, 1944, my mother died of hunger, total exhaustion, and lice. My mother had fought so long for her own life and mine, but could hold on no longer. She was forty-five years old — I was thirteen at the time. By then I had almost no hope that I would survive.

A week after my mother's death, we were told that those who had no shoes or who could no longer work could stay in the camp. I was barefoot and so I stayed in the camp. When the others had left the camp, the rest of us were counted. They chopped off a shock of our hair, so we wouldn't be mistaken for workers. Then we were led to the train station — or so they told us. We marched all day and all night. And I didn't have any shoes.

Suddenly we were ordered to turn around, and we had to go back the same long, weary way. I don't know how long it took, because I hadn't seen a watch in years. Those who were still in the camp were very surprised to see us return. They thought we would be murdered. But we evidently did march to the train station, except there was no longer a train station, nor were there any trains. The Red Army was very close by. We could hear the thunder of their cannons.

When I returned from this "excursion," I could no longer stand up. I couldn't support myself on my feet, which were black and festering. The camp physician wrote down my number and said that they would have to amputate my feet, that they would never heal. But there was no longer any chance of getting away from the place, since all the roads were closed because of the approaching front line.

I had wonderful friends in the camp — Gita Torbe, Eva Pollak, Resi Schwarz. They helped me so much. Without them I wouldn't have survived it all.

On January 20, 1945, we were given orders to get ready to march. This applied of course only to those who were able to walk. No one knew where they were headed. The Russians were close by. Anyone who could walk left the camp. I stayed behind, lying on the straw. And then the very worst part began.

The SS men began "inoculating us for typhoid," so they said. In reality it was phenol that they were injecting. But they did it clumsily, or didn't have enough injections. At any rate I wasn't given one, and no one died of it.

The very same evening they then ordered us to go to the camp cemetery, where trucks would be standing ready to transport the sick. I couldn't stand on my feet, so I stayed behind in the camp, lying all alone in deep straw.

Meanwhile, my comrades had marched to the cemetery where the trucks were supposed to be waiting for them. But it was a lie, of course. There were no trucks. And on the way to the cemetery the SS men shot them all. They beat some of them to death with their rifle butts to save on bullets. The blows weren't always fatal. Despite everything, a few of them managed to survive.

Meanwhile, I lay hidden in the straw. The Germans didn't find me. They were in too much of a hurry! That night, it was January 21, 1945, something incredible happened. The Germans simply ran away!

The next morning the few survivors came back to the camp. Among them were my comrade Anita Fischer and her mother. They had spent the night lying on the road unconscious and had now come back to the camp. [Anita's name now is Anita Franková, and she works at the Jewish Museum in Prague.] We had nothing to eat, and those who could still walk went into Gutau to beg for food. A lot of Poles helped them and even let them into their homes. But I only know what I was told, since I couldn't stand up, and I had to make do with what they brought me. The Lithuanian women, who had more energy, cooked potatoes on top of the stove and gave me the hot water. It tasted wonderful.

The next day a Red Army soldier, maybe twenty years old, suddenly appeared in our shed. He greeted us, but we couldn't understand him. Then came a military doctor who treated my feet, which had turned completely black. After a few days we were quartered in the house of the mayor, who presumably had fled. The war wasn't over yet. But you could feel the end was near.

Theresienstadt, December 23, 1944 (from Otto Pollak's diary)

The first Slovak-Hungarian transports have arrived. Four hundred people. Nine who had died on the way were carted away. As a Christmas present we are given three ounces of bacon, a white roll, a pound of potatoes, and a boullion cube. What might my poor child have gotten? It has been two months to the day since Helga left.

December 24, 1944

An Aryan transport with furniture and archives arrives from Hungary. Also members of the Hungarian government, or so it is said.

December 31, 1944

Nine o'clock in the morning. Meet with

blue-eyed, blond Eva Winkler, Helga's friend, who I assumed was a *mischling.* Her father is a carpenter. Evidently that's why she wasn't included in the October transports.

January 1, 1945

Driving snow this morning. I'm constantly thinking about my child. In the afternoon Helga's friends Marianne Deutsch and Anna Flachová come by with their good wishes. It hurts more than it helps, because Helga isn't here.

January 5, 1945

Frieda's thirty-fifth birthday. How is she doing, I wonder? Does she think we're still alive? In her last Red Cross letter she wrote: Take care of little Helga until I'm able to see her again. If Frieda only knew that my only child was taken from me on October 23rd and that I no longer have any way to watch over my precious girl. I'm constantly plagued by my conscience asking whether I shouldn't have left with my child after all, whether I didn't betray Frieda's last words of advice by putting Helga in the care of her counselor. The head of Helga's home advised me not to go on the transport. R. Sticker and Dr. Altenstein told me that we wouldn't be able to stay together and our only time together would be on the trip itself and that my sacrifice would be in vain. All these objections wouldn't have kept me from joining my child on her journey into the unknown if I had both legs and could have carried my own baggage. I know what moral, psychological, and material support I provided for my child in Theresienstadt.

The transport of October 23, 1944, carried 1,707 prisoners away from Theresienstadt, among them Helga Pollak, Handa Pollak and her aunt Hanička, the counselor Ella Pollak, Eva Stern, Laura Šimko, Kamilla Rosenbaum, and Greta Hofmeister.

"None of us knows how long we were in Auschwitz," Helga Pollak says as she describes her experiences.

From the moment the train came to a halt beside the ramp, most of us were in shock. Had it been three days, or maybe six? At any rate, they were days without any food, any warmth, any blankets, any mattresses. We now lay jammed together on wooden bunks, six to a bunk that was made to hold four. No one paid any attention to us, and no one spoke to me.

I walked around the barracks and

wept. A *kapo* asked me why I was crying, and I said, "I want to be with my mother." And the *kapo,* a woman, asked me where my mother was, and I replied, "In England." She was so surprised that she gave me half a head of cabbage and a packet of margarine. I shared it with the people on my bunk. We were given something to eat, but we had no dishes, no spoons and things of that sort. And so we had no way to hold our food, which was always soup.

Once, at some roll call or other, a band marched passed us. They were playing music! I thought I must be in a madhouse, I've gone completely crazy. Another time the camp elder, Edith, a Slovakian woman, came in and asked us if we were hungry, and we all said we were. Then she asked who would help fetch a bucket of soup. There were several volunteers, and four in our group went with her. Eva Stern and her sister Doris were among them. They did not came back. Four other women brought the bucket back.

Then Mengele came into our barracks, and we had to walk backward past him completely naked, with our hands raised. He selected several of us, either pregnant women or those who were too old or too thin. And then it was off to the baths again. And then we stood all day in rows of five and waited.

When it got dark, we were rushed to a train. Many transports were processed there, and I was in a panic for fear I might lose my group. We walked past tables and someone handed us bread and sausage. Once we were in the dark, we all sat down on the floor. I ate my bread and sausage right away, because I told myself that this way no one could take it away from me, which is what had happened to the food I brought with me from Theresienstadt. It even happened with a couple of chocolate drops that I hadn't eaten because I wanted to bring them to my niece Lea. But they took all my things away the moment we arrived, and then, too, I never saw Lea in Auschwitz.

Handa Pollak has never forgotten her arrival in Auschwitz, either.

After the first selection that took place immediately on arrival, we were sent to the showers and what happened there came as a horrible shock. It was as if we were in some awful nightmare. We had to undress and were shaved. The moment the women were shaved bald I no longer recognized them — they were like a band of monkeys. What I saw weren't familiar human beings. I could somehow make out familiar voices, but couldn't attach them to faces I knew. I became hysterical. No one could calm me down. I began to do strange things. We were given a jacket, but to me it seemed like trousers. I wanted to slip into the sleeves as if they were trouser legs. And when that didn't work I grew more hysterical. I'm actually a very calm and composed person. But that night . . . It's a wonder that I didn't go mad.

We were given a few pieces of clothing — a light dress, a pajama jacket, a pair of socks. But no underwear, and it was October. We were in Poland, and it was very cold. We grabbed shoes at random from a big pile, without any regard to size or whether they matched. The shoes I got were much too big. But that wasn't so bad. It was much worse if someone got shoes that were too small.

Then we were taken to our block, with its three-tiered bunk beds. But whereas we had slept two to a bunk in Theresienstadt, here it was six, all under one blanket. Anyone who wanted to roll over had to ask the others first; it would have been impossible otherwise. That's how close we lay to one another.

After a week there was another selection. We had to undress and march past an SS doctor, with our hands raised. I had no problem passing, because I was tall for my age. But as Tella walked past him, she had to stand still. It was a frightening moment. We didn't know whether she would make it. He checked her over. Tella was very thin. He hesitated. Then he let her pass.

We were taken to another camp, close to the Auschwitz train tracks. We were given underwear and a piece of bread. And then we were loaded onto trains again. They took us to Germany, to Oederan in Saxony, near Chemnitz. There we were brought to a factory. It was directly beside the tracks, which meant that trains could be easily loaded and unloaded. And there we got off.

In January 1945 the SS ordered ten wooden barracks to be built in Theresienstadt. Children were also put to work constructing them. Flaška had to break up the ground with a rake, but her gloves had so many holes that she froze terribly.

No one knew why these barracks were being built. All anyone knew was that the SS attached great importance to them, because they drove the prisoners to work at a feverish pace. Little Marta Fröhlich pushed heavy carts of loamy soil up a narrow wooden ramp, sometimes under the watchful eye of Commandant Rahm, who stood nearby, legs astraddle. "I always trembled when I saw him. One time my cart upended, and everything fell out. I was horribly afraid." But her comrades quickly came over and helped her deal with the accident, and nothing happened.

In February 1945 more mysterious construction projects, closely guarded by the SS, were begun. Sealed storerooms were to be built in the casemates of the fortress, and next to them, in a section of the ramparts, a "duck pond" was to be created. At least that's what they were told. But the engineers managing these projects soon became convinced that they were for something quite different: a deadly trap into which the SS would drive the prisoners the moment the planned liquidation of the ghetto had arrived. There was talk of gas chambers; ever since the arrival of the

Slovak-Hungarian transport on December 23, 1944, everyone in the ghetto knew what awful things had been happening elsewhere. And so the prisoners began to sabotage the construction work. But these efforts were of little consequence because of new developments, of which the prisoners were becoming increasingly aware.

Aware of their imminent defeat, the Germans were growing uneasy, and they were divided about how the remaining prisoners at Theresienstadt should be handled: Kill them all and liquidate the ghetto? Or create alibis and hide the evidence?

"One day I saw smoke somewhere and I went to find its source," Horst Cohn recalls. "And then I saw six SS men burning filed papers out in an open field. One of them turned around and saw me. And all six of them instantly pulled out their pistols and fired at me. I ran away as fast as I could, at the speed of lightning, but in a zigzag, hitting the ground again and again, like the way the rabbit gets away from the fox in the story. Then I reached a house and hid. I've always said that the Brothers Grimm saved my life."

In early February 1945 there suddenly came word that a transport with twelve hundred prisoners was to be sent to Switzerland. "Are they crazy?" Ela can clearly remember even today how outraged her mother was. "They can't believe we're going to fall for that! That a transport is actually going to Switzerland! After all that has happened! After so many people were forced to leave and not one of them has ever returned!" Ela and her mother did not volunteer for that transport.

Among those who were put on the list for this transport were Eva Winkler and her family — but not because her parents were anxious to get on it. Karl Rahm had personally added their names. Up to the last moment the Winklers doubted that this transport was really going to Switzerland and fearfully awaited their departure. "But when we saw that we were traveling on a real passenger train and not in those cattle cars," Eva says, "we gathered fresh hope that it might perhaps be true."

This time they were not disappointed. The train was bound for Switzerland and brought its passengers, among them Horst Cohn and his parents, safely over the border. Postcards that arrived in Theresienstadt a few days later confirmed the incredible news for those left behind. Was their long-awaited liberation actually close at hand?

The drone of airplanes, which could be

heard ever more frequently now, bolstered their hopes. As did the shiny silver strips, more and more of which rained down on the ghetto — they came from Allied planes dropping strips of tinfoil to avoid being picked up on German radar screens. The residents of the ghetto took notice. Two of these tinfoil strips can be found in Vera Nath's album, along with the words "Forbidden to pick these up."

When Adolf Eichmann showed up yet again in Theresienstadt on March 5, 1945, he ordered a new "beautification." The cemetery was to be tidied up and decorated with little gravestones; the prisoners' quarters were to be whitewashed, the kitchens cleaned, the coffeehouse, the stages, and the house of worship all reopened. What was the point? Did this herald the end of the war? All signs pointed in that direction.

In mid-April, Theresienstadt was treated to yet another big surprise. The Danes were told to get ready to go home. The news spread like wildfire. And on Friday, April 13, 1945, between eight and ten in the evening, several white Red Cross buses drove up, all of them fitted out luxuriously. The Swedes escorting these buses even distributed food, cigarettes, and sweets among the other prisoners and made no attempt to hide their disdain for the Nazis. Paul Rabinowitsch, the trumpeter from *Brundibár,* climbed aboard one of the buses along with his mother and stepfather, as did 412 other Danes. He couldn't believe his good fortune. "Those left behind stood there waving and weeping," he would write decades later. "They had felt somehow safe as long as the Danes were there. But what would become of them once the Danes were gone?"[2]

Those left behind did not know what their liberation would be like. But their belief that it was going to happen very soon grew stronger with every day — as did the bonds of friendships among the four remaining girls of Room 28: Ela, Flaška, Marta, and Marianne.

As she watched the Danes depart, Ela recalled a song that she most likely heard in the early days of her confinement in the ghetto, when she was still in the Hamburg Barracks. She remembers it to this day, and mentions it in commemoration whenever she gives a talk about Theresienstadt. Ilse Weber, a poet and children's book author who had been deported to Theresienstadt in 1942 and who died in Auschwitz in 1944, would sing it as she played the music on a guitar.

You and I, what friends we are
You and I, how close we are
Theresienstadt is where we met
And there shook hands
You and I what friends we are
Something we'll not forget.
You and I, what friends we are
You and I, how close we are
One day the gate will open wide
The night will pass, the sun will rise
You and I, what friends we are
Our friendship will abide.[3]

Judith Schwarzbart arrived in Auschwitz on October 28, 1944, along with her parents, Julius and Charlotte Schwarzbart, and her sister, Ester. At the first selection upon their arrival, she saw her father for the last time. A few days later, she was loaded onto a work transport together with her mother and sister and two thousand others. The trip lasted two to three days, and then they arrived at Kurzbach, a small town in southwestern Poland, north of Wroclaw. "There we had to dig trenches to stop tanks," she recalls.

These were deep ditches, and it was very cold, and all we had on were summer dresses. Somehow we managed it in

November, but then it turned so cold that the ground froze. It was terribly hard to get a shovel into it — we had already dug very deep holes. It got colder and colder. We were given some sort of coats. Most were old rags, too long for some, too short for others, and wooden slippers.

We were housed in wooden barns, a thousand women to a barn. We had only a light blanket — and it was the middle of the winter! When our shoes got wet, they stayed wet, and we had to work with wet feet. When it began to snow they sent us into the forest, where we had to drag whole trees to the trenches in order to camouflage them. I don't think they were ever used, because it was already too late. There was an SS man there, a sadist. The women knew that I was fourteen, and so they always sent me into the middle, where the work wasn't as hard. But the SS man kept calling me out and putting me up front, where it was hardest. The dragging left me with a bad back that I still have today.

I don't remember what they gave us to eat; it certainly wasn't much. I think there was no breakfast all, and a watery soup in the evening — after working ten hours in the freezing cold. One evening I slipped out into the fields and hid some corn in my blouse — I was lucky no one caught me. I was always hungry. And once as we were marching along a street four abreast, I saw a door open and someone threw us something. I picked it up — it was a piece of bread, and we shared it. You simply can't imagine what that piece of bread meant to us!

One day we suddenly heard detonations and shots nearby. We hoped the front line was getting closer and that we would soon be liberated. But we were wrong. It was mid-January 1945, and instead of sending us to work they sent us off into who knew where. It was freezing, there was snow everywhere, and we marched on foot for days. At night we were herded into barns or pigsties that had already been abandoned. We didn't get anything to eat, but in the empty sties we almost always found some potatoes or turnips intended for the pigs. We didn't care. The main thing was we had something to eat. And it was warm in the stalls. All the same, many women died on the way.

Finally we arrived in Gross-Rosen. We

were brought to the washrooms, and were given different clothes and something to eat. Then they loaded us onto cattle cars, and our journey into the unknown continued. At the train station in Weimar the train came to a halt, and bombs fell from the sky. It was dreadful. The cars were sealed, we couldn't get out, and the station was in flames. The Germans guarding us jumped from the train and took cover under the cars, while there we were in open cars watching airplanes diving at us with a hellish racket and dropping their bombs directly overhead. Horrible. You just can't imagine it. Three women in our car died.[4] I don't know if they died of shock or from bomb fragments. The corpses stayed in the car until we reached Bergen-Belsen.

If until then I had thought that nowhere could be more horrible than where I was, I was mistaken. The worst was Bergen-Belsen. No human being can imagine what Bergen-Belsen was, what it was like there! It was a starvation chamber. We got a ladleful of water once a day, with a few tiny pieces of turnip floating in it — and that was for three people, plus a slice of bread for each. In the morning, again for three people, there was a ladleful of "coffee" — some dark fluid. We sometimes fought — over a piece of turnip! Can anyone imagine that — fighting over a piece of turnip? I'm ashamed of myself now — but that's how it was. We fought over every spoonful of soup! We didn't fight because we were angry with each other, but over a turnip, over a spoonful of soup.

We lay three to a wooden bunk. People were dying all around us, dying en masse. What an awful thing to be speaking to someone who suddenly falls over dead — it's indescribable. A woman I knew, Suse Hoffmann from Brno, who was the same age as my brother, died right beside me — fell over dead. And once again, roll calls — where we stood outside for hours, no matter what the weather. All I can say is that I am here thanks to my mother and sister. I don't know how often I fainted during those roll calls. Sometimes my mother braced me up from behind, sometimes my sister, so that I wouldn't fall over and end up in sick bay. No one came back from there.

It was mid-April 1945 when the Germans fled. They didn't even leave us watery soup or a piece of bread. When the British arrived, we heard that the Germans had prepared bread for distribution, but that the camp elders had forbidden the handing out of the bread. It was handed out in one barracks — and they all died because the bread had been poisoned by the Germans, or so it was said. That's what I was told. I don't know if the story is true or not.

At any rate, for those last twenty-four hours, we didn't have any bread or any water — nothing. I wanted to drink from the well, but there were many, many people around it, because it was the only one. There were fights and brawls, and you couldn't possibly get through. It was only later that I learned that many people came down with typhoid as a result of drinking the water.

We left the camp in April, and we ate the buds off the trees. I told my sister, "Come here, eat it. It's wonderful. It tastes like almonds." Bergen-Belsen was a horrible camp. I don't know whether enough is known about it. The only thing people know is what was filmed, the footage that the British made. Those truckloads of corpses with dangling arms and legs — that was Bergen-Belsen.

■ ■ ■ ■

On April 16, 1945 — in the presence of leading representatives of the Hungarian Jewish Relief and Rescue Committee (Va'ad Ezra V'hatzolah) and a negotiator named Reszo (Rudolf) Kastner[5] — Eichmann's henchmen Hermann Krumey and Otto Hunsche delivered to camp commandant Karl Rahm orders from Himmler to surrender Theresienstadt without a fight. Rahm, Kastner reports, was thoroughly surprised. His comment upon hearing Himmler's orders was, "I no longer understand this world."[6]

The German front lines had fallen apart, the camps in the East were liberated, one after the other; the great retreat had begun — prisoners, soldiers, SS, refugees of every sort streamed toward the West. But the Allies had not yet reached Theresienstadt, and despite Himmler's orders, the SS saw no reason to give up their control of the camp. And so they were still there when the first prisoners from the death camps in the East reached Theresienstadt.

"Dear God, what is happening here; I can't even describe it," Eva Ginz, Hanka's friend from Prague, wrote in her diary on

April 23. "One afternoon [Friday, April 20] I was at work, when we saw a freight train passing. People stuck their heads out of the windows. They looked simply awful. Pale, completely yellow and green in the face, unshaven, like skeletons, sunken cheeks, their heads shaved, in prisoners' clothes . . . and their eyes were glittering so strangely . . . from hunger. I immediately ran into the ghetto (we were working outside) to the station. They were just getting out of the trucks, if you could call what they did getting out. Only a few managed to keep on their feet (their legs were just shanks covered with skin); the rest were lying completely exhausted on the floor of the trucks. They had been on the road for a fortnight and had been given almost nothing to eat. They were coming from Buchenwald and from Auschwitz. . . . Then one transport after the other began to arrive. Hungarians, French, Slovaks, Poles (they had been in concentration camps for seven years) and some Czechs as well."[7]

"One very cold day in April 1945," Eva Herrmann recalls, "thousands of people arrived. Many of them were wearing wooden slippers. When so many people in wooden shoes are moving along slowly it makes a dreadful noise, a kind of monotone clacking sound. We heard it at times during the night. And so we got up and followed the noise and watched and waited until the people arrived. We could see that there were all kinds of people from everywhere. They looked awful."

"We heard shots in the distance," Flaška remembers. "We thought the army would be moving in. But it was the poorest of the poor who arrived, specters. It was horrible — many of them simply fell down on the street and lay there. They were emaciated, sick, starved, just rags on their bodies."

"In April 1945, people from the death marches began coming back," says Ela. "At first it was just men. But then one day a transport with women arrived, and we asked them where they had come from, and they didn't know themselves! From then on I always stood and watched when people came back. They always passed by where we were working. They could barely walk! They just dragged themselves along, they looked so horrible, like skeletons — completely starved, exhausted."

"I was standing on the street beside Kursawe when the first prisoners from the concentration camps came back," recalls Willy Groag. "They were in an inhuman condition, just skin and bones, their heads shaved. I was horrified; we were all horrified. And I can still see how terrified Kursawe looked. It really was incomprehensible. We couldn't believe that these were our friends, our closest friends."

"The town's heart stood still," Alice Ehrmann noted in her diary on April 20, 1945. "And now they're here. Stinking, vermin-ridden cattle cars, with stinking, vermin-ridden people in them, half alive, half dead, or corpses. They were pressed to the windows, horrible faces, bones and eyes. What had kept us trembling in fear, for months, was coming directly toward us."[8]

"When new people arrived," Marianne Deutsch recalls, "my father, who worked in the Central Registry, had to enter people's names in the files. And so he went out to these people and had a kettle of soup brought out to them. They fell on it like madmen. And my father said, 'They must be from an insane asylum,' and sent for doctors. The doctors determined that they were normal people, but that they had been through horrible things."

It was not just that these people had survived the death camps. Shortly before the Allies reached the camps, the SS had driven them westward, in the direction of concentration camps at Gross-Rosen,

Ravensbrück, Sachsenhausen, Buchenwald, Bergen-Belsen, Dachau, and Mauthausen. But those camps were by then terribly overcrowded and the roads could not handle such a huge stream of refugees. The SS didn't know what to do with their prisoners, so they would ruthlessly shoot and kill those who could not keep moving or who had caught their eye for whatever reason. Finally they started directing some of these "death marches" toward Theresienstadt.

On April 22, 1945, Benjamin Murmelstein, who still held the post of chief elder, let it be known that Paul Dunant, a delegate of the International Red Cross, had been present at a meeting of the Council of Elders. He had formally announced that the Theresienstadt camp could count on help from the Red Cross and that he was commissioned to establish and maintain a direct and permanent connection with that institution. "This is in fact the expected takeover by the Red Cross, even though the Germans are still here," Erich Kessler wrote in his diary that day.[9] The hour of liberation was now palpably near.

But there was still one last ordeal to face at Theresienstadt. The SS was still running the camp. Even though they were getting ready to pick up and leave, carting away everything that could be carted away, and even though their ranks were gradually diminishing, the hard core — Hans Günther, Karl Rahm, Rudolph Haindl, Ernst Möhs — was still there. Using whatever authority they still exercised, they blocked any help being offered to those returning and prevented emergency measures from being taken, such as inoculations to stop typhoid and other epidemics from spreading to the rest of the population. It was impossible to isolate the sick from the healthy. Medicines were in short supply, there were too few nurses, and there was not enough food for the approximately thirteen thousand thoroughly exhausted people who had been arriving since April. Many of them died shortly before liberation became a reality.

Hanka Wertheimer and her mother had been transported to Hamburg in July 1944 with a working brigade. Along the way several cars were uncoupled and shunted in a different direction. Miriam Rosenzweig and the counselor Eva Weiss were in one of them, and they were sent to Christianstadt, a secondary camp at Gross-Rosen not far from Wroclaw. Hanka, however, ended up in Hamburg. The city had been badly ravaged by bombs, and the women were put to work clearing rubble and rebuilding.

Hanka recalls:

We were given a special uniform, beige overalls and a pastel blue headscarf. And that's how we marched through the streets. We were always five abreast and sometimes sang songs like "After Every December Comes the Month of May."

Of course the residents of Hamburg had to be given some explanation about who we were, and so they were told we were convicts and came from a prison. That's how we were presented — as criminals, as murderers and thieves. That's what was printed in the newspaper, too.

We built streets in a new settlement in Hamburg-Neugraben. Sometimes we scavenged for food in garbage cans and made soup of it — we had a place to cook. When people saw us looking for scraps in their garbage, they sometimes put out something edible for us, wrapping it in newspaper and laying it next to the garbage cans, and then we'd find maybe a potato, or an onion, or a piece of bread. Then we'd cook our soup. Those were the best soups!

We had a guard from the Wehrmacht. He was very fat and, in comparison to the others, very nice. We even called him Papa.[10] I remember a Frau Schmidt as well. She had read in the paper that we were criminals. And my mother, who spoke very good German, told her, "Do you believe everything in the paper is true? Do you believe that my thirteen-year-old daughter killed somebody or committed some other awful crime?"

The "Wehrmacht Papa," who guarded us all by himself, let us speak with people a little, and so gradually we came into contact with the local population. A lot of us could speak German. Gradually people realized that we weren't criminals. And many of those who had had their homes bombed and had very little left themselves were really quite nice to us.

I think we were in three different places in Hamburg — in Veddel, in Neugraben, and in Tiefstack, which were all camps attached to Neuengamme. For a while we worked in an oil factory. I remember that we got a very good soup every day at noon. The soup was so good because there were other workers in the bombed-out factories we were there to repair — Germans, French, Italians, all prisoners of war. Good soup was sent to these factories, and we were given some of it. It tasted wonderful. . . .

We were always closely guarded, of course. One day, the SS men found a letter one of us was trying to smuggle out. It had been written by a Hana. All the Hanas had to step forward. My mother was terribly frightened for my sake and told me, "You stay here, because your real name is Hanneliese." They found the Hana they wanted. They shaved her head and sent her to Auschwitz.

Winter came on, and it turned very cold. We didn't have any stockings and wore wooden shoes that let the snow in. Many of us got sick. And our overalls were all that we had. I don't even know if we ever washed them. I only know that there were frequent air-raid alarms. The British dropped bombs, the Americans dropped bombs, and large sections of Hamburg lay in ruin and ashes.

I was always happy when there was an air-raid alert — because I thought that every bomb brought the end of the war just that much closer. We often fled to an aboveground bunker. These buildings weren't really meant for us prisoners. But the Germans who guarded us couldn't leave us by ourselves. So they took us along. And we were always put on the top, the eighth floor, where it was most dangerous, of course. The Germans were right below us, so that we couldn't run away.

I liked going to the bunker. I could finally get some real sleep. I was always very, very tired — I remember that. We usually had to get up very early to go to work. And we came back late in the evening. I got far too little sleep. But if there were bombs, I could get some real sleep. It's strange — I was probably too tired to be afraid. And too young. I told myself, "I haven't committed any crime; why should anything happen to me?" What I really wanted to do was stay in my bunk and sleep. But sometimes my mother would make me join her in the basement, where we were better protected. Nothing ever happened to us, although sometimes bombs fell very close. . . . Then in April 1945, we were taken to Bergen-Belsen. . . . It's really not that far away. But it took us seven days by train, because so many trains were going to Bergen-Belsen. Hundreds of cars, thousands of prisoners from every point on the compass. . . .

"In late April there were suddenly hundreds of people returning to Theresienstadt," Ela says, describing all this as if it had happened yesterday. "I was on the lookout for familiar faces. Suddenly I recognized my friend Helga, and I called out, 'Helga! Helga!' I flung off my wooden shoes, which were much too big for me, and ran to her father and shouted, 'Helga is here! Helga is here!' I bellowed it like a madwoman and ran back so that I wouldn't lose sight of Helga and could greet her before she had to be put under quarantine, because they were all ill. And so I found my Helga again."

"I heard Ela shouting," Helga recalls. "She couldn't get to us because we were separated from everyone else right away and led to the West Barracks. While we were standing there waiting to see what would happen next, a distant relative suddenly came up and brought me a bag of something to eat that my father had sent — my father couldn't walk very fast and so had sent his cousin. No sooner had we reached in for a bite than the bag was gone. Some Polish and Slovak women standing next to us simply ripped it from our hands."

It was the end of April when Helga, Handa, and Tella arrived in Theresienstadt. Placed in the West Barracks, where the children of Bialystok had once been housed, they were handed something to eat, treated by doctors, and given beds. "When these poor devils were brought into the hospital ward and saw beds with white sheets, pillows, and blankets, they began to weep," Erich Kessler noted in his diary. "They were undressed and washed. Their backs were covered with a layer of dirt as thick as your finger. Then they were given a soup that been specially prepared so as not to overtax their stomachs."

When Helga had regained her energy somewhat, she asked for a piece of paper and a pencil and wrote these lines to her father:

Theresienstadt, April 1945

My beloved Papa,

I still can't believe that I am here with you. I'm so incredibly happy that I can't even express it. That I can be a normal human being again is a feeling you can't imagine. The concentration camp is behind me now. And the only good thing about that is that I shall now treasure everything in my life. Papa, you can't imagine what a feeling it is to be clean, with your own clean clothes on your body. Without a white cross on your back. To have your own bed, a blanket, a pillow, and to have peace and quiet and not have to be so terribly hungry. I always used to believe that a person needed to be rich, too. Now I see just how little a person actually needs. When I wake up in the morning and roll over and can stay in bed until nine o'clock, I am so grateful that I don't have to get up at four-thirty, that no one is shouting at me, that I won't be punished by having to stand for two hours of roll call the way I had to in Oederan. I don't have to stand in wet snow anymore — three to four hours long. And we were grateful just to have a coat and a sweater, and shoes and socks, although the socks were much too short and shoes too small. In Auschwitz we didn't even have that. All we had were wooden slippers that were falling apart, and filthy clothes that were too small for me. I want so much for this quarantine to be over soon. I'm so afraid we'll come down with something here yet. Please, Papa, come to see me; we can talk over the fence if you have them send for me. Daddy, my dearest. I want to be with you so much! Try to get me out of here.

Please bring me my tattered washcloth and soap. The man from Kyjov, Markus, or whatever his name is, is living in the Sokolovna. Please go to him and come with him to the fence. Our window is right across from a bench. There are too many people up front, and we wouldn't have any privacy there, and they won't let you in the back part of the building here. But because he lives here, they'll let you get closer with him along. And bring some paper for me to write on and fight for me to be moved.

Papa, please send word whether the coat I brought with me can be repaired. If only it were just a little shorter. And bring clothes from Frau Bader — maybe Frau Bader will have a blouse for me or some underwear. I don't even have a knife here; I forgot to bring it and left it with you. And Papa, see to it that I get out of here. A hundred million kisses, and a big hug,

Your one and only Helga

The counselor Eva Weiss had been taken from Auschwitz to a forced labor camp at Christianstadt, where she worked for several months in a munitions factory. Life became a little easier for her. Although there was always a severe shortage of food, her life was no longer in danger. Things changed, however, at the end of January, when gunfire was first heard in the distance. On February 2, 1945, she was forced to join one of the death marches.

Eva recalls:

It was cold, the ground was covered with snow, and we dragged ourselves along. We weren't the only people on the road. We saw all sorts of vehicles along the way, Germans and Poles who were traveling in the same direction we were. The Russians were evidently closing in at great speed, causing panic and confusion. It looked as if it might be possible to flee, but if escape was to be possible it had to be planned down to the smallest detail. Since I didn't have the courage to run away all by myself, I wanted to talk a friend into joining me, someone who looked a little like me, not too Jewish — and that was Ruth Iltis.

We had one whole day and night to plan our escape down to the last detail. We decided to pass ourselves off as sisters of German-Polish descent, just simple girls. We invented names — Annie and Gertrud Hinze. The next day, when we got the chance, we disappeared behind some firs in a little patch of woods, hoping no one would notice. Shots were fired in our direction, but they didn't hit us. And after that, they didn't follow us. And so we found ourselves in unknown terrain on a cold day in February.

Eva and Ruth, now called Annie and Gertrud Hinze, first made their way to a farm, and from there they were sent to the "employment office" in the town of Weisswasser. People bought their story. They were given documents and an address where they could work as cleaning ladies. When they got to the place, they were in for a big shock.

We stared at the sign over the door: HITLER YOUTH HOME. What should we do? It was getting darker and colder and we were getting hungrier and hungrier. We rang the bell. The door opened, and we were received by a motherly woman. She gave us a room, just for us two. We were also given a key and could lock the door. We were told we would be put to work cleaning up the kitchen the next day, doing the least pleasant tasks.

The Youth Home was full of young boys in uniform, with flags, swastikas, and similar items everywhere. We pretended to be very simple girls, a little dumb and uneducated. The boys especially liked Ruth, now Annie, who was very pretty, but we kept our distance and kept to ourselves. There was always the great danger that they might find out who we really were. A few days later someone said we needed to have a medical checkup, and we were terribly afraid that our tattooed numbers would be discovered. What should we do? We tried cutting them out, but that wasn't as easy as we thought, and our only choice was to burn them off. We had a stove with a fire. And while Adolf Hitler looked on — his picture was on the wall — we each laid a hot ember on our numbers. It crackled and burned and hurt, but we were doing it to save our lives. Afterward I went to the nurse and said that I had burned myself, and she gave me some salve and a bandage, which I then shared with Ruth. She couldn't possibly show up with the same injury without arousing suspicion.

A few weeks later, we were summoned to SS headquarters and assumed that our charade was all over. But we were well treated as cleaning ladies, and eventually sent to a village near the Czech border, where we remained until early May.

Meanwhile, we had our roles down pat, and our relationship to the boys training for the front lines had become friendlier. We were even promoted to cooks, and to our great joy we now had enough to eat.

As the Russians got closer the Germans started to panic and ran away from the Russians and toward the advancing Americans — "from Ivan to the Amis," as they said. We joined them in hopes of soon reaching the Czech border. When we saw a road sign with the word "Liberec," we simply vanished in that direction. It was May 3, 1945. Ruth knew the name of an acquaintance of her father's in Liberec, and we knocked on the door. We were welcomed and treated with genuine Czech hospitality. Then we started out for Prague.

On our way there we experienced what for us was the only air raid of the entire war — a small German plane at low altitude swept wildly back and forth across the area, but kept coming back heading directly for us, and we had to take cover in a ditch. When the scare was over, we were covered in mud. We first had to clean up and so went to the nearest inn, where friendly people helped us. The people there started asking us questions, and we told them about our experiences. But when we told them about Auschwitz we could sense they didn't believe us.

The next day someone saw to it that we didn't have to continue on foot, but could ride to Prague. We sat on the trunk of a car that was decorated with lots of flowers and Czech flags. Some people tossed more flowers to us. To this day I don't know who organized the trip. I only know: The hour of liberation had come.

In late April 1945, after a separation that had lasted half a year, Helga and her father were reunited at the very same wooden fence that had sealed the Theresienstadt ghetto off from the outside world for three and a half years and that was now supposed to keep the healthy from the sick. "Helga's father was so happy," Handa says, describing this reunion. "He wanted to give Helga the best that he had, and that was a little jar of butter. Helga hid it in her blouse, but we couldn't resist. We knew that we shouldn't eat the butter right away. But we each took a teaspoonful and then another — without bread, about two ounces for each of us. And had terrible diarrhea as a result. We were lucky that it was no worse than that."

Their girlfriends were happy as well, and they also wanted to make sure the returnees had food, especially some of the good soup that Ela's mother had kept in reserve for just this moment. But after learning how dangerous fat was, they managed to get some sugar for the time being. Handa and Helga were so emaciated and weak that their friends had to do something to coddle them.

"Shortly after my return," Handa recalls, "a woman suddenly came running toward me with a cry of joy. It was Jitka, my governess from Olbramovice. She had been deported to Theresienstadt toward the end of the war. She began to weep, and I asked her, 'Why are you crying? I'm here, and I'm alive.' 'But you used to have such pudgy little hands,' she replied, 'and look at them. They're just skin and bones.' "

On April 29 word spread through the ghetto that the SS would have to leave the town within forty-eight hours. So now they would finally have to prepare for their departure, those gentlemen of the SS: Rahm, Haindl, Bergel, Möhs, and the rest of the pack. "Dunant is here, he's in the Council of Elders, without any Germans," Alice Ehrmann wrote on April 30. And one day later: "Capitulation — Churchill presenting it to the House of Commons . . . ? The excitement is getting unbearable. I just want to sob or die. Things just can't get more intense; they have to come to a breaking point."

"On May 2 the black SS flags and the swastikas were raised at half-mast over the Little Fortress. And we all knew on the spot what that meant," Erich Kessler noted. "We also received confirmation that Hitler had put an end to his cursed life."[11]

On May 3, 1945, the International Red Cross, under the direction of Paul Dunant, took Theresienstadt and the Little Fortress under its protection. "The SS finally has to make its exit," wrote Erich Kessler. "The news is that Goebbels has been found dead. Rumor has it that peace is already here. Those who come from Prague are to return home within four days."[12]

These were days for holding your breath. The end was in sight and yet all were surrounded by death. "We were told to be careful, to keep the windows closed, and not show ourselves at the windows," says Handa, who was quartered with Tella in what had previously been Room 1 in L 417. "There were still SS men and snipers who were firing at random."

Handa could watch the exciting events on Market Square from her room, and she had a good view of the main road through town. Even so, it was difficult to understand what was going on there. There were throngs of people everywhere — prisoners, German soldiers, Czech policemen. A great deal of traffic was moving in all directions — trucks packed full of hundreds of black boxes, people from Prague and other towns coming to fetch their relatives, the vehicles of the Wehrmacht driving through town on the way to Prague.

"On May 4 I was awakened very early by a strange noise," Handa recalls very clearly. "It was as if a huge swarm of bees was flying this way — *buzzzz.* I didn't know what it was. I risked looking out the window. I didn't see anything. But the noise got louder and louder. Finally I saw Russian tanks with a lot of people riding on them. They were former Theresienstadt prisoners on their way back to the ghetto, who had run into the Russians on the road. They were shouting to their friends and weeping at the same time."

The Russian troops drove on toward Prague as well. And there were still scattered Wehrmacht units moving through Theresienstadt, with shots fired now and then.

"On May 5, 1945, which was my sister's birthday," Ela says, describing the day, "there was a great shout as the Czech police entered town under the old Czech flag. They drove through the streets. There was jubilation everywhere. We really celebrated."

Bearing the flag of Czechoslovakia and singing a potpourri of national anthems, people stormed the commandant's headquarters, and Rahm and Haindl fled. The Czech police took command of the town.

But in the barracks there was still hunger and death, and in Prague there was still fighting going on. Endless columns of tanks continued to roll through Theresienstadt, the sounds of rifles and machine guns were still being heard, transports of prisoners were still arriving, and SS men were still trying to escape.

On May 6 Otto Pollak wrote to his daughter, who was still under quarantine:

My one and only child,

I received the sweet lines you wrote from the West Barracks and was saddened at first to know that you will be leaving me again. I didn't sleep much last night either, because there was so much to think about and I didn't have my little sparrow beside me.

After much consideration, I've come to the decision to let you depart along with your friends who shared your fate in Oederan. I do this because I assume your transport will be under the protection of the Red Cross and that Switzerland will be the place chosen for your recuperation. I have nothing so beautiful to offer you for the next few years, my sweet darling, and I hope that you will enjoy the love and care of the Swiss in full measure. Do all you can to get out of quarantine, because I have so many things I want to talk over with you and want us to be able to say goodbye before you leave.

If you can't come to me, Frau Sander and I will pack your suitcase for you. And I have a little handbag with toilet articles and some food for the trip to give you as well. I brought your diary out into the light of day today. It is in good shape. So for now, my little child, I send you lots and lots of kisses and remain,

Your Daddy

On the evening of May 7, almost the entire population of Theresienstadt gathered in the main square in order to finally hear the news with their own ears: Germany had surrendered unconditionally. The surrender documents had been signed the night before in Reims, France, by Colonel-General Alfred Jodl. This time there was no jubilation. The war was over, but there could not be any real talk of peace as yet. The very next day, the population was warned to exercise the utmost caution.

On May 8 the thunder of cannons could still be heard almost the entire day. But then the tension faded. Standing at an attic window in the Dresden Barracks, Vera Nath looked down at the streets below: "It was already late evening," she recalls. "Around nine o'clock. Suddenly we saw a woman with a red flag, and we ran downstairs. The barricades to the ghetto had been opened. The Red Army was entering. They were all just children, fifteen-, sixteen-, and seventeen-year-old boys. We cheered them; what else could we do? We stood outside for hours and watched. Everyone sang the 'Internationale' — in German, Czech, Polish, Hungarian, all blended together."

! ! GENERAL WARNING ! !

In view of the hostilities occurring in close proximity to Theresienstadt, the following directives are to take effect immediately:

1) The streets are to be used only for official business. And in no case are the ramparts and walls or roads leading around town to be used, beginning at the Litoměřice Gate, Bodenbach Barracks, Dresden Barracks as far as the Sluice Mill, plus all roads leading to Bauschowitz–Litoměřice and all roads leading around the Fortress; moreover, everyone should avoid the vicinity of these roads.
2) It is forbidden to loiter near windows and doors or in the courtyards of houses and buildings! At the sound of gunfire, people should take cover against the wall nearest to the windows to avoid being hit by gunfire penetrating windows or doors.
3) Until further notice, children are to

stay indoors!

4) If artillery fire should be heard, everyone should immediately take cover in the cellars of residences and larger buildings. Supervisors and directors in all buildings are to make sure that the entrances to cellars are kept open for immediate entry at all times. In such event, at least two men are to stand guard at the cellar entrance.

5) No open fires whatever are permitted until further notice!

6) If gunfire is heard, all streets and public areas are to be evacuated at once and cover taken in houses or beside walls.

Už od rána bylo slyšet dělové rány

Theresienstadt, 8. Mai 1945

!! W A R N U N G A N A L L E !!

Mit Rücksicht auf die gegenwärtigen Kriegereignisse in der allernächsten Nähe von Theresienstadt werden mit sofortiger Wirksamkeit folgende Anordnungen getroffen:

1) Das Betreten der Strassen darf nur aus dienstlichen Gründen erfolgen! Keinesfalls dürfen die Schanzen und Wälle sowie die Umgehungsstrassen, beginnend vom Leitmeritzer Tor, Bodenbacher Kaserne, Dresdner Ka - serne bis zur Schleusenmühle, weiters die Strassen in der Richtung Bauschowitz – Leitmeritz, sowie alle We- ge, die um die Festung führen, betreten werden, bezw. ist auch die Nähe dieser Verkehrswege zu vermeiden.

2) Der Aufenthalt bei und in der Nähe der Fenster und Türen sowie auf den Höfen der Häuser und Gebäude ist verboten! Sobald Schüsse hörbar sind, ist neben den Fenstern an der Mauer derart Schutz zu suchen, dass der Schutzsuchende durch Geschosse, die durch das Fenster oder durch die Tür eindringen, nicht getrof- fen werden kann.

3) Kinder haben bis auf Weiteres die Häuser nicht zu verlassen!

4) Im Falle dass Artilleriegeschützfeuer hörbar wird , sind unverzüglich die Keller der Wohnhäuser bezw . Gebäude aufzusuchen. Die Hausverwalter bezw. Gebäu- deleiter haben dafür Sorge zu tragen, dass die Kel- ler jederzeit unverzüglich geöffnet werden können . Vor jedem Eingang der Keller sind in diesem Falle mindestens 2 Männer als Wache aufzustellen.

5) Das Anzünden von offenen Feuern hat bis auf weiteres unbedingt zu unterbleiben!

6) Im Falle dass Schüsse hörbar werden, sind sämtliche Strassen und öffentlichen Plätze sofort zu räumen und Deckung in den Häusern bezw. hinter Mauern zu suchen.

Dr. Fo Eaeck, Dr.Alfred Meissner, Dr.Heinrich Klang,Dr.Eduard Meyers.

vždy blíž a blíž — až večer v 9 h jel první ruský tank kolem Terezínské ohrady

May 8, 1945, General Warning

Epilogue

EVA WEISS and her friend Ruth Iltis were among the first survivors of German concentration camps to experience the end of the war in Prague. There they anxiously awaited their relatives and friends. "But only a few returned," recalls Eva. "And all of them had a sad tale to tell. Everyone knew of many others who would never return. It was a time of highs and of very deep lows."

Since no one from her immediate family in Brno was still alive, Eva remained in Prague. There she met her future husband, a Czech who had emigrated to England and had marched into Prague with the British army's Czech Brigade. When he returned to London a year later, Eva could not accompany him because she had no valid papers. Not until three years later did she manage to acquire a joint passport, which was issued to an Aliyah group and allowed her to travel to Israel, where the couple was

Eva Weiss Gross

reunited. They were married in Kibbutz Givat Chaim Ichud. After a few months they moved to England, where she began a new life.

Eva lived in London for many years and now resides near Winchester in the south of England.

HANKA (CHANA) WERTHEIMER only barely survived the hell of Bergen-Belsen. Fourteen thousand people died there in just the first five days after liberation, which had occurred on April 15, 1945, and another

Hanka Wertheimer Weingarten

fourteen thousand perished in the weeks that followed, among them Hanka's mother, Lily Wertheimer, who succumbed to typhus on May 16, 1945.

Hanka remained in a hospital in Celle, Germany, until July 1945, and was then moved to a hospital in Plzeň. With her strength for the most part restored, she traveled on to Prague. "I went directly to Žitná 38," Hanka remembers. "Our Mařka was still living in the same little bachelor flat. She broke down in tears when she saw me. If she had met me on the street, she said, she wouldn't have recognized me. I weighed only seventy-seven pounds, and was ill and deeply unhappy."

Hanka had lost almost her entire family apart from her sister, who had been able to make it to Palestine in time, as did her mother's brother. Of her father's eleven siblings, only two brothers had been able to save themselves by emigrating to South America.

Mařka gave back to Hanka the apartment that Hanka's mother had once rented in Mařka's name. It was not far from Wenceslas Square and soon became a regular meeting place for Hanka's friends: Handa Pollak, Ela Stein, Eva Seger, Stepan Krulis, Yehuda Huppert (Polda), and Jirka Brady, the brother of little Hana, who had perished in Auschwitz.[1]

In the first years after liberation it seemed unimaginable to Hanka and her friends that they could ever be friends with people who had not been through what they had. They could not picture marrying anyone who was not one of them. Images of the camps stayed alive in their minds for a long time. "It was such a strong force inside us," Hanka says. "While we were in the camps, when we closed our eyes we saw bread. After the war, when we closed our eyes, we saw the concentration camp."

Hanka and her friends often walked along the Old City Ring, past the Tyn Church, to the Old Town Hall with its astronomical clock, always keeping an eye out for some familiar soul who might suddenly emerge from the crowd. She thought about her friend Polda, but she could not bring herself to start a search — for fear that she would receive bad news. Then one day Polda crossed her path, and Hanka was happy to see him again and to know he was alive.

Hanka's time in Prague after liberation proved short. Handa Pollak and she had just enrolled in school when Hanka was diagnosed with tuberculosis. She was placed in a sanatorium that was run by Zionists in Davos, Switzerland, where the beds were intended solely for members of the Zionist organization Hechalutz. She remained there for more than two years, during which time she attended middle school. In 1948 she returned to Prague.

In the meantime, her friends had moved off in various directions. Jirka went to America and Stepan to Australia; Ela, Handa, Eva, and Polda immigrated to Palestine. In 1949 Hanka also found her way at last to the place she had so long yearned for — Israel.

In Kibbutz Hachotrim Hanka met her future husband, with whom she spent many interesting years in places as varied as the United States, Bulgaria, Singapore, India, and Italy. She has three sons and now lives with her husband in Tel Aviv.

JUDITH SCHWARZBART and her sister, Ester, also escaped the "death mills" of Bergen-Belsen (to use the title of director Billy Wilder's 1945 documentary). Like Hanka, they lost their mother shortly after liberation. Charlotte Schwarzbart died in a

Judith Schwarzbart Rosenzweig

hospital in Celle, Germany, on May 5, 1945.

In mid-July 1945 Judith and her sister returned to their Moravian homeland. Their brother, Gideon, was waiting for them in their parents' house in Brno-Jundrov. He had found the house uninhabited and stripped of its furniture, apart from some things he discovered smashed and shattered in the courtyard. Except for a Passover plate and an old clock, which neighbors gave back to them, there was nothing left of their parents' possessions.

The three siblings — Ester, nineteen; Gideon, seventeen; and Judith, fifteen — were on their own. Their parents and other relatives had perished. They were receiving just enough government money to get by. They attended school, but the cold winter of 1945–46 was a terrible one. "We did our homework," Judith recalls. "My sister was studying for her graduation exams, and I can still see how a glass of water, which was always at her side and which we always kept wrapped in a cloth, turned to ice — that's how cold it was. There was no wood or coal. I would have emigrated right then if I could have. But my brother and sister held me back until I was eighteen. I finished high school, moved to Hachsharah [a program/community that prepared people for immigration to Israel], and then on to Palestine in 1948."

At six o'clock in the morning on May 15, 1948, Judith arrived in the harbor of Jaffa, on one of the first three ships to dock in the newly founded state of Israel. They were greeted by rounds of gunfire coming from Arab planes that swept over the harbor. That was the beginning of her new life.

When one of Judith's aunts who had immigrated to Palestine before the war asked her what had actually happened to her, Judith began to relate her experiences. But no sooner had she started than she was interrupted by these words from her aunt: "Oh, don't start exaggerating. It can't have been that bad." And so for decades Judith said nothing about those times. She became a pediatric nurse and married in 1951. She has three children and makes her home in Haifa.

EVA WINKLER experienced the end of the war with her parents and her brother Jiři in Switzerland. In July 1945 they returned to their home, first to Miroslav and then to Brno. They, too, waited in vain for the return of other family members. "It was a terrible time," she says. "The war was over, and we then learned what had happened —

Eva Winkler Sohar

that my grandparents, almost all of my aunts and uncles and their children, and many of my friends had not survived the Holocaust."

Over the next few years Eva attended school in Miroslav and Brno and graduated from a technical high school. She never really felt at home again in Czechoslovakia. "There were many Czechs who had collaborated with the Germans. Anti-Semitism lived on. I had a teacher who made things unpleasant for me because he couldn't bear the fact that I, as a Jew, was the best in the class. I also often had a feeling I was being followed, that someone was walking behind me."

In 1949 she and her brother immigrated to Israel. Her parents had hoped to follow them. But then came Communist rule, the Iron Curtain, and the borders were closed. Not until the death of Eva's father in 1968 did her mother move to Israel with her youngest son, Pavel.

Eva spent several years in Kibbutz Hachotrim, the same kibbutz where Hanka and Handa lived. She married, had two children, and now lives with her husband in Haifa.

At her first opportunity, MARTA FRÖHLICH traveled with her brothers and sisters to Pisek, where her mother still lived. "She was wearing a lovely pink dress when we arrived," Marta recalls. "She was crazy with happiness! She kissed us and danced with us."

But no sooner had her father returned from Theresienstadt than he started making trouble and was again abusive to his wife and children. Only after Jenda, who was now eighteen years old, returned home in September 1945 and resolutely stood up to his father did these violent episodes become less frequent. But there was no changing their father. All four of Marta's siblings im-

Marta Fröhlich Mikul

migrated to Israel in the late 1940s. Marta alone remained behind with her mother, whom she loved dearly. Marta married, has three children, and now lives in Cheb.

VERA NATH, along with other children from Theresienstadt, including Flaška, arrived in Štiřin, Lojovice, on June 6, 1945. The Christian humanist Přemysl Pitter had turned an old castle there into a sanatorium for children.[2] After a few weeks, Vera returned with her parents and sister to Prague, where they searched in vain for other rela-

Vera Nath Kreiner

tives who might be alive. The trail for most of them ended in Auschwitz and Lodz. Only two cousins had been able to immigrate to Palestine in time. Her mother's older brother, Eugen Kolb, a well-known Zionist from Budapest, had been aboard the Kastner Transport to Switzerland in late 1944 and later made his way to Israel.[3]

On October 28, 1948, Vera left for Israel, and was followed by her parents a few months later. She married, has two children, and now lives with her husband in Ramat Gan.

Ela Stein Weissberger

ELA STEIN lived for a while with her aunt in Kolín, and then joined her mother and sister in Prague. Only a few members of her large extended family survived the Holocaust — sixty-two of them were among its victims, including her uncle Otto Altenstein.

"After the war I was terribly afraid that I could not be like other children," Ela remembers, "that they would all point at me and say, 'Look, she was in a concentration camp.' But I wanted more than anything to go to school again. I wanted to learn. Even today I still tell children, 'Don't tell me you don't like school.' For me the most wonderful thing was to attend school again, to sit on a school bench and listen to the teacher without fear."

In 1949 Ela was able to fulfill her long-standing wish to immigrate to Israel. There she served in the army for two years, married in 1953, and moved with her husband to the United States in 1958. She has two children and lives in New York State. In recent years, performances of *Brundibár* have brought her all across the United States, where she is an honored guest as an eyewitness to history. She has made it her mission to keep alive the memory of her friends from Theresienstadt.

MARIANNE DEUTSCH was happy beyond belief finally to rejoin Memme, her governess. She lived in Olomouc with her parents and Memme for several years, attending a commercial high school and then pursuing her profession. She married in 1954 and moved to Ostrava with her husband. But before the Soviet Union and its allies could march into Prague in August 1968, bringing the Prague Spring to an abrupt end, she and her husband decided to leave their home and take their ten-year-old son, Peter, with them. "We didn't want to make the same mistake our parents had, who didn't take 'little corporal Hitler' seriously," she says. "We didn't want our children to grow up with their spirits broken. So we left everything behind, apart from two suitcases, and fled to what was then West Germany, by way of Austria." There Marianne and her family built a new life for themselves.

MIRIAM ROSENZWEIG was liberated from Bergen-Belsen in 1945. Seriously ill with typhoid, she was hospitalized for a few weeks and then taken to Sweden, where she spent a year in a hospital recovering from tuberculosis. She then returned to Prague

Miriam Rosenzweig Jung

and immigrated to Israel in 1948. She also lived at Kibbutz Hachotrim for a while and, later, in Haifa. She married, and in 1959 moved with her husband and two sons to California, where a third son was born. She lives, as she says, a pleasant life in Orange County. "I don't concern myself with the past much," she says. "But now that the youngest of us are growing old, like many others I feel that our past should not be forgotten. We kept silent for many years. But now the time has come to speak about our experiences during the war, before it is too late."

EVA ECKSTEIN lost her mother and her two sisters, Hana and Herta, in Auschwitz. She was transported from Auschwitz to Freiburg, near Dresden, where she was put to work in the airplane industry. After the deadly air raid on Dresden in February 1945, the prisoners were loaded onto open cattle cars and transported in the direction of Czechoslovakia. After a week's journey with almost nothing to eat, they arrived somewhere near Plzeň, where the train halted for a long time. Over the objections of the SS, local women forced their way over to the prisoners, demanded that the cattle-car doors be opened, and brought soup to

Eva Eckstein Vit

the starving women. The journey continued and finally came to an end at the Austrian concentration camp of Mauthausen, which was already under the protection of the Red Cross and was liberated by the Americans on May 4.

Eva returned alone to her hometown of Louny, where she found nothing as it had been. The grocery store and the house that her parents had owned ended up in the hands of collaborators. In 1946 her fiancé, Hermann, reappeared, and they were married a year later. Eva lived in Louny with him and their two children through all the difficulties of the Communist regime. In 1968, while Soviet tanks were putting an end to the reforms of the Prague Spring, she and her husband seized the opportunity to leave the country on a tourist visa to Sweden. Sweden became their new homeland, and Eva still lives there today.

EVA STERN lost nearly her entire family in the Holocaust. She and her sister Doris eventually immigrated to Israel, where she now lives. An abyss lies between her current life and the years between 1939 and 1945, about which she prefers not to speak.

EVA LANDA's odyssey did not come to an end with the war's end on May 8, 1945. Leaving Gutau, the Polish village where she was liberated by the Red Army in January 1945, she was first taken, still half frozen, to a military hospital in Eylau, in what had been German East Prussia. In April 1945 the hospital was closed, and she was sent farther to the east, eventually ending up in Sysran, an old Russian town on the Volga, not far from Kujbyšev, which is now called Samara.

On that journey, Eva met a man who would change her life: Dr. Mer, the head of

Eva Landa, now Evelina Mer

the train's medical staff and a major in the Soviet army. He took a great interest in his patients, especially in Eva, whom he immediately took to his heart. Dr. Mer, himself a Jew, had lost his parents to the Nazis and lived with his wife in Leningrad. They had no children.

He decided to adopt Eva. "He suggested it to me at once," Eva recalls. "But I didn't want any part of it. I wanted to return to Prague. He told me I had no home in Prague, that I would be put in an orphanage. We were en route for almost three weeks, and Dr. Mer managed to persuade me. I thought that somehow I would be able to return to Prague after the war."

On April 23 they arrived in Sysran, where Eva spent several more weeks in the hospital. Because Dr. Mer's military ambulance train had farther to go, he asked the head doctor at the hospital, Leonid Ostrower — who was both a doctor and a writer — to see to it that Eva would be left where she was if the patients should be transferred elsewhere. A few weeks later, the patients were indeed moved to a civilian hospital, but Eva was left behind alone, among strangers whose language she did not understand.

By May 8 Eva's feet had healed — they did not have to be amputated. For the first time in a long time, she went to the movies.

Eva remained in Sysran until the end of August, when a telegram arrived from Dr. Mer, informing her that he himself could not come for her, but that he had arranged for her trip to Leningrad. And so Eva undertook another arduous journey, this time in the direction of Leningrad, where she finally arrived on August 31, 1945. "It was early in the morning on a rainy day," she recalls. "There was no one there to meet me. My telegram had never arrived. But I did have an address — Dostoyevsky Street 36. And there I would spend the next eleven years of my life."

Cut off from her homeland and roots, Eva began her new life in distant Leningrad (now St. Petersburg) with an entirely new identity — as the daughter of Dr. Mer and his wife. She had no success in trying to learn about the fate of her immediate family, her relatives, or her friends. The letters she wrote to the Red Cross went unanswered.

For Eva's adoptive parents, any talk about her past was taboo. She was to act as if her childhood — the years before 1945 — had never happened. The fact Eva was a Jew, a survivor of the concentration camps Theresienstadt and Auschwitz, was a stigma that had to be concealed in the anti-Semitic Soviet Union. Just to speak of it was dangerous, and Eva was warned never to do so. When she returned to school in 1947, she told no one of her past. Nor did she say a word about it when a relative of Dr. Mer talked about her own experiences in Bergen-Belsen. And how did Eva live with this?

"That's the sort of question to which I have no answer. I don't know. I wrote to my friends Marta and Anita, but I never received an answer. I had no idea where they were. I lost all contact. And so I simply accepted what had happened, and what was still happening, as facts. Maybe I even actively participated in this game. I was young. I was back in school. I wanted to make up for all that I had missed. I wanted to get a good education; I always wanted that. I learned a great deal, and was rewarded for my efforts. In 1950 I finished school with honors for the best essay — in Russian! I was proud of that. I had new friends. I never spoke about the past."

In 1953 Eva married a Russian-Jewish architect. She received her doctorate in German studies and became a university lecturer. In 1960 she finally succeeded in obtaining a visa for a trip to Czechoslovakia. The decisive factor for her had been a book she came across, *The Death Factory: Documents on Auschwitz,* by Ota Kraus and Erich Kulka. She wrote the authors a letter, which they arranged to have published in various Czech newspapers, and to which friends and one distant relative in Prague responded. She then received the invitation that enabled her to take a journey into her past. She traveled there alone in 1960, leaving her husband and four-year-old daughter at home.

Once in Prague, Eva was confronted with

the shocking news that she had long ago been declared dead, and that the assets of her parents and grandparents — including real estate of considerable value — had been inherited by a distant cousin of her father.

In 1990 her son, Viktor Nimark, a painter and architect, moved to Germany. Her daughter remained in Russia with her family. Since then Eva, whose husband died in 1985, has been making three cities her home: St. Petersburg, Prague, and Frankfurt.

Handa Pollak Drori

HANDA POLLAK had been taken from
Auschwitz to Oederan in Saxony, together
with Tella and Helga Pollak, and she remained there as a worker in a munitions
factory until mid-April 1945. The company,
Agricola Refrigeration Machinery, Inc., was
an extension of the Flossenbürg concentration camp. As the war's front lines moved
closer, the workers were supposed to be
taken to another camp. But one camp after
another was being liberated, and roads and
railways were in a state of chaos. They were
shunted from place to place in open cattle

cars for weeks on end, until they finally wound up in Theresienstadt.

Handa and Tella returned to Prague on May 12. There they waited in vain for Karel Pollak; they had no better luck with inquiries sent to Olbramovice. Still hoping for his return, Handa spent a few weeks in Olbramovice with a family that had once been friends with her father.

Handa will always remember with profound horror the moment when she finally learned of her father's fate. It was in the loft of a barn where Handa was hiding from the Russians together with the daughter of the family with whom she was living. Tella had been in Olbramovice the day before. She had wanted to tell Handa about her father, but couldn't bring herself to do it and had told the family instead, which is how the daughter learned of it. It was from this girl that Handa had to learn the awful news. "Your father's kicked the bucket," the girl hissed. "And if you cry, I'll slap you like you've never been slapped before."

Karel Pollak had died in a secondary camp attached to Dachau on March 9, 1945, "of despair," as a man who was with him to the end later reported. "After his bout with typhoid," Handa says, "my father, my robust father, had become a specter. He was so weakened that he believed that if he was in such a state, there was no chance that we were still alive. He lost all hope and didn't know for whom he should go on living."

Of the thirty-one members of her immediate family who had been deported by the Nazis, Handa was the only one to survive. Tella wanted to rebuild her own life in Prague as a piano teacher, and she saw to it that Handa returned to high school and learned to play the piano. Handa's uncle, Karel Ančerl, was looking after her, too. But Handa did not feel that anything was keeping her in Prague. She was drawn increasingly to Hanka Wertheimer's circle of friends, many of whom wanted to immigrate to Palestine. "I was not very much of a Zionist, but I wanted a new beginning," she says.

In February 1949 Handa immigrated to Israel as part of a Youth Aliyah group. Tella followed her not long after. Handa found a new home at Kibbutz Hachotrim, where she and her husband still live today.

After she was released from quarantine, HELGA POLLAK was not sure whether she should go to a sanatorium in Switzerland. Then came a surprise — a cousin from Ky-

Helga Pollak Kinsky

jov arrived on a Russian truck, and from that moment on she was certain that she would greatly prefer to go home with her father. "Besides which," she says, "I had found a louse on my pillow, and I said to myself, 'I'm not staying one day longer. I have survived all this, and I'm not going to die of typhus. I'm leaving.' The train to Brno was already there. And the three of us took it to Brno, and from there to Kyjov." Soon they were faced with a terrible fact: Sixty-three members of Otto Pollak's family would never return — not Aunt Marta or Uncle Fritz, not her cousin Joši or little Lea.

In 1946 Helga's greatest wish was fulfilled: She joined her mother in London. There she graduated from high school and attended college. In 1951 she married an emigrant from Rössl in former East Prussia, who had escaped the Nazis by moving to Bangkok and building a new life there. Helga first moved to Bangkok with him, then to Addis Ababa. This retreat to the Far East satisfied a very basic need. "For a long time after liberation, I didn't want to speak German. Or even think of building a house or buying one. For years I wanted to be prepared to leave Vienna at the drop of a hat."

Gradually her life began to take a more normal course. In 1957 Helga, her husband, and their two children returned to Vienna. They wanted to provide the finest possible education for their daughter, who had been born deaf, and Vienna offered the best educational opportunities for her. Another reason for their return was that Helga wanted to be near her beloved father, who lived in Vienna until he passed away in 1978.

Two documentary films by the American filmmaker Zuzana Justman include segments on Helga's story: *Terezin Diary* (1989) and *Voices of the Children* (1997).

Ever since the first staged reading of *Helga's Diary: A Girl of Room 28,* in Freiburg, Germany, in 2002, Helga Pollak has frequently accompanied me on the traveling exhibition "The Girls of Room 28, L 410, Theresienstadt," to performances of the children's opera *Brundibár,* and to other related events, where she offers her personal eye-witness account and reads from her diary. In May 2005 Helga was a guest of the Theodor Heuss Gymnasium in Freiburg for the premiere of the play *Ghetto Tears 1944: The Girls of Room 28,* directed by Elmar Wittmann. The model for the main character is the diarist Helga Pollak.

ANNA FLACH ("Flaška") was fortunate in that her parents and siblings survived the Holocaust. But she never again saw most of her relatives.

A new life began for Flaška in Brno. She devoted herself to music and became a pianist, singer, and professor of song and piano at the Brno Conservatory and the Janáček Academy. In 1955 she married the oboist Vitešlav Hanuš; each has shared in the other's brilliant musical career. They have been guest performers together at countless concerts both at home and abroad

Anna Hanusová-Flachová

— in Beijing from 1959 to 1961, in Beirut from 1966 to 1969, and in Sydney in 1968 and 1969.

Their son, Tomáš Hanuš, who was born in 1970, is an internationally renowned conductor. He founded the New Czech Chamber Orchestra and is permanent conductor of both the Prague Chamber Orchestra and the Slovak Philharmonic Orchestra in Bratislava. In 2007 he was appointed music director of the National Theatre Brno.

Anna, who remains devoted to promoting music, belongs to the Dvořák Society in

Brno while continuing her work as an educator. She is deeply committed to preserving the memory of Theresienstadt composers, especially Pavel Haas, who was born in Brno. Her unflagging efforts have resulted in many musical events. Over the last few years she has often served on the jury of the annual Verfemte Musik (banned music) instrumental and vocal competitions in Schwerin, Germany, which are sponsored by the Jeunesses Musicales of Mecklenburg-Vorpommern and the Schwerin Conservatory.

Anna also serves on the board of the Theresienstadt Initiative in Prague.

Since the touring exhibition "The Girls of Room 28, L 410, Theresienstadt" first opened in Schwerin, Germany, on September 23, 2004, with the assistance of the Stiftung Erinnerung, Verantwortung, und Zukunft (the Foundation for Remembrance, Responsibility, and Future) and the Verfemte Musik festival, Anna has frequently been invited to appear as a witness to history. In the course of the many events and activities connected with this project, Anna and the other girls have not only shared their experiences, especially with the younger generation, but experienced wonderful moments together and made friends in many parts of Germany, the Czech Republic, and Austria. One particular highlight was the opening of the exhibition at the Deutsche Bundestag in conjunction with National Holocaust Memorial Day in January 2008; eight of the girls from Room 28 were invited to Berlin to participate.

What Anna has said about her motivation for involvement applies equally to all the girls: "I see it as my duty to speak about our experiences in the Holocaust, all the more in view of the growing chorus of voices denying, ignoring, or belittling it. I do not want those years to be forgotten or denied."

ACKNOWLEDGMENTS

My God, my God
May these things never cease:
The sand and the sea
The rushing of the waters
The lightning in the heavens
The prayer of man

— Hannah Senesh

More than ten years have passed since I first met the Girls of Room 28 and we began to hatch the plan of writing a book to commemorate the murdered children of Theresienstadt and the adults who lovingly and selflessly devoted themselves to the well-being of all the children there. I was also intent on relating the background and tragic story behind the first performances of the children's opera *Brundibár,* which is how my own interest in this project began.

I would like to thank Frank Harders-Wuthenow, the music publisher who in

1994 first brought to my attention Hans Krása's children's opera and steered me toward a course on which I have remained ever since. Never has a project mesmerized me as this one has. Today I know why: It offered challenges, experiences, encounters, and friendships that have enriched my life and expanded my horizons.

I would never have been equal to these challenges had a series of individuals not stepped forward time and again to support the project. In 1999 Thomas Rietschel, then secretary-general of the Jeunesses Musicales Deutschland (JMD), got hold of my book proposal and decided to invite the Girls of Room 28 and me to Weikersheim, where the JMD is based, so we could work on the book together. In 1996 Rietschel had launched an educational *Brundibár* project and thus played an essential part in making this children's opera known throughout the world.

An invitation ensued to Schwerin, where the director of the Jeunesses Musicales Mecklenburg-Vorpommern, Volker Ahmels, had started an international competition for young musicians called Verfemte Musik (Forbidden Music). From the very beginning, the Girls of Room 28 project was part of the cultural and historical program accompanying this competition. It was in Schwerin that the exhibition "The Girls of Room 28, L 410, Theresienstadt" first opened on September 23, 2004. Since then, it has made its way throughout Germany and Austria. Thanks to an American donor, Dr. Alfred Bader, there is now a Czech version as well, organized by the Jewish Museum in Prague/Brno.

On October 3, 2002, there was a staged reading in Schwerin from the then-unpublished manuscript of the book. To our happy surprise, a guest at the reading, Barbara Zeisl-Schönberg, professor emerita of German at Pomona College and the daughter of the Viennese composer Ernst Zeisl, who had emigrated to the United States, spontaneously offered to translate the manuscript into English — and did so because, as she told us, she wanted to help us bring the book to the United States. Many thanks, dear Barbara, for your selfless, wonderful dedication!

I am also deeply indebted to Susan Cernyak-Spatz, survivor of Auschwitz and associate professor emerita at the University of North Carolina, Charlotte. She translated portions of an early draft of the manuscript into English, and thus buoyed the hopes of the Girls of Room 28 that this book might someday appear in English.

Trevor Glover went to great lengths to help us achieve this goal. Aware of the compelling nature and significance of the children's opera *Brundibár,* he embarked from his home in London on a fervent search for an English-language publisher at a very early stage of the project. Unfortunately, he was not able to place the book at that time. Still, his belief in it was not in vain — it helped me move the project ahead. I am deeply sorry that I can thank him only in my thoughts. Trevor died on September 12, 2007.

This trip down memory lane leads me right back to when the American journalist and author Peter Wyden was an integral part of my life. I owe so much to him, and it pains me to have to express my thanks to him posthumously as well. I began working with him in 1984 in Berlin, compiling information and conducting countless interviews, most of them for two of his books: *Wall: The Inside Story of Divided Berlin* and *Stella: One Woman's True Tale of Evil, Betrayal, and Survival in Hitler's Germany.* I learned what it meant to work with source material, to carry out meticulous research, and to stick to the facts — and just how much tenacity, stamina, and creativity are required to tackle a big subject and to put a book out. It saddens me to realize that my good friend and mentor will not be there when this book comes out in America.

In Germany I was told that I had little cause for hope that this book would ever be published in the United States. But here it is, thanks to Sebastian Ritscher at the literary agency Mohrbooks in Zurich, to my devoted American literary agent, Alison Bond, and to my wonderful editor at Schocken Books, Altie Karper. Thank you so much! You have made me and the Girls of Room 28 very happy. And although it took several years for the book to find a home with an American publisher, the dream has become a reality, a result of the dedication on the part of these editors and agents, and of Shelley Frisch, an outstanding translator who rendered the text in her native English and whose great care, attention to detail, and exquisite sensitivity to the story and the people involved gave it an authentic tone. Many thanks, dear Shelley! The girls no longer have to await the outcome with baited breath — they can now revel in the finished product.

I can still hear their eager questions: When will the book be finished? Who will publish it? We're not getting any younger, Hannelore! Our conversations kept circling around a single question: When? It was certainly a long and difficult process to turn an idea into a full-fledged book. I try not to recall every twist and turn in this arduous route — just the positive outcome. And it was worth every bit of the effort! I really got to know the Girls of Room 28. No matter how impatient they grew, no matter what doubts gnawed at them, no matter what difficulties they faced, they always stuck by me unconditionally. We grew to be a strong group. This has been the finest part of this project. And so to the girls I say: Thank you. Thank you for your wonderful cooperation. Thank you above all for your unshakable confidence, without which I could never have written this book!

I would be remiss if I failed to mention another mundane but essential source of assistance — the financial support I have received for this book. I have lost count of how many publishers and potential sponsors I contacted, how many grant applications I submitted in the course of this project. I only know that now and then good fortune came our way, and at each happy financial juncture the project leaped ahead. I therefore offer my heartfelt thanks to the Maria Strecker-Daelen Foundation, the

Foreign Office of Germany, the German-Czech Fund for the Future, the Robert Bosch Foundation, and the Walther Seinsch Memorial Fund.

That I was finally able to devote myself to writing the manuscript for ten uninterrupted months was made possible by a generous grant from the commissioner for the Office of Government Affairs for Culture and Media in Germany, and the advocacy of ministry secretary Dr. Matthias Buth, supported by Dr. Hanna Nogossek, now at the German History Museum in Berlin (DHM). I am very grateful for this help from the German government, which allowed me to complete the decisive last step.

My cordial thanks go to the staffs of various archives, especially to the Jewish Museum in Prague and to Alisah Schiller and Anita Tarsi of the Archive Beit Theresienstadt in Givat Chaim Ichud, Israel. Sadly, my thanks to Anita Frank and Alisah Shek come too late for these lovely women to read them in print.

I also mourn the death of people whom I interviewed and who became very precious to me: Willy Groag (1914–2001), who conveyed such a vivid picture of his experiences in Prague and Theresienstadt and of life in the Girls' Home; the violinist Paul Kling (1928–2005), who became a steadfast friend from the time we first met in 1996 in New York, and whose love for music and nobility of spirit became a source of inspiration; and Thomas Mandl (1929–2007), who impressed me with his outstanding memory and his philosophical and kind nature. The death in 2007 of Paul Aron Sandfort (aka Paul Rabinowitsch), the trumpeter in *Brundibár* and a close friend, greatly saddened us all.

I also want to thank pianist Edith Kraus in Jerusalem and Alice Sommer in London, whose one-hundredth birthday on November 26, 2003, I will never forget. Nor will I forget the moment when Anna Hanuš thanked her for the lifelong inspiration she has received from Alice's music, particularly her concert of Chopin études in Theresienstadt. This precious moment was caught on film for a documentary about the Girls of Room 28, directed by Bill Treharne Jones and edited by Paul A. Bellinger, both of London. I trust that this film, large parts of which were shot in Spindlermühle, Prague, Theresienstadt, and London, will eventually find the support it needs to be completed and shown. Thank you, Paul and Bill, for your unwavering faith and for your commitment.

I was unfortunately unable to include all the stories I heard, but everyone who shared their experiences with me made an essential contribution to the project as a whole. I would like to thank Eva Herrmann, Dagmar Liebl, Greta (Hofmeister) Klingsberg, Ruth Brössler, Zdenka Fantl, Margit Silberfeld, Zvi (Horst) Cohn, Leopold Lowy, and George Brady.

Special thanks go to Helga Hosk-Weiss, who once lived next door to the Girls of Room 28. It was in 1996, in her apartment in Prague and at the invitation of Ela Weissberger, that I first met several of these women. Helga Hosk-Weiss is a wonderful painter. As a child she drew what she saw in the ghetto, which is why the touring exhibiton is called "Draw What You See." Her paintings can be seen throughout the world. I was pleased to read in a German review of my book: "The [children's] drawings in particular, of which those by twelve-year-old Helga Weiss of Room 24 in the same Home have become the best known, can now be viewed against the horrific backdrop of daily life in the ghetto from the perspective of an unbiased child."

A complete list of everyone who is inextricably linked with this book project needs to include a tribute to two individuals who accompanied us from beginning to end, and whose presence at the annual meetings in Spindlermühle was key to our success: Micky Kreiner and Abraham Weingarten, the husbands of Vera and Hanka. Their devotion and amiability, and their joy in spending time with us and in working on our project, helped spur us on to achieve our goal. Thanks, dear Micky! Thanks, dear Abraham!

I owe a debt of gratitude to historian Vojtěch Blodig of the Theresienstadt Memorial, who responded to all my inquiries and offered valuable insights. He also checked the historical accuracy of the manuscript. Thank you, Dr. Blodig, for your invaluable assistance!

Last but not least, I would like to thank all the people who accompanied me on the long road I have traveled, and who always offered their kind support when I needed it, in particular Tilman Kannegiesser and, again, Frank Harders-Wuthenow, both of the musical agency Boosey & Hawkes in Berlin, as well as my dear friend Eva Wuthenow. And I cannot fail to mention still others who helped breathe life into this book: Nicolette Richter, who was the first to volunteer to proofread the manuscript long before there was the prospect of a publisher; Annette Anton, my enormously capable German literary agent; and Klaus Fricke and Jürgen Bolz, my editors at Droemer Verlag and Aufbau Verlag, which published a new German edition in 2008.

This English-language translation was greatly enhanced by two people. My heartfelt thanks go to Ernest Seinfeld of Connecticut, a survivor of Theresienstadt and Auschwitz, who offered valuable suggestions. I am equally grateful to Gabriel Fawcett, a young British historian, translator, and historical tour guide who is based in Berlin. I only wish I had meet him earlier. Gabriel assisted me in proofreading the English translation and displayed an extraordinary feel for language and knowledge of history. The book has benefited from Gabriel's advice on how the girls' story fits into the larger context of the Holocaust and World War II.

A very personal thank-you goes to my daughter, Hester, who is now seventeen years old. Since the age of four, she has lived with the melodies of *Brundibár* and with a mother who has always been busy doing research, making phone calls, traveling, and writing a book. It certainly hasn't been easy for her. But whenever I found my spirits flagging, she came through miraculously, urging me on by saying, "Mom, you can do it." How could I have disappointed her? Thank you, sweetheart.

NOTES

* Hannah Senesh was born in Budapest in 1921. A Zionist, she arrived in Palestine in September 1938. She joined the active resistance to the Nazis and participated in a parachute drop over Yugoslavia on March 13, 1944. The goal of her squadron was to liberate Allied pilots whose planes had been shot down over enemy territory. When Hannah crossed the border into Hungary she was captured by the Germans and sent to a prison in Budapest, where she was executed on November 4, 1944. In Israel, Hannah Senesh is regarded as a national heroine.

ONE: SPINDLERMÜHLE, CZECH REPUBLIC, AUTUMN 2000

1. The Bielefeld production was the first postwar production of *Brundibár* on a major stage. The translation of the text by

Frank Harders-Wuthenow and Michael Harre is now the authorized version, published by Boosey & Hawkes/Bote & Bock Music Publishers, and the basis for more recent productions of the opera. It is an unusual success story that owes a great deal to the Jeunesses Musicales Deutschland (JMD) and especially to the commitment of its former general secretary, Thomas Rietschel. In 1996 the JMD initiated the pedagogical *Brundibár* Project, which had an enormous impact throughout the world. It must also be noted, however, that even before there was a score or piano reduction or a text of *Brundibár*, Veronika Grüters, a nun and music teacher at the St. Ursula Gymnasium in Freiburg, worked with a group of students and went to great lengths to stage the opera in July 1985. In May 1986 this same ensemble toured Israel, giving four performances of *Brundibár*. Veronika Grüters had discovered the opera by way of the film of *Brundibár — die Kinderoper von Theresienstadt* [*Brundibár — the Children's Opera of Theresienstadt*], Cineropa-Film (Munich, 1955), directed by Walter Krüttner.

2. The feature is now available on a CD produced by Austrian Radio (ORF): Edi-

tion Abseits, EDA 015-2, together with a second CD of the opera *Brundibár* in co-production with Southwest German Radio (SWR), in a 1997 production directed by Friedemann Keck.

3. Fredy Hirsch's speech on the one-year anniversary of the Boys' Home L 417, mid-1943. Typescript, Jewish Museum in Prague, Terezín Collection, Inv. No. 304/1.

4. Ibid.

5. Livia Rothkirchen, "Der geistige Widerstand in Theresienstadt" ["Intellectual Resistance in Theresienstadt"], in *Theresienstädter Studien und Dokumente 1997*, ed. Miroslav Kárný, Raimund Kemper, and Margita Kárná (Prague: Edition Theresienstädter Initiative Academia, 1997), pp. 118–40.

6. "Musik in Theresienstadt" ["Music in Theresienstadt"], in *Theresienstadt*, ed. Rudolf Iltis, František Ehrmann, and Ota Heitlinger, trans. Walter Hacker (Vienna: Europa Verlag, 1968), pp. 260–63.

TWO: SAYING GOODBYE

1. Kyjov is the Czech name of this town, Gaya the German name. These double names come from the period of the Austro-Hungarian Empire, during which

many cities bore both a German and a Czech name. Each cultural community used the variant appropriate to it. During the period of German occupation, German names were in official use. After 1945, these place-names reverted to their Czech version. In this translation Czech names have been used throughout, except when official German documents are quoted or when German names, especially those of concentration camps, are the more common usage in the English-speaking world.

2. "Sudetenland" was the term used by the German population for those parts of Bohemia and Moravian-Silesia that had been settled by Germans. It does not represent any historical, geographical, or cultural entity as such. The name is derived from the Sudeten Mountains, part of the Iser mountain range. The term "Sudeten Germans" first gained political currency with the increasing strength of the Sudetendeutsche Party, and then began to replace the competing term "German Bohemians."

3. Hans Safrian, *Eichmann und seine Gehilfen* [*Eichmann and His Helpers*] (Frankfurt: S. Fischer, 1995), p. 115.

4. *Deutsche Politik im "Protektorat Böhmen*

und *Mähren" unter Reinhard Heydrich 1941–1942,* ed. Miroslav Kárný, Jaroslava Milotová, and Margita Kárná (Berlin: Metropol, 1997), pp. 137ff.

5. Ibid., p. 150.

6. Jochen Von Lang, *Das Eichmann-Protokoll. Tonbandaufzeichnungen der israelischen Verhöre* (Munich: Ullstein, 2001), pp. 93–94.

THREE: DAILY LIFE IN THE CAMP

1. Miroslav Kárný, "Jakob Edelsteins letzte Briefe" ["Jakob Edelstein's Last Letters"], in *Theresienstädter Studien und Dokumente 1997,* pp. 216–29.

2. Tomáš Garrigue Masaryk (1850–1937), philosopher, president of the Czech Republic, 1918–35.

3. "Berichte zum ersten Jahrestag der Theresienstädter Heime in L 417" ["Reports on the First Anniversary of the Theresienstadt Homes in L 417"], in *Theresienstädter Studien und Dokumente 1998,* ed. Miroslav Kárný, Raimund Kemper, and Margita Kárná (Prague: Edition Theresienstädter Initiative Academia, 1998), p. 150.

4. Ibid.

5. From the testimony of Zeev Shek before

the Commission for the Concentration Camp of Terezin, June 29, 1945, in Kurt Jiri Kotouc et al., *We Are Children Just the Same:* Vedem, *the Secret Magazine by the Boys of Terezin,* trans. R. Elizabeth Novak (Philadelphia: Jewish Publication Society, 1995).

6. Ibid.

7. Typescript of the "Report on the First Anniversary of the Theresienstadt Homes in L 417," by Dr. Rudolf Klein, Jewish Museum in Prague, Terezin Collection, Inv. No. 304/1.

8. "Theresienstädter Kindertagebücher, Helga Kinsky, Helga Weissová-Hošková, Charlotte Verešová," in Iltis, Ehrmann, and Heitlinger, eds., *Theresienstadt,* pp. 114–24.

9. Typescript of a submission to an essay contest held on the anniversary of the Girls' Home L 410, October 18, 1943. The young author's initials are R.G.; Memorial and Archive Beit Terezin, Givat Chaim Ichud, Israel.

10. "Theresienstadter Kindertagebücher." Taken from the diary of fourteen-year-old Šary Weinstein of Prague (she later went by the name Charlotte Verešová). She lived in another room of the Girls' Home.

11. In addition to this adaptation and stag-

ing of the Esther story, there was a more elaborate production for adults directed by Norbert Fried, with music by Karel Reiner.

12. "Kurt Singer: Musikkritischer Brief Nr. 4, Verdi's *Requiem*" ["Kurt Singer: A Music Critic's Letter No. 4, Verdi's *Requiem*"], in Ulrike Migdal, ed., *Und die Musik spielt dazu. Chansons und Satiren aus dem KZ Theresienstadt* (Munich: Piper, 1990), pp. 169ff.

13. As we learn from Kurt Singer's report, Tella (Ella Pollak) usually accompanied these productions. He writes: "Presumably Schächter would have speeded up the tempo of the *Dies Irae* if he had had an orchestra instead of a piano (placed in an inconvenient spot, but played excellently by Miss Pollak)."

14. Rosa Engländerová, "Unsere Aufgabe, unser Weg" ["Our Task, Our Path"], in *Theresienstädter Studien und Dokumente 1998*, pp. 169–71.

15. Egon (Gonda) Redlich, "Die dreifache Aufgabe der Jugendfürsorge" ["The Threefold Task of Youth Welfare"], in *Theresienstädter Studien und Dokumente 1998*, pp. 154–56.

16. See Kotouc et al., *We Are Children Just*

the Same.

17. Typescript of a submission to an essay contest held on the anniversary of the Girls' Home L 410, October 18, 1943. Memorial and Archive Beit Terezin, Givat Chaim Ichud, Israel.

18. William L. Shirer, *The Rise and Fall of the Third Reich* (New York: Simon & Schuster, 1960), p. 939.

19. Willy Groag in a conversation with the author in Israel, 1999. Willy Groag died on October 10, 2001.

20. Von Lang, *Das Eichmann-Protokoll,* pp. 221–22.

21. Ruth Bondy, "Es gab einen Kameraden. Die Kinderzeitung *Kamerád* im Ghetto Theresienstadt" ["There Once Was a Comrade. The Children's Periodical *Kamerád* in Theresienstadt Ghetto"], in *Theresienstädter Studien und Dokumente 1997,* pp. 248–61.

22. Web site of the House of the Wannsee Conference, Memorial Center: www.ghwk .de/deut/ausstellung2006.htm.

23. Gerhart M. Riegner, "Die Beziehung des Roten Kreuzes zu Theresienstadt in der Endphase des Krieges ["The Relationship Between the Red Cross and Theresienstadt in the Final Phase of the War"], in *Theresienstädter Studien und Do-*

kumente 1996, ed. Miroslav Kárný, Raimund Kemper, and Margita Kárná (Prague: Edition Theresienstädter Initiative Academia, 1996), pp. 19–30.

24. As Bernd Biege reports in his book *Helfer unter Hitler. Das Rote Kreuz im Dritten Reich* [*Helpers Under Hitler: The Red Cross and the Third Reich*] (Reinbek: Kinder Verlag, 2000), Ernst Robert Grawitz, chief medical officer of the SS, confidant of Heinrich Himmler, and active as well as passive participant in criminal experiments conducted on human beings, was executive president of the German Red Cross from 1937 to 1945. He wrote the rules by which selections were made in concentration camps. Thus, it was Grawitz who ordered the immediate death of 70–80 percent of the Jews arriving at these camps — above all the ill, the frail, the aged, and small children.

25. *Theresienstädter Studien und Dokumente 1994,* ed. Miroslav Kárný, Raimund Kemper, and Margita Kárná (Prague: Edition Theresienstädter Initiative Academia, 1994), document section, unpaginated.

26. The *Patria* never arrived at its destination. Since the British had refused entry into the harbor, the ship exploded just off the Israeli coast. There were many casual-

ties. Flaška's sister survived and swam ashore, but the events surrounding her arrival remained a lifelong trauma.

27. Sokol (Czech for "falcon") was a Czech athletic club founded in 1862 as part of the Czech nationalist movement. After the occupation, it was closed to Jews, and in 1941 the entire organization was declared illegal and dissolved.

FOUR: ISLAND IN A RAGING SEA

1. Rudolf Franěk, "*Brundibár,* der Brummbär" ["*Brundibár,* the Grumbler"], in Iltis, Ehrmann, and Heitlinger, eds., *Theresienstadt,* pp. 272–78. After the war, Rudolf Freudenfeld changed his name to Rudolf Franěk.

2. Honza Holub played the ice-cream vendor. Unfortunately, the casting information is incomplete.

3. Kotouc et al., *We Are Children Just the Same,* pp. 154–55.

4. According to Vojtěch Blodig, historian for the Theresienstadt Memorial, within thirty-six hours 6,422 people from the Sudeten Barracks and the Bodenbach Barracks were resettled. The vacated rooms were used as a depository for the secret files of the Reich Security Main Office.

This institution was given the name Berlin Branch Office and was separate from the rest of the camp.

5. Manfred Grieger, "Anton Burger — ein österreichischer Dienstmann" ["Anton Burger — an Austrian Henchman"], in *Theresienstädter Studien und Dokumente 1995,* ed. Miroslav Kárný, Raimund Kemper, and Margita Kárná (Prague: Edition Theresienstädter Initiative Academia, 1995), pp. 241–48.

6. Karel Berman, "Erinnerungen von Karel Berman" ["Recollections of Karel Berman"], in Iltis, Ehrmann, and Heitlinger, eds., *Theresienstadt,* pp. 254–58.

7. "Theresienstädter Kindertagebücher," pp. 114–24.

8. On the night of August 15, 1943, the SS began liquidating the ghetto of Bialystok, a city in northeast Poland with a high percentage of Jewish inhabitants. (In 1913, 48,000 of the 61,500 residents were Jewish.) From the start of the German occupation on June 27, 1941, to August 1943, approximately 20,000 Jews had already been shot dead or deported and murdered in the death camps. The remaining 30,000 Jews in the Bialystok ghetto were murdered on the spot between August 16 and August 20, 1943, in the

course of a futile attempt at resistance, or brought to Auschwitz, Treblinka, Majdanek, or labor camps at Ponoatowa and Blizyn, where they met their deaths. Twelve hundred children, accompanied by 25 adults, were brought to Theresienstadt on a train. The adults were immediately sent on to Auschwitz. On October 5, 1943, the children, plus 35 escorts, left Theresienstadt on Transport Dn/a for the same destination. Immediately upon arrival, both the children and their escorts were murdered in the gas chambers.

9. Ruth Bondy, "Chronik der sich schliessenden Tore" ["Chronicle of the Closing Gates"], which quotes the *Jüdisches Nachrichtenblatt* [*Jewish Newspaper*] of March 22, 1940, in *Theresienstädter Studien und Dokumente 2000,* ed. Miroslav Kárný, Raimund Kemper, and Margita Kárná (Prague: Edition Theresienstädter Initiative Academia, 2000), pp. 86–106.

FIVE: LIGHT IN THE DARKNESS: *BRUNDIBAR*

1. Adolf Hoffmeister in the film *Brundibár — die Kinderoper von Theresienstadt* (Munich, 1966). Produced by Cineropa Film; directed by Walter Krüttner.

2. "Berichte zum ersten Jahrestag der Theresienstädter Heime in L 417": Hans Krása, "*Brundibár,*" in *Theresienstädter Studien und Dokumente 1998,* pp. 178–80.

3. Franěk, "*Brundibár,* der Brummbär," pp. 254–58.

4. Typescript of a lecture by Professor Israel Kestenberg, 1943. Original in the Jewish Museum in Prague, Terezin Collection, Inv. No. 304/1.

5. "Berichte zum ersten Jahrestag der Theresienstädter Heime in L 417": Friederike Brandeis, "Kinderzeichnen" ["Children's Drawings"], in *Theresienstädter Studien und Dokumente 1998,* pp. 175–78. Unless otherwise noted, the quotations that follow are also taken from this source.

6. Elena Makarova, *Friedl Dicker-Brandeis. Ein Leben für Kunst und Lehre* (Vienna and Munich: Christian Brandstätter Verlag, 2000), p. 21.

7. Edith Kramer in a conversation with the author in Berlin on July 19, 2001. Edith Kramer, who emigrated to New York in 1938 and made a name for herself there as an art teacher and painter, has been especially active in keeping the artistic legacy of Friedl Dicker-Brandeis alive. In her first book, *Art Therapy in a Children's*

Community (1958), she formulated the theoretical basis for her work, making her, along with Elinor Ulman and Margareth Naumburg, an American pioneer in this pedagogical discipline. The fact that Edith Kramer dedicated her second book, *Art Therapy for Children,* to Friedl Dicker-Brandeis suggests what a strong influence her teacher had on her own development.

8. Georg Schrom in a lecture given as part of the symposium "Art, Music and Education as Strategies for Survival," Moravian College, Bethlehem, Pennsylvania, February 10, 2000.

9. Makarova, *Friedl Dicker-Brandeis,* p. 130.

10. Ibid.

11. Ibid., p. 131.

12. In his daily order of July 7, 1943, camp commandant Burger threatened the harshest punishment for unreported pregnancies. For a while all pregnancies were terminated with abortions. Later the commandant reserved for himself the decision as to whether a pregnancy was to be aborted or carried to full term. Most pregnant women, however, could expect to be put on the next transport to the East. A total of about 350 involuntary abortions were carried out. Of 207 children born in the camp, 25 survived.

13. On January 10, 1942, nine ghetto prisoners were hanged for infractions against camp rules; seven more hangings followed on February 26, 1942. Most of them had smuggled or tried to smuggle illegal letters or news out of the camp. One had secretly met with his non-Jewish wife, who had come to see him at the camp. After February 1942, there were no more executions in the ghetto, although individuals were taken to the Little Fortress and murdered there.

14. Alice Herz-Sommer in an interview with the author, summer 1999. Additional quotations are also based on this interview.

15. Elsa Bernstein, *Das Leben als Drama: Erinnerungen an Theresienstadt* (Dortmund: Edition Ebersbach, 1999), p. 114.

SIX: APPEARANCE AND REALITY

1. Otto Pollak, diary entry. Presumably, "Monte Terezino" is the bastion on the ramparts. On July 11, 1943, Otto Pollak noted: "The first time on the bastion with Ornstein and Rühlmann from Berlin. Beautiful view of Litoměřice."

2. Miroslav Kárný, in "Jakob Edelsteins letzte Briefe," in *Theresienstädter Studien*

und Dokumente 1997, pp. 216–29. Jakob Edelstein and his family were shot dead in Auschwitz-Birkenau on June 20, 1944.

3. Kotouc et al., *We Are Children Just the Same,* p. 127.

4. Viktor Ullmann, "Kritik Nr. 8, Musikalische Rundschau," in *26 Kritiken über musikalische Veranstaltungen in Theresienstadt,* ed. Ingo Schultz (Hamburg: Bockel Verlag, 1996), pp. 51–55.

5. Von Lang, *Das Eichmann-Protokoll,* p. 225.

6. There was, in fact, a concentration camp for political prisoners at Heydebreck, Upper Silesia. But Eva is correct. The reality was that "to go to Heydebreck" meant "to go to the gas chambers." As part of the deception of prisoners, the camp high command told them that the mass murders they were planning were merely a transport to the labor camp at Heydebreck.

7. "Prominent" people were those designated as such by the SS or the Council of Elders. They were given so-called privileged quarters and enjoyed some protection from being transported. Ultimately, however, such status was of use to only a very few. In the end, they were treated just like all other prisoners and were put on transport lists.

8. Jindřich Flusser, "Lebwohl, Theresien-stadt" ["Farewell, Theresienstadt"], in Il-tis, Ehrmann, and Heitlinger, eds., *Theresienstadt,* pp. 302–6. The number given for the town's population at its highest level is incorrect. Up to fifty-eight thousand people actually lived in Theresien-stadt.

9. "Theresienstädter Kindertagebücher," pp. 114–24.

10. Gonda Redlich's diary, quoted by Vojtěch Blodig in his *Ammerkungen zu Maurice Roussels Bericht, Theresienstädter Studien und Dokumente 1996,* p. 304 n. 16.

11. Rumors (*bonkes*) about a visit by a delegation of the International Committee of the Red Cross began circulating with the first orders for beautification in December 1943, but no one knew when it would occur. Himmler officially agreed to an inspection of the Theresienstadt Ghetto for the Elderly in May 1944. A letter dated May 18, 1944, sent by the Reich Security Main Office to Colonel Niehaus of the German Red Cross, said that Himmler "had approved an inspection of the Theresienstadt ghetto and of a Jewish labor camp by you and a representative of the International Committee of the Red Cross. Also taking part in the inspection

will be representatives of Denmark and Sweden. The date for this inspection is sometime in early June 1944." Quoted in *Theresienstadt Studien und Dokumente 1994,* document section. Historians concur that the term "Jewish labor camp" referred to the family camp at Auschwitz-Birkenau, which itself was planned as part of a Nazi propaganda campaign.

12. See H. G. Adler, *Theresienstadt 1941– 1945, Das Antlitz einer Zwangsgemeinschaft, Geschichte, Soziologie, Psychologie* (Tübingen: J. C. Mohr, 1956).

13. Of note in this context is Cara De Silva's *In Memory's Kitchen: A Legacy from the Women of Terezin* (Lanham, Md.: Rowman & Littlefield, 2006), a collection of traditional Bohemian, Moravian, Austrian, and German recipes that were exchanged among the women of Theresienstadt to satisfy their hunger, at least in their fantasies. They had neither the ingredients nor a place to cook or bake the foods in these recipes.

14. Heinrich Taussig, born in 1923; Bernhard Kaff, born in 1905 in Brno. Neither survived. Viktor Ullmann also wrote about a Beethoven concert given by Bernard Kaff. See "Kritik Nr. 19" in Ullmann, *26 Kritiken,* p. 76.

15. "Theresienstädter Kindertagbücher," pp. 114–24.
16. Ibid.
17. Eva Herrmannová in an interview with the author in Prague, 1998.
18. See Herbert Thomas Mandl, *Die Wette des Philosophen. Der Anfang des definitiven Todes* (Munich: Boer Verlag, 1996), p. 106.
19. Franěk, "*Brundibár,* der Brummbär."
20. Maurice Rossel's report and other documents were first published in their entirety in *Theresienstädter Studien und Dokumente 1996,* pp. 284–301, with an introduction by Miroslav Kárný, pp. 276–82, and detailed notes by Vojtěch Blodig, pp. 302–20. Unless otherwise noted, all other quotations by Maurice Rossel are taken from this report.
21. Claude Lanzmann in a conversation with Maurice Rossel, published in *Theresienstädter Studien und Dokumente 2000,* pp. 168–91. Lanzmann conducted this conversation for his documentary film *Shoah* (1985), but it was not used in the film. It was first published in *Un vivant qui passe Auschwitz, Theresienstadt 1943–1944* (Paris: Editions Mille et une nuits/ Arte Editions, 1997).

22. The deportees' baggage was confiscated by the SS at the "sluice" and then plundered. What was left landed in the *Kleiderkammer;* it was very strictly inventoried and then distributed among the prisoners and/or sold in shops for ghetto currency.

23. Karel Kursawe, born in 1892; member of the SS camp high command and director of camp agriculture.

24. Eva Herrmannová in an interview with the author in Prague, 1998.

25. From the program of a 1995 production of *Brundibár* by Jeunesses Musicales Deutschland; premiered at the Staatsoper Unter den Linden, Berlin.

26. Käthe Starke-Goldschmidt, "Die Zentralbücherei des Ghettos Theresienstadt" ["The Central Library of the Theresienstadt Ghetto"], in Iltis, Ehrmann, and Heitlinger, eds., *Theresienstadt,* pp. 185ff.

27. Hans Höfer, "Der Film über Theresienstadt" ["The Film About Theresienstadt"], in Iltis, Ehrmann, and Heitlinger, eds., *Theresienstadt,* pp. 194ff.

28. Eva Herrmannová in an interview with the author in Prague, 1998.

SEVEN: GHETTO TEARS

1. See Ullmann, "Kritik Nr. 16," in *26 Kritiken.*
2. Ullmann, "Kritik Nr. 24," in *26 Kritiken.*
3. See Zdenka Fantlová, *My Lucky Star* (New York: Herodias, 2001).
4. Paul Kling (1928–2005) in conversations with the author in New York and Berlin, 1997 and 1998.
5. Leo Haas, "Die Affäre der Theresienstädter Maler" ["The Theresienstadt Painters' Affair"], in Iltis, Ehrmann, and Heitlinger, eds., *Theresienstadt,* pp. 170ff.
6. *Mitteilungen der Jüdischen Selbstverwaltung* [*Communications of the Jewish Self-Administration*], no. 45, September 17, 1944, taken from the literary estate of Otto Pollak; also quoted in Otto Pollak's diary entry of Saturday, September 16, 1944.
7. Miroslav Kárný, "Die Theresienstädter Herbstransporte 1944" ["The Theresienstadt Transports in the Fall of 1944"], in *Theresienstädter Studien und Dokumente 1995,* pp. 7–37.
8. Ibid. Kárný's essay provides solid evidence that Himmler's chief motive in ordering these transports was to weaken resistance in Theresienstadt, to eliminate

all potential for resistance, and to counter what he feared most, an uprising. At the same time he could then carry on unhindered with his camouflage of Theresienstadt and garner any political capital such a deception might yield.

9. Felix Weiss was a cousin of Otto Pollak and a member of the fire department in Theresienstadt. He died in January 1945 in a concentration camp in Bavaria.

10. Kárný, "Theresienstädter Herbstransporte 1944," pp. 7–37.

11. Eva Herrmannová in an interview with the author in Prague, 1998.

12. Mica was important for the manufacture of munitions. It had to be splintered into very thin pieces and weighed, both processes demanding good light and exceptional dexterity. After September 1944, more than a thousand women were put to work fracturing mica.

EIGHT: LIBERATION

1. Horst Cohn, a resident of Israel, in a conversation with the author in Schwerin, Germany, January 2001.

2. Paul (Sandfort) Aron, *Ben: The Alien Bird,* trans. Paul Aron and Alex Auswaks (Jerusalem: Gefen Books, 1999), p. 295.

3. Irena Lauscherová, "Die Kinder von

Theresienstadt" ["The Children of Theresienstadt"], in Iltis, Ehrmann, and Heitlinger, eds., *Theresienstadt,* p. 111.

4. Among the dead was the Viennese pianist Renée Gärtner-Geiringer (1908–1945). Flaška's sister Lizzi, who was on the same train, tripped over the dead body of Gärtner-Geiringer as she left the cattle car after the bombardment.

5. In their attempt to save Hungarian Jews, Rudolf Kastner and Joel Brand were involved in controversial dealings with the Nazis. On April 5, 1944, when Kastner and Brand first met with Dieter Wisliceny, who was part of Eichmann's Section IV B 4, Wisliceny demanded $2 million in exchange for the lives of 800,000 Hungarian Jews. After the first partial payment, a rescue operation was set in motion for a selected group of 1,700 Jews, who, after extended incarceration at Bergen-Belsen until late 1944, finally did make it to Switzerland. As part of those April negotiations, Eichmann offered Joel Brand another deal: the release of one million Jews in exchange for ten thousand trucks and other goods from the West. This offer of "blood for goods," as it was called, was rejected by the Allies. Kastner nevertheless continued negotiations, which the Al-

lies supported for tactical reasons. Accused of betraying Jews and collaborating with the Nazis, Kastner was later tried in Israel in 1954–55. Kastner's legal appeal was still pending when he was shot and killed on the street by nationalist extremists in Israel on March 15, 1957. Kastner's good name has now largely been restored. Those whom he saved have erected a monument in his honor.

6. *Der Kastner-Bericht über Eichmanns Menschenhandel in Ungarn* [*The Kastner Report Concerning Eichmann's Traffic in Human Beings in Hungary*] (Munich: Kindler, 1961), pp. 323–27.

7. Kotouc et al., *We Are Children Just the Same,* pp. 72–73. Eva Ginz is the sister of Petr Ginz, the editor of *Vedem.*

8. Alice Ehrmann, "Ein Theresienstädter Tagebuch, October 18, 1944–May 19, 1945" ["A Theresienstadt Diary"], in *Theresienstädter Studien und Dokumente 1994,* pp. 171–205. The author was born on May 5, 1927, and arrived in Theresienstadt on July 13, 1943. There she became friends with Zeev Shek, a committed Zionist leader. In 1947 they married, and in 1948 she followed him to Palestine. Alisah Shek is one of the cofounders of the archives and memorial Beit Terezin, at Gi-

vat Chaim Ichud, Israel, where she lived until her death in 2007.

9. *Theresienstädter Studien und Dokumente 1995,* pp. 306–24. Erich Kessler was born on June 14, 1912. He lived in Prague until he was deported to Theresienstadt on February 9, 1945, along with other Jews living in (as the Nazis called it) a *Mischehe* (mixed marriage).

10. According to information provided by Karl-Heinz Schultz, chairman of the Friends of the Neuengamme Concentration Camp Memorial, "Papa" was a customs agent who had been reassigned to guard prisoners on September 13, 1944. He was killed in an air raid on Hamburg-Tiefstack.

11. Erich Kessler in *Theresienstädter Studien und Dokumente 1995,* pp. 306–24.

12. Ibid.

EPILOGUE

1. Hanka Brady's story is told in the book *Hana's Suitcase,* by Karen Levine (Morton Grove, Ill.: Albert Whitman & Co., 2007).

2. Přemysl Pitter (1895–1976) was a Christian humanist who devoted his life to social work with children. Pavel Kohn has written a book in his honor: *Schlösser der*

Hoffnung. Die geretteten Kinder des Pře-mysl Pitter [*Castles of Hope: The Rescued Children of Přemysl Pitter*] (Munich: Langen Müller, 2001).

3. Eugen Kolb (1898–1959) was an art critic, art historian, and journalist; from 1952 to 1959 he served as director of the Helena Rubenstein Museum in Tel Aviv.

BIBLIOGRAPHY

The following three publications were especially rich sources of information and inspiration:

Theresienstadt. Ed. Rudolf Iltis, František Ehrmann, and Ota Heitlinger. Trans. Walter Hacker. Vienna: Europa Verlag, 1968.

Theresienstädter Studien und Dokumente. Ed. Miroslav Kárný, Raimund Kemper, and Margita Kárná. Prague: Edition Theresienstädter Initiative Academia, annual volumes starting 1994.

Kotouc, Kurt Jiri, et al. *We Are Children Just the Same:* Vedem, *the Secret Magazine by the Boys of Terezin.* Trans. R. Elizabeth Novak. Philadelphia: Jewish Publication Society, 1995.

Adler, H. G. *Theresienstadt 1941–1945, Das Antlitz einer Zwangsgemeinschaft. Geschichte, Soziologie, Psychologie.* Tübingen: J. C. Mohr, 1956.

———. *Die verheimlichte Wahrheit. Theresienstädter Dokumente.* Tübingen: J. C. Mohr, 1958.

Blodig, Vojtěch. "The Genocide of the Czech Jews in World War II and the Terezín Ghetto." In *Art, Music and Education as Strategies for Survival: Theresienstadt 1941–1945,* ed. Anne D. Dutlinger, pp. 144–61. New York: Herodias, 2001.

———. "Die letzte Phase der Entwicklung des Ghettos Theresienstadt." In *Theresienstadt in der Endlösung der Judenfrage,* ed. Miroslav Kárný, Vojtěch Blodig, and Margita Kárná, pp. 267–78. Prague: Panorama, 1992.

———. "Terezín in the 'Final Solution of the Jewish Question.'" In *The Holocaust Phenomenon: Conference Report of the International Scientific Conference,* pp. 87–91. Prague, 2000.

Bondy, Ruth. *"Elder of the Jews": Jakob Edelstein of Theresienstadt.* New York: Grove Press, 1989.

Chládková, Ludmilla. *Das Ghetto Theresienstadt.* Terezín: Verlag Nase Vojsko, 1991.

De Silva, Cara. *In Memory's Kitchen: A Legacy from the Women of Terezin.* Lanham, Md.: Rowman & Littlefield, 2006.

Drori, Hana, and Jehuda Huppert. *Theresienstadt. Ein Wegweiser.* Prague: Vitalis, 1999.

Karas, Joža. *Music in Terezin, 1941–1945.* New York: Beaufort Books, 1985.

Die Kleine Festung Theresienstadt, 1940–1945. Exhibition catalogue. Prague: Památník Terezín, 1996.

Kuna, Milan. *Musik an der Grenze des Lebens.* Frankfurt: Zweitausendeins, 1993.

Migdal, Ulrike, ed. *Und die Musik spielt dazu. Chansons und Satiren aus dem KZ Theresienstadt.* Munich: Piper, 1990.

Schwertfeger, Ruth. *Women of Theresienstadt: Voices from a Concentration Camp.* New York: Berg, 1989.

Ullmann, Viktor. *26 Kritiken über musikalische Veranstaltungen in Theresienstadt.* Ed. Ingo Schultz. Hamburg: Bockel Verlag, 1996.

AUTOBIOGRAPHICAL LITERATURE ON THERESIENSTADT

Aron, Paul (Sandfort). *Ben: The Alien Bird.* Trans. Paul Aron and Alex Auswaks. Jerusalem: Gefen Books, 1999.

Bernstein, Elsa. *Das Leben als Drama: Erinnerungen an Theresienstadt.* Dortmund: Edition Ebersbach, 1999.

Bor, Josef. *The Terezin Requiem.* New York: Alfred A. Knopf, 1963.

Elias, Ruth. *Die Hoffnung erhielt mich am Leben.* Munich: Piper Verlag, 1988.

Fantlová, Zdenka. *My Lucky Star.* New York: Herodias, 2001.

Kantor, Alfred. *The Book of Alfred Kantor.* New York: Schocken Books, 1987.

Klüger, Ruth. *Still Alive: A Holocaust Girlhood Remembered.* New York: Feminist Press, 2003.

Koenig, Ernest. *Im Vorhof der Vernichtung. Als Zwangsarbeiter in den Außenlagern von Auschwitz.* Frankfurt: S. Fischer, 2000.

Mandl, Herbert Thomas. *Durst, Musik, Geheime Dienste.* Munich: Boer Verlag, 1995.

———. *Die Wette des Philosophen. Der Anfang des definitiven Todes.* Munich: Boer Verlag, 1996.

Meyer, Alwin. *Die Kinder von Auschwitz.* Göttingen: Lamuv Verlag, 1990.

Oppenhejm, Mélanie. *Theresienstadt: Survival in Hell.* Trans. Dina Ullendorff. London: Menard Press, 2001.

Ross, Carlo. *Im Vorhof der Hölle.* Munich: dtv, 1994.

Salus, Grete. *Niemand, nichts — Ein Jude.* Darmstadt: Darmstädter Blätter, 1981.

Scheuer, Lisa. *Vom Tode, der nicht stattfand.* Reinbek: Shaker Verlag, 1998.

Spitzer, Federica, and Ruth Weisz. *Theresienstadt. Aufzeichnungen von Federica Spitzer und Ruth Weisz.* Ed. Wolfgang Benz. Berlin: Metropol, 1997.

Troller, Norbert. *Theresienstadt: Hitler's Gift to the Jews.* Trans. Susan E. Cerynyak-Spatz. Chapel Hill: University of North Carolina Press, 1991.

Utitz, Emil. *Psychologie des Lebens im Konzentrationslager Theresienstadt.* Vienna: Verlag A. Sexl, 1948.

Vrba, Rudolf. *Als Kanada in Auschwitz lag. Meine Flucht aus dem Vernichtungslager.* Munich: Piper, 1999.

CHILDREN'S PAINTING IN THERESIENSTADT

Dutlinger, Anne D., ed. *Art, Music and Education as Strategies for Survival.* New York: Herodias, 2000.

Makarova, Elena. *Friedl Dicker-Brandeis. Ein Leben für Kunst und Lehre.* Vienna and Munich: Christian Brandstätter Verlag, 2000.

Volkavkova, Hana. *I Never Saw Another Butterfly.* New York: Schocken Books, 1994.

Vom Bauhaus nach Terezin. Friedl Dicker-Brandeis und die Kinderzeichnungen aus dem Ghetto-Lager Theresienstadt. Exhibition catalogue. Frankfurt: Das Jüdische Museum, 1991.

Weissová, Helga. *Zeichne, was Du siehst. Zeichnungen eines Kindes aus Theresienstadt.* Göttingen: Wallstein, 1998.

GENERAL LITERATURE ON THE HOLCAUST

Aly, Götz, and Susanne Heim. *Vordenker der Vernichtung.* Frankfurt: S. Fischer, 1993.

Benz, Wolfgang. *Der Holocaust.* Munich: C. H. Beck, 1997.

Berkley, George E. *Vienna and Its Jews: The Tragedy of Success, 1880s–1980s.* Lanham, Md.: Madison Books, 1988.

Biege, Bernd. *Helfer unter Hitler. Das Rote Kreuz im Dritten Reich.* Reinbek: Kindler Verlag, 2000.

Deutsche Politik im "Protektorat Böhmen und

*Mähren" unter Reinhard Heydrich 1941–
1942.* Ed. Miroslav Kárný, Jaroslava Milotová, and Margita Kárná. Berlin:
Metropol, 1997.

Deutsche und Tschechen. Ed. Walter Ko-
schmal, Marek Nekula, and Joachim Ro-
gall. Munich: C. H. Beck, 2001.

Encyclopedia of the Holocaust. Ed. Israel
Gutman. 4 vols. New York: Macmillan,
1995.

Friedrich, Otto. *The Kingdom of Auschwitz.*
New York: HarperCollins, 1994.

Gilbert, Martin. *Auschwitz and the Allies.*
New York: Holt, Rinehart & Winston,
1981.

Hilberg, Raul. *The Destruction of the European Jews.* 3rd ed. New Haven, Conn.:
Yale University Press, 2003.

———. *Perpetrators Victims Bystanders: The
Jewish Catastrophe, 1933–1945.* New York:
HarperCollins, 1993.

Jüdische Schicksale. Berichte von Verfolgten.
Vienna: Dokumentationsarchiv des öster-
reichischen Widerstandes, 1992.

Kárný, Miroslav. "Nisko in der Geschichte
der Endlösung." *Judaica Bohemia* 3, no. 2
(1987): 69–84.

Longerich, Peter. *Die Wannsee-Konferenz
vom 20. Januar 1942, Planung und Beginn
des Genozids an den europäischen Juden,*

Gedenk und Bildungsstätte Haus der Wannsee-Konferenz. Berlin: Edition Hentrich, 1998.

Müller-Tupath, Karla. *Verschollen in Deutschland. Das heimliche Leben des Anton Burger, Lagerkommandant von Theresienstadt.* Hamburg: Konkret Literatur Verlag, 1994.

Ondrichova, Lucie. *Fredy Hirsch. Eine jüdische Biographie 1916–1944.* Constance: Hartung-Gorre-Verlag, 2000.

Safrian, Hans. *Eichmann und seine Gehilfen.* Frankfurt: S. Fischer, 1995.

Shirer, William L. *The Rise and Fall of the Third Reich.* New York: Simon & Schuster, 1960.

Von Lang, Jochen. *Das Eichmann-Protokoll. Tonbandaufzeichnungen der israelischen Verhöre.* Munich: Ullstein, 2001.

Wlaschek, Rudolf M. *Juden in Böhmen. Beiträge zur Geschichte des europäischen Judentums im 19. und 20. Jahrhundert* Munich: Oldenbourg, 1997.

UNPUBLISHED DOCUMENTS AND MANUSCRIPTS

The Diary of Helga Pollak, © private property, represented by the author.

The Poetry Album of Anna Flachová © private

property, represented by the author.

The Document Album of Vera Nath © private property, represented by the author.

Všechno, the Notebook of Handa Pollak, © private property.

Reports by the members of the Youth Welfare Department of Theresienstadt. Typescripts, Jewish Museum, Prague.

Essays by the girls of Girls' Home L 410, written October 18, 1943. Subject: "What has made the deepest impression on you since you have been living in the Girls' Home?" Archives Beit Theresienstadt, Israel.

BRUNDIBÁR

Hans Krása (music) and Adolf Hoffmeister (text), *Brundibár,* represented by the music agency Boosey & Hawkes, Berlin, London, New York. www.boosey.com.

Brundibár: Eine Oper für Kinder von Hans Krása & Brundibár und die Kinder von Theresienstadt. Feature von Hannelore Wonschick. EDITION ABSEITS, 1999. Double CD with the opera and a radio documentary on the history of the opera with recorded recollections by survivors of Theresienstadt. www.room28projects .com.

ILLUSTRATION PERMISSIONS ACKNOWLEDGMENTS

The author and the publisher wish to thank the Girls of Room 28 for supplying many photographs and documents from their personal collections for publication in this book:

Anna Hanusová-Flachová: pp. 18, 19, 148, 156, 193, 470, 500, 501
Helga Kinsky: pp. 39, 41, 52, 68, 81, 373, 425, 426, 475, 483, 497
Eva Stern: p. 91
Handa Drori: pp. 108, 163, 190
Eva Gross: pp. 115, 247, 411, 562
Vera Kreiner: pp. 119, 134, 196, 258, 387, 422, 560, 572
Judith Rosenzweig: pp. 198, 201, 566
Ela Weissberger: pp. 245, 349
Hanka Weingarten: p. 261
Marianne Deutsch: p. 333
Evelina Mer: p. 356
Marta Mikul: p. 362

Eva Sohar: pp. 364, 569
Eva Vit: p. 383
Miriam Jung: p. 472

p. 29: Still from the propaganda film *Theresienstadt: Dokumentarfilm aus einem jüdischen Siedlunzgsgebiet Theresienstadt: Documentary of a Jewish Settlement.* Photograph © Národní Filmovy Archiv v Praze National Film Archive in Prague.

pp. 72, 76: © Židovské Muzeum v Praze.

p. 78: © Archive Beit Theresienstadt, Givat Chaim Ichud, Israel.

pp. 94, 103: From *Zeichne was Du siehst: Zeichnungen eines Kindes aus Theresienstadt/Terezin. Draw What You See: Drawings of a Child of Theresienstadt/ Terezin* by Helga Weiss. Göttingen: Wallstein Verlag, 1998.

pp. 126, 129: © Židovské Muzeum v Praze.

p. 150: *Moon Landscape,* 1942–44, by Petr Ginz. Drawing, pencil on paper. Gift of Otto Ginz. Reprinted by permission of the Yad Vashem Art Museum, Jerusalem.

p. 158: Private collection.

p. 184: Private collection.

p. 212: Reprinted by permission of the Theresienstadt Memorial.

p. 228: From *Zeichne was Du siehst: Zeichnungen eines Kindes aus Theresienstadt/*

Terezin. Draw What You See: Drawings of a Child of Theresienstadt/Terezin by Helga Weiss. Göttingen: Wallstein Verlag, 1998.

p. 239: © Židovské Muzeum v Praze.

p. 266: Private collection.

p. 269: Reprinted by permission of the Theresienstadt Memorial.

p. 272: © Židovské Muzeum v Praze.

p. 275: Reprinted by permission of the Theresienstadt Memorial.

p. 312: © Beit Theresienstadt Archive, Givat Chaim Ichud, Israel.

p. 321: © Židovské Muzeum v Praze.

p. 333: © George Brady, Canada.

p. 336: © Alice Sommer.

p. 339: © Chava Linden.

p. 370: Private collection.

p. 394: Watercolor sketch from *The Book of Alfred Kantor: An Artist's Journal of the Holocaust,* by Alfred Kantor and John Wykert. New York: Schocken Books, 1987.

pp. 443, 446: © Židovské Muzeum v Praze.

p. 508: Reprinted by permission of the Theresienstadt Memorial.

pp. 563, 571, 573, 575, 577, 579, 584, 587, 590: © Hannelore Brenner-Wonschick.